SPINNING INTELLIGENCE

RMD—*To Anna: for the good times, and with love.*
MSG—*To my lovely wife Denise.*

Spinning Intelligence

Why Intelligence Needs the Media, Why the Media Needs Intelligence

Editors

Robert Dover and Michael S. Goodman

Columbia University Press
New York

Columbia University Press
Publishers Since 1893
New York   Chichester, West Sussex
Copyright © 2009 C. Hurst & Co (Publishers) Ltd
All rights reserved

Library of Congress Cataloging-in-Publication Data

Spinning intelligence : why intelligence needs the media, why the media needs
intelligence / editors, Robert Dover and Michael S. Goodman.
    p. cm.
    ISBN 978-0-231-70114-3 (alk. paper)
    1. Government and the press. 2. Espionage. 3. Spies in mass media. I. Dover, Robert,
1977– II. Goodman, Michael S. III. Title.

PN4735.S67 2009
070.4′4932712—dc22

                    2009014170

∞

Columbia University Press books are printed on permanent and durable
acid-free paper. This book is printed on paper with recycled content.
Printed in India

c 10 9 8 7 6 5 4 3 2 1

References to Internet Web sites (URLs) were accurate at the time of writing. Neither
the author nor Columbia University Press is responsible for URLs
that may have expired or changed since the manuscript was prepared.

CONTENTS

CONTENTS

ACKNOWLEDGEMENTS

We would like to thank Michael Dwyer and his colleagues at Hurst for their help, assistance and support in producing this book.

RMD—I would like to thank Pierre Lethier, Andrew Monaghan and Sarah Massingham for their helpful critiques of my chapter, Juliet Parker for introducing me to the wonders of pilates and thus making writing all day at a desk far more pleasant, Wurzel for his good ideas, and the Economic and Social Research Council for funding the workshop that accompanied this book under the Research Workshops' Grant titled 'Intelligence and Government in the 21st Century'.

MSG—I would like to thank Richard J. Aldrich, Trish Hayes at the BBC Written Archives Centre, and West Ham United FC. Thanks also to Humpty Dumpty for his endless assistance and addiction to emails. I am especially grateful to Denise for keeping me sane and ensuring that I always have a smile on my face.

Scire loqui decus est; decus est et scire tacere

INTRODUCTION

INTELLIGENCE IN THE INFORMATION AGE

Robert Dover and Michael Goodman

When Donald Rumsfeld uttered his famous 'known-knowns' retort to criticisms about the intelligence leading up to the Gulf War many commentators scoffed. But his comments were remarkably apt: 'Reports that say that something hasn't happened are always interesting to me, because as we know, there are known knowns; these are things we know we know. We also know there are known unknowns; that is to say we know there are some things we do not know. But there are also unknown unknowns—the ones we don't know we don't know.' The knowledge that is produced by intelligence agencies and by the media is commonly assumed to be certain and thus fits into the category of 'known knowns', but in reality intelligence work and investigative journalism are often working at the level of known unknowns—that is trying to piece together knowledge on that which is obscured and mysterious. What this book seeks to do is explore the fluid, contradictory and occasionally supportive relationship between intelligence agencies, governments and the media and how they bridge the gap between the unknown and the known.

While intelligence has always been described as the missing dimension in international relations, this cannot possibly be the case today. It might be underexplored and under-examined by the public, politicians and academics, but it is directly in front of us. In every part of society, and in all our social interactions, intelligence has a role to play in conditioning the political and social environments in which we live.

1

Since the turn of the century a plethora of intelligence reforms have been introduced across the western world that have the potential—if misapplied—fundamentally to change the relationship between the citizen and the state. Plans to introduce identity cards in the United Kingdom (to help with the fight against terrorism), the logging and storing of people's movements on public and private transport across Europe and North America, and, in the case of air travel, across the globe, have brought the citizen in much closer contact with the state. Formerly it was possible for an individual effectively to opt out of contact with the state if he or she remained on the right side of the law and did not holiday abroad, for example. Today, this is simply not possible and, as a result, we have to be aware of debates over the substance and form of intelligence activity, what oversight we and our elected representatives have over those agencies and whether the threats we face are sufficient to warrant an amendment to our social contracts with our governments. Some recent developments, like the networks of CCTV cameras, the tracking of an individual's movements on mass transit systems using payment card information and face-recognition CCTV, right down to the logging and storing of information on all of our social, economic and sexual preferences through internet trails, store card data and email and telephone communications (as currently practised in the US, UK and France) all have the potential to affect our everyday social interactions and relation with the state.

The desired outcome of these developments is to enhance the security of our societies, to protect our core values, and to free us from the oppressive yoke of jihadi and other terrorist groups. The unintended consequence of these policies has been to narrow down the range of political views that any individual can hold and act upon. This is not necessarily a bad thing, but it is notable that, as of early 2009, several ministers in Gordon Brown's cabinet—in particular—cut their teeth in the radical politics of the 1970s and 80s, before coming round to more mainstream political views. Late teenage political rebellion is often a core feature of an individual's political development and it may be being effectively stymied and criminalised through more intrusive levels of intelligence activity and policing. We are not arguing for the radicalisation of the youth—far from it—but merely note the historical change.

The terrorist attacks perpetrated against New York and Washington in 2001, Madrid in 2004 and London in 2005 were all media events. 9/11 is—in the minds of the majority—something they saw live on television or in the immediate aftermath. The image of the second tower when the second plane struck, juxtaposed against the shots filmed from the other side of Manhattan of the two towers standing but billowing with smoke, are indelibly printed on the consciousness of the west. Similarly, the evocative image of a red London bus torn asunder by a bomb (that had been destined for a tube train) in July 2005 became 'the' defining image of the London bombings. And intelligence surrounded the London bombings in the public consciousness. The Joint Terrorism Analysis Centre (JTAC) reduced the terrorist threat warning in June 2005, something that demonstrated in July 2005 the difficulty of pin-pointing accurate intelligence. The capture of the 21/7 bombers in London (and one subsequently in Rome) was a curious media event: television camera crews were on site, albeit unable to get close enough to film the operation, thus providing a semi-detached, real-time view. Intelligence-led operations remained at the very forefront of the British news agenda for months after the London bombings, including in the unfortunate targeting and killing of an innocent Brazilian who was mistaken for a suicide bomber. The *9/11 Commission* in America, and the *Butler* and *Hutton Reports* in the UK opened the world of intelligence up for the general public in a way that has only been echoed by the *Scott Report* in the UK (1996) and the US *Church Committee* (1975). What distinguishes the contemporary and historical examples are the now ubiquitous twenty-four hour rolling news channels and the internet, which have opened up for the public the possibility of almost limitless exposure to the machinations of the committees and thus of the workings of the intelligence machinery.

The use of intelligence materials to justify the war against Saddam Hussein's Iraq has heralded another development in the relationship between intelligence, the media and the general public. The presence of US Secretary of State Colin Powell at the UN in February 2003, presenting the case against Iraq, premised on what we now know to be faulty intelligence, gave the viewing public a sense of ownership over these materials. We were asked to judge and acknowledge their validity—and the consequent decision to invade Iraq—and as a result news outlets published more and more source documents, be it through their primary publication routes, or on their websites. Every man or woman began to think of themselves as government intelligence analysts—particularly when the perception began to creep in that the government specialists had got their assessments wrong. Furthermore, books like Omar Nasiri's *Inside The Global Jihad* and Ed Hussain's *The Islamist* have given the public insights into the 'jihadist mindset' and the opportunity to reflect on how best to deal with it.[1] So, the new phenomenon of the arm-chair analyst has further complicated and deepened the tripartite relationship between intelligence agencies, media outlets and the public, raising ever more important questions about where the media gets its information from, and how and why it disseminates it. Following on from books like *Flat Earth News*, by Nick Davies, and *Thinker, Faker, Spinner, Spy* edited by William Dinan and David Miller this book explores the relationship between the media and intelligence agencies, and the extent to which they rely on each other.[2] Examples of this range from helpful stories being planted in the press, agencies helping filmmakers construct narratives about threats and how to depict espionage, through to the tensions between a newspaper's desire to publish information that government agencies would rather they did not.

Flat Earth News and similar books remind us of another, perhaps surprising, element of the relationship between the media and intelligence, which is just how similar the jobs of journalist and intelligence field officer are. The methods are—in many ways—quite close. The cultivation of sources, and of trust, small payments to smooth the passing of information or the betrayal of an asset's employers, of surveillance and interception are all common to both professions. Notable intelligence professionals sometimes traverse both roles, as did South Africa's recently retired Intelligence Co-ordinator Barry Gilder over the course of a long career. The difference between the two is clearly wrapped up in questions of structure and scale—the journalist can afford to make mistakes (apologies can be issued, falsehoods forgotten, or damages paid out) whilst the intelligence officer, in the right circumstances, can be literally responsible for life and death decisions. Both professions are engaged in the production of knowledge, but what happens to that knowledge after it is produced differs markedly from one to the other.

Journalists and intelligence officers also enjoy a somewhat privileged position when it comes to accountability and oversight. Journalists are confined by the civil and criminal law codes on libel and unduly affecting judicial proceedings, and they are also confined—individually—by the freedoms their editors afford to them, the editorial line imposed by the owners, and the sales figures of the paper. The oversight mechanisms are therefore mostly issues of internal discipline, rather than formally constructed ones, as is often the case in times of total war, with the exception of the D-Notice committee that is conspicuous in war time, but in the background at all times. For intelligence officers, they face the legal constraints set out by their political masters, their own career aspirations, which may limit certain types of behaviour, and the internal oversight mechanisms within the agencies. Theirs is a far more controlled environment the notion of 'rogue spooks', as portrayed on television and at the cinema, is wildly off the mark. But neither measure up to publicly held assumptions of 'democratic accountability' that set standards of openness and transparency enjoyed or endured by other public bodies. And this is a product of necessity, for the most part. Intelligence would not, and could not, function under conditions of openness—its function is to discover the information of others while concealing their own position and that of their government. For the media, their lines of accountability are driven by the reality of their position as private profit-seeking entities—again it is a publicly driven perception that they are, in some way, accountable as public servants.

This *ménage à trois* of spooks, hacks and the public is worthy of serious attention, because it is a relationship of such great dependencies, synergies and feed-back loops. Intelligence and the media operate within the realities established by the societies from which they spring. They can shape the nature and form of these societies, and it is this dynamic that this book explores.

Coming in from the cold

The intelligence services and the media have had a troubled and varied past. Let us take an example. British intelligence has had a long history of interacting with the media. In fact it would not be extravagant to argue that without a public discussion of the 'threat', then no modern British intelligence system would have come into being. Writing in the late nineteenth and early twentieth century, one of the most popular authors of the day was William Le Queux. Le Queux was a journalist cum author who managed to write a staggering average of four novels per year. In 1906 he published *The Invasion of 1910*, a fanciful account of the German invasion of Britain. It was a runaway success and was followed by further books that detailed the devilish Germans and the threat they posed to British security. In effect Le Queux generated mass hysteria, where the perceived fictional German menace became intertwined with its real, yet unfulfilled, potential. Public concern became political reality, and in late 1909 the government decided to create what would become MI5 and MI6—one intelligence organisation to look at the internal threat, the other to look externally.

From that point onwards British intelligence developed a shadowy, mysterious demeanour, with a common policy 'neither to confirm nor deny' any rumours that might appear. It was not all secret though. Almost from the outset, the presence of the Joint Intelligence Committee as the central coordinating body was publicly confirmed—its first airing was a talk by Major

General Hastings Ismay at the Royal United Services Institute (RUSI) in 1938. Furthermore, upon the death of its secretary, in 1945, the chairman of the JIC published an obituary in *The Times*, outlining what an excellent job he had done. These were atypical aberrations, yet they signalled a steady expansion of intelligence collection and assessment.

With the end of the Second World War a series of 'Official Histories' were commissioned. One notable exception was the decision to produce a history of the Special Operations Executive (SOE), the shadowy wartime organisation designed, in Churchill's words, to 'set Europe ablaze'. This history, produced by Professor M.R.D. Foot, took two years to write and five years to clear for publication. The decision in the mid 1970s to release the fact that British intelligence read wartime German codes was revolutionary, not just in comprehending the conduct of the conflict, but also in understanding the significant role that intelligence could play in international affairs. As part of the Second World War volumes, a further series was commissioned on the role of British intelligence. These histories were, again, quite revolutionary at the time, for not only did they highlight the successes and failures of British intelligence, but they also revealed the myriad agencies that existed (no comment was offered as to whether these bodies continued in their wartime guise). The first three volumes were produced and published relatively speedily; the fourth and fifth, on counter-espionage and deception accordingly, were held up for a number of years, with Professor Michael Howard's volume finally appearing ten years after its completion.

The first official recognition of the intelligence services' post-war role was Lord Franks' report into what had gone wrong with the Falklands War. Here reference was made to the Joint Intelligence Committee and its role in warning (or not, as it turned out) about acts of aggression. More farcical still was the fiasco over the publication of Peter Wright's 'memoir' *Spycatcher*. Wright, who had been refused permission to publish his book in Britain, eventually found an Australian publisher. The ensuing legal battle saw the Cabinet Secretary, Sir Robert Armstrong, fly to Australia to play his part in the drama. In commenting on the book, Armstrong was forced to concede that MI5 did exist for the period of Wright's employment, but could neither confirm nor deny whether it had existed before or after.

The impact of the Cold War refusal to acknowledge the existence of the intelligence agencies led to a growth industry in turgid books that revealed 'the truth', yet a careful examination of their footnotes (or lack thereof) revealed the hollowness on which such claims were based. The public clamour was for greater openness, greater clarity, and greater stories about the intelligence world, a gap that was filled by a vast espionage literature, characterised, most famously, by those diametrically opposed yet most impressive caricatures of the genre—James Bond and George Smiley.

With the end of the Cold War came greater openness. Starting in 1989 and continuing in 1994 Britain's intelligence agencies stepped out of the dark, becoming avowed one by one. The head of MI5 was photographed and even published her own memoir. Finally, in the twenty-first century, official websites appeared, and plans to publish several intelligence 'official histories' were made public. Is the circle now complete? Not exactly. With the release of intelligence documentation into the archives still patchy and incomplete, the gaps will have to be filled in other ways. Moreover, with the public desire to know what is happening, and the battle against terrorism being increasingly fought in the public *and* secret intelligence spheres, there will remain room for conjecture and hyperbole. This is not necessarily a bad thing.

Journalists and spooks: blood brothers; separated at birth?

The terms 'globalisation' and 'information age' have become ubiquitous in modern parlance. They seek to sum up the interconnectedness of the world—something assisted by fast internet connections, cheap air travel and the acceptability of moving around the globe with fewer barriers than ever before. These globalising trends have assisted the spread of American and European business practices and finance, cultural and social norms and western style democracy. But with this opening up of new frontiers to the west have come attendant dangers—domestic adversaries, as well as those in the developing world, have also harnessed these technologies, financial techniques and fundamental openness to attack the west.

The challenge to western intelligence agencies from globalisation has come in the form of identifying, containing and rolling back threats from a multitude of sources able to move more freely across the globe, who are able to train and finance each other via the internet rather than necessarily in person, and to make sense of and analyse truly staggering amounts of information that is exchanged and traded in the form of electronic mail and internet VOIP telephone calls (which are notoriously difficult to intercept). The enormous advances in computing technology also allow large amounts of information (the sort of amount that in paper form would have previously been stored in a warehouse) to be moved around in wafer—thin memory devices—something that caused the British government successive embarrassment in 2007 and 2008 as many have gone missing or been stolen. The corollary is that the adversary too can move around large amounts of information and that security breaches are very serious indeed.

Globalisation can also be thought of as a multitude of transnational pressures, be they from civil society, transnational corporations, or social trends that interact with states as they cross their jurisdictions, but also outside those geographically limited areas as states seek to protect their core interests in the wider world. Despite the gradual emergence of a functioning transnational civil society since the naval age (beginning in c.1600), which was given an enormous boost by the technological revolution following the fall of communism in 1991, the state remains a key actor within the international system and state responses to a globalised media and the security challenges that flow from the information age still dominate. To reflect this reality *Known Knowns* contains chapters that explore this situation in the United States, the United Kingdom and Canada, which form the central section of the book.

Scott Lucas and Steve Hewitt explore the relationship between the American intelligence agencies and the media around the pivotal point of 9/11. They demonstrate both the checks and balances the media placed on the Administration, but also the useful function the media serves for various government departments executing the war on terror and involved in selling the Iraq war to American and coalition publics. Tony Campbell—the former head of Canadian intelligence analysis—highlights the problems and tensions there have been in the relationship between Canadian intelligence and the media particularly since 9/11 and the perception that the government has sought to manipulate the media for its own ends. Completing the tour of the western part of the Anglosphere, Michael Goodman and Nick Wilkinson consider two elements of the situation in the United Kingdom. Wilkinson—as a former *Secretary* of the *D-Notice committee*—spent five years adjudicating on issues of balance between the news media's right to publish pieces of interest contrasted against national security interests. In a curiously English pattern the *D-Notice Committee* does not have judicial powers, relying instead on the binding conventions of self-regulation (a fear on the part of the media outlets of being legally regulated), thus Wilkinson is able to comment on the relationship between these two sides, posing the question that Tony Campbell also raises, of whether the two sides are 'bedmates or sparring partners'? Michael Goodman deals with a far clearer case of 'bedmates' when he considers a brief history of the British Broadcasting Corporation's (BBC) Monitoring Service. Bankrolled by the UK's Foreign and Commonwealth Office, the Monitoring Service served a crucial function in providing sensitive intelligence information to the British and American governments, and thus also helped to preserve the 'special relationship' between the two. The British government's influence over the Monitoring Service was never hidden, but the extent to which the government had control of the service was and is novel in an international context. This was public service in the name of the government, and whilst providing an excellent two-way transmission belt between Britain and the wider world it has been controversial precisely because it provides an intrusive form of open source intelligence-gathering.

One of the interesting elements of the information age is the so-called '24-hour news cycle', which is epitomised by the Cable News Network (CNN), Fox News, and in the UK by BBC News 24, and Sky News. These channels, alongside constantly updating web-based news sites, provide a demand side pressure on politicians to provide instant responses to emerging stories, but also on journalists to constantly update their stories and to find new angles on what they are reporting. These developments have moved intelligence agencies on both sides of the Atlantic closer to media outlets in the sense that part of managing their own relationship with the public is conducted via mass-media outlets. As Sir David Omand points out in his chapter, the management of government secrets and operational information is a crucial and sensitive part of this relationship—failure to manage this relationship properly can result in embarrassment for the government but also have serious operational impacts. His view is particularly interesting because of the role he played within government—as the co-ordinator of governmental intelligence—Omand sat at the apex of competing political, bureaucratic and journalistic pressures and has reflected on these relationships at length.

Another dimension in the relationship between intelligence agencies and the media is the similarity of their operational methodologies. Journalists and spies are two distinct kinds of knowledge producers—they both often operate without the consent of the people they are seeking information about and then produce knowledge for distinct purposes, something that Wyn Bowen's chapter traverses, showing the use of open source intelligence on the work of nuclear weapon counter-proliferators. We can observe a kind of intelligence cycle within the journalistic trade and also a clarity of method that rings true within government spying as well.

Strictly speaking, there is a large degree of separation between the agencies and media outlets. As Richard Aldrich correctly notes in his chapter, the main line of accountability intelligence agencies face today is from the media, be it the traditional media or online media driven by pressure groups and non-governmental organisations. Taken further we can see in Gordon Corera's chapter on counterinsurgency and counter-terrorism that the messages carried by the media, the way they report incidents in Afghanistan and Iraq, and the jihadist use of online media all contribute to the information war being waged between the Allies and Muslim extremists. As Corera notes, this information war is not an esoteric scuffle occurring at the margins of the conflict—it is central to the containment of radical Islam and the jihadist threat—and therefore it is an actual battleground on which the war on terror is being fought. And it is here that Patrick Porter intervenes with his chapter on what he describes as the cultural turn in the war on terror. Not only is this an information war but, he argues, it is also being fundamentally tested at the cultural level as western states struggle to understand cultural difference and how to programme their intelligence and military campaigns to take into account this cultural dissonance.

Examples within this volume abound of media outlets of various kinds being used to transmit official messages or to shape the public debate. Chapman Pincher, as a veteran journalist of some fifty years standing, demonstrates this from his own experiences and in an overt way. His description of running false stories in the *Daily Express* to mislead the Japanese government over British nuclear bomb tests in the Pacific exemplifies how the media can be used to facilitate and advance a covert operation; the UK Foreign Office's defunct and re-established 'Information Research Department' is another example of such practices. The other element of Pincher's chapter that really comes to the fore is the extent to which political, media and intelligence elites are recruited from the same social and educational establishments and backgrounds. This common demographic served Pincher well in navigating around 'the establishment', but it raises question marks over the distinctiveness of these communities; a separation that is at the heart of how they are discussed publicly and in academic publications. Robert Dover and Pierre Lethier, in their chapters on intelligence and popular culture, also suggest that cinematic and televisual depictions of intelligence have been influenced and occasionally led by British, American and French intelligence agencies. The utility of these mass-media portrayals of intelligence has been to educate the public about the work of the agencies, the sorts of threats faced by the state and to shape the discursive ground on which government policies are mapped—the most obvious examples of which were throughout the Cold War (which Lethier covers) and during the so-called 'global war on terror' (which Dover deals with).

INTRODUCTION

This volume provides crucial insights into a complex series of relationships between governments, intelligence agencies and various kinds of media that, in themselves, overlap and intertwine in ways that are not immediately obvious. These complex relationships—characterised by the bifurcated and simultaneous need to provide oversight on the activities of government, whilst providing a supportive role of not jeopardising the national interest have, to a large extent, shaped the international system, and domestic debates about national security. This interesting dynamic—being both led by and shaping events—is at its most acute in the case of popular dramas like *24* and other cinematic efforts, where the gap between fact and fiction is wafer—thin, with intelligence agencies being able to create new realities with the freedoms afforded to them under the war on terror. Given the salience of the globalised, information age, the nature and qualities of the interactions between intelligence and media outlets is worth extended examination, it will help to shape the way our governments and we think about security, our relationship with the state and also what we think is acceptable in the fight against Islamic extremists. As Sun Tzu remarked, 'if you know neither yourself nor your enemy, you will always endanger yourself'.

1

REGULATION BY REVELATION?

INTELLIGENCE, THE MEDIA AND TRANSPARENCY

Richard J. Aldrich

Editors' Notes: Richard Aldrich's current interest in the relationship between globalisation and intelligence is reflected in this chapter. Using the United States as the focus of his study, Aldrich debunks the myth that intelligence agencies and the media lead separate existences. He argues that they have similar operating methodologies and a symbiotic relationship that has been enhanced and reworked by globalisation. His chapter also examines the role that the media, freedom of information and non-governmental organisations play in effectively regulating the activities of intelligence agencies, as he puts it 'regulation by revelation'.

Despite the prolific press coverage of the intelligence services since 9/11, the interaction of this secret realm of government with the media has received little sustained analysis. This chapter focuses primarily on the example of the United States and argues that the relationship between intelligence and the media is long-standing and remarkably close, with its origins lying far back in the first decade of the Cold War. Initially, many writers and journalist willingly co-operated with the intelligence services in the expanding realm of cultural warfare. Thereafter, during the last two decades of the Cold War, other journalists developed a counter-culture of revelation, focusing the spotlight of investigative journalism upon what they considered to be governmental miscreants. Yet even where the relationship was prickly, there remained an underlying appreciation that the journalism and espionage were cognate activities and shared common professional ethics, including the diligent protection of sources.

It is suggested here that more recent changes in this relationship are best understood through the prism of globalisation. In the early 1990s, many western governments wrongly believed that the exponential increase in global trade was contributing to an era of democratic peace and accordingly cut their intelligence budgets by a quarter. They also believed that the intelligence services were now unimportant enough to be made more transparent and to be opened up to increased media coverage. In the United States, both the White House and the CIA made extravagant promises of declassification regarding their recent history. In Europe, the intelligence services embraced a complex culture of avowal and regulation. However, in reality, the 1990s were a period of unprecedented growth for transnational threats, including the 'new terrorism', which also found it convenient to ride the wave of globalisation.

Accordingly, after 9/11, governments quickly sought to re-expand their intelligence services and to tighten state secrecy. Some have argued that this new era of intense security represents a crisis for civil rights in which western democracies are subjected to hyper-surveillance from unaccountable intelligence agencies. Others argue that the media, including new forms of reporting on the Internet, have ensured that the intelligence services are now subject to a 'reverse gaze'. With formalised national systems of intelligence accountability looking weaker, informal accountability through revelations provided by a globalized media in tandem with activists and whistleblowers, may become more important. Certainly, in the United States, nascent legislation that was in preparation in 2008 suggests that prominent American politicians had accepted that this was all but inevitable. Predictably perhaps, executive administrators and the agencies evinced less enthusiasm.

Government secrecy and transparency

When President Lyndon B. Johnson signed the United States Freedom of Information Act on 4 July 1966 he was probably unaware of the transformation in governmental style that was being unleashed. Thereafter, the scandal of Watergate, together with associated intelligence inquiries that began in 1975, led to the strengthening of the Freedom of Information Act under

President Jimmy Carter in 1976. Increased transparency was intended to work together with media scrutiny to provide an additional source of oversight. This was underlined in 1974 when Potter Stewart, a US Supreme Court Justice, explained that he saw the main purpose of the First Amendment as being an attempt to create a fourth estate, that operated outside government and functioned as a vital check on the official elements of governments. Stewart buttressed his arguments by referring to several recent cases in which the US Supreme Court had sanctioned the role of the press as a brake on officials, the most important being the controversy over the Pentagon Papers in 1971. This focused on top secret files relating to the origins and conduct of the Vietnam War which were initially revealed by the press. Nixon had asked for restraining orders but the high court decided otherwise.[1]

Over time, the result of the Freedom of Information Act has been a growing cascade of government openness, with approximately sixty countries around the world emulating the United States and adopting some form of 'right to information' legislation. By the 1990s, the impact of the Internet was also making this information more widely available, allowing it to be accessed by NGOs, the press and campaign groups. Journalists have used such freedom of information provisions frequently when seeking to write about the intelligence services, despite the caveats that exist in most legislation concerning matters of national security. Some have argued that there now exists a growing climate of expectation of some government transparency, even to a degree in the realm of intelligence.

The broad increase of government openness over the last half century, and especially since 1989, is an accepted trend that commands more or less universal assent among academic analysts. Precisely what the most important drivers are is more open to question, but many would point to, among other things, emerging communication and information technologies, the widespread adoption of democratic institutions, the rise of NGOs dedicated to government-watching and the global reach of mass media organizations. Particularly important has been the 'demassification' of the media that is associated with the Internet, allowing issue-based campaign groups and watch-groups to co-ordinate their activities across continents and permitting individuals access to the rapid distribution of information in an unregulated manner.

Interpretations of the long-term effects of this ongoing digital revolution upon government, and especially upon national security agencies, range from the optimistic to the darkly distopian. Few commentators have sought to offer a definitive judgement, since so much of this vast terrain is constantly shifting.

Some have regarded the likely outcomes of new information technologies to be largely positive and straightforward, arguing that they will increase the visibility of all areas of government. This school of thought is not unconnected with those who enjoy an optimistic outlook on globalisation generally. Offering a sort of Whig history for the twenty-first century, they presume an unstoppable tide of democracy, peace, prosperity and openness. At the opposite end of the spectrum, others have presumed that nothing as important as global communications will remain free in the hands of anarchic individuals for long and see information technology as part of the rise of semi-authoritarianism. They would suggest that information technology is used by officials to flood the media with volumes of bland and useless information, reducing the power of the individual citizen. These arguments, whatever their texture, are exceedingly complex and difficult to substantiate, since they are connected at many points to assertions about the increasing interdependence of a deregulated world economy and promises about the withering away/re-invigoration of the state.[2] At every level the pundits are divided on the information revolution. The same is true at a more work-a-day level for the operations of the intelligence services themselves. Some would argue that secret services have been given a boost by the enhanced surveillance and data-processing capabilities of new information technologies. Meanwhile others would argue that the information leviathans of the state struggle to stay abreast of the exponential flow of person-to-person communications through an ever proliferating range of innovative devices.[3]

For many, this is more a story of structure than agency. The impact of technology, notably the prevalence of inter-governmental email and word processors, is also making transparency harder to achieve. Modern government information is vast in its scale and in the speed of its flow; it is also often disaggregated and unstructured. Increasingly, there is no central point of administration and no latter-day equivalent of the main case file. For formal set-piece government inquiries, with large teams of lawyers and investigators, this can be a bonus, as underlined by the Hutton Inquiry. This investigation unearthed a stream of email correspondence, liberally sprinkled with expletives, that civil servants never expected to see the light of day. The lesson that Whitehall's intelligence officers took from the Hutton Inquiry was that everything should be presumed to be disclosable. Yet, for the individual journalist, or the average citizen, extracting meaningful information requires ever greater resources and knowledge of a complex government information system. Alastair Roberts argues that while new technologies should, in theory, increase transparency as the record of activity becomes more comprehensive, the difficulties of navigating the ocean of digitised government information become more challenging and can be exploited by government to create new kinds of obscurity. This also applies to historical research on issues of intelligence and security, since archivists in repositories are increasingly baffled about how to warehouse the terabytes of electronic data, mostly emails, that are coming to them from government departments.[4]

Given their post-9/11 security frame of mind, governments are hardly likely to rush to extend information equivalence to journalists, activists, or ordinary citizens. However, one might argue that in certain areas, especially the international realm, a degree of informal accountability imposed on intelligence services through revelation is the only kind of accountability that exists. Since the 1990s, and especially since 9/11, intelligence, security and policy agencies have rapid expanded the scope of their international co-operation, often working as multinational teams on particular operations. These relationships are not the classic security alliances of the Cold War period, restricted to the mature democracies that are typified by alliances such as NATO in the 1980s. Instead, they often involve improbable partners from the security agencies of countries such as Sri Lanka, Egypt and Ghana. The chances of formal bodies charged with the accountability of intelligence and security agencies being able to introspect into such shared activities is highly remote. Moreover, since 9/11 we have seen stronger government outsourcing of activities to large-scale private security corporations such as Aegis, Blackwater and Halliburton which, as businesses, are notably opaque. Parliamentary bodies find them hard to scrutinise. And yet, the scale of available information leaking into the public domain about some of these activities is considerable.[5]

Given that the formal mechanisms of global and regional governance are relatively weak and have little purchase in this area, the remaining option is global civil society and the untidy business of accountability through 'revelation' by a mixture of journalists, activists and NGOs.[6] How far have these admittedly abstract arguments been paralleled by practical examples? This essay reviews the experience of the United States during the Cold War, the post-Cold War 1990s and then events subsequent to 9/11.

The Cold War

Perhaps the most common misperception concerning modern intelligence agencies is that they have attempted to live in the shadows. They are often interpreted as seeking to conceal themselves from the press and doing their best to avoid contact with the media. The reality is rather different. Over more than fifty years, intelligence agencies have been concerned to shape public perceptions of intelligence, partly because they have substantial budgets to defend. Indeed, much of what we know about modern intelligence agencies has in fact been placed in the public domain deliberately by the agencies themselves, or through other government departments, often using the medium of the press. Moreover, during the Cold War, governments also launched major operations in the realm of propaganda and cultural warfare that have required close co-operation with—even co-option—of the press, academia, cultural organisations and other elements of civil society. For many years, the available forms of non-official cover for western intelligence officers wishing to operate in the Middle East or Asia was mostly limited business, journalism or archaeology. Therefore the worlds of intelligence and the media intersect at many points

Arguably, the intelligence agencies of the United States have always enjoyed a remarkably close relationship with the press, which in part explains the peculiar transparency of the American intelligence community. The fact that we know more about the American intelligence community than almost any other is commonly assumed to reflect a written constitution that provides journalists wishing to write about intelligence with a remarkable degree of formal constitutional protection. However, no less important is the long-standing determination of elements within American intelligence to court the press. This is, in turn, reflects the politicised nature of the American intelligence community. In contrast to most other national communities, where the senior figures tend to be intelligence officers with a lifetime of service, in the United States, political figures are often appointed at the top. These figures have less personal investment in smooth inter-community co-operation and are more likely to 'try and cut their opponents off at the knees'. In addition, the ample budgets enjoyed by US agencies have allowed more active turf-fights between the agencies. The press has often been the happy beneficiary of these Beltway Battles that have spilled onto the front pages of American news-papers. Inter-agency rivalry is a frequent cause of intelligence agencies briefing against each other.[7]

This phenomenon was apparent as early as the autumn of 1945. Those who wished to perpetuate the wartime intelligence organisation know as the Office of Strategic Services (OSS) were stymied in part by an organised series of leaks to the press by military intelligence, designed to conjure up the idea of the creation of an 'American Gestapo'. OSS veterans retaliated by organising a series of books and then Hollywood films detailing the daring exploits of their wartime colleagues. By 1947, many former OSS personnel we being inducted into the new CIA and, here again, the outlines of its activities could be followed in the press. Remarkably, the first 'history' of the CIA appeared as early as 1953, only six years after the formation of the agency, entitled *The Cloak and Dollar War*. Written by a hostile leftwing British journalist, it drew most of its material from a forensic reading of *The Washington Post* and *The New York Times*. At that time, it would not have been possible to piece together an outline history of a national intelligence agency from the press in any country other than the United States.[8]

The CIA was both subject and object for the American press. It is now clear that as early as 1948, when Frank Wisner was appointed director of what was to become the Office of Policy Coordination (OPC), the press was a key vehicle for covert propaganda. Almost immediately, Wisner established operations designed to exert influence within the American media. Key players included Thomas Braden and Cord Meyer who in turn co-opted respected members of *The New York Times*, *Newsweek*, *CBS* and other mainstream media outlets. Leading journalists who participated in these activities included Joseph Alsop, whose writing appeared in some two hundred different newspapers. Some journalists worked for the CIA on a paid basis, but the majority co-operated freely, at the same time hoping for access to privileged information to help them with their work.[9] Liaison between journalists and the CIA immediately prior to a foreign assignment was especially common. Although the primary purpose of this network was externally focused, seeking to influence foreign governments with regard to anti-communism, or indeed other aspects of American foreign policy, there was a constant backwash into the American domestic media, often known as 'blowback'. The CIA planted stories about both the Soviet Union and China, accepting that this material might, for example, feed back into analyses by the State Department. Efforts to smear the Soviet Union by exaggerating its support for rebel groups engaged in terrorism in the 1980s constitutes a notable example.[10]

Predictably perhaps, the CIA took a profound interest in books and press articles about the Cold War battles between the intelligence agencies themselves. Of those sponsored by the CIA—and sister services like MI6—a number were about the so-called intelligence war. In the United States, this included the *Penkovsky Papers*, which was largely ghost written by the CIA. In Britain this included Alexander Foote's 'autobiography' entitled *A Handbook for Spies*, which is thought to have had strong input from MI5 and was said to have been cleared for release by the Chief of MI6. Numerous other defectors on both sides of the Iron Curtain were assisted in publishing their memoirs.[11] No less important was the concerted effort to pre-empt negative publicity about intelligence and to prevent secrets escaping into the public domain, often into the hands of investigative journalists.

During the first two decades of the Cold War this had not been a problem, but by the late 1960s, encouraged by a more critical political climate, investigative journalism directed at intelligence was growing. The first significant example arose in 1963, when the CIA discovered that Random House planned to publish a book about the CIA entitled *Invisible Government* by David Wise and Thomas Ross, covering many of the Agency's early covert actions. When the authors refused to implement deletions, the CIA considered an operation designed to buy up the whole print run of *Invisible Government*, but it became clear that Random House would simply print a second edition. There was anxiety at a high level and in 1964 DCI John A. McCone advised President Lyndon B. Johnson that the consequences were likely to be 'very serious'.[12] Contemporaneously, the CIA tried to stops Edward Yates from making a documentary on the CIA for the National Broadcasting Company (NBC). This attempt at censorship failed and NBC went ahead and broadcast the critical documentary. The appearance of this material in the public domain opened the floodgates to journalistic emulators and over the next decade many more books and press articles focused on intelligence.

The extent of the links between the CIA and the press were only uncovered during the Congressional hearings by the Select Committee to Study Governmental Operations with Respect to Intelligence Activities in 1975. Senator Frank Church showed that it was routine CIA policy to employ journalists and authors on a clandestine basis to feed information to the foreign media as part of a clandestine propaganda war with the Soviet Union. The CIA worked with organisations like the Information Research Department (IRD) in the UK, buying up the rights of books which made appropriate arguments, translating them and then allowing overseas publishers to license them for free. Church asserts that more than a thousand books were sponsored by the CIA before the end of 1967. Keeping this material out of American domestic circulation was almost impossible and so overseas propaganda also washed into the domestic realm. Church's 1976 report asserted:

The CIA currently maintains a network of several hundred foreign individuals around the world who provide intelligence for the CIA and at times attempt to influence opinion through the use of covert propaganda. These individuals provide the CIA with direct access to a large number of newspapers and periodicals, scores of press services and news agencies, radio and television stations, commercial book publishers, and other foreign media outlets

Church's report suggested that this programme had cost the CIA approximately $265 million a year.[13]

Public reactions in the wake of these revelations were intensely hostile, as indeed they were against all forms of covert actions. In the same year that Senator Frank Church's report appeared, George Bush, who had replaced William Colby as Director of Central Intelligence, unveiled a new policy. He insisted that henceforth the CIA would not 'enter into any paid or contract relationship with any full-time or part-time news correspondent accredited by any US news service, newspaper, periodical, radio or television network or station.' However, he insisted that the CIA would continue to work with journalists on an unpaid and voluntary basis, and in practice this represented the majority of past relationships.[14]

The 1980s saw a continued expansion of both journalistic and increasingly serious historical writing about the American intelligence services. This was in part fuelled by the Freedom of Information Act which had allowed researchers partial access to large quantities of intelligence material. There was also some recognition within government that the detailed coverage of intelligence that was increasingly achieved by journalists was only possible because officials were informally handing material to the press in vast quantities. Partly in response to this, in 1982 the Congress passed the Intelligence Identities Protection Act, which forbade the publications of material that would identify undercover intelligence officers and their agents working for the United States.[15] However, in contrast to Britain, legal action was rarely taken against leakers and journalists continued to write books and articles about recent American intelligence activities more or less with impunity. The revelations about the Glomar Explorer operation to recover a sunken Soviet submarine was but one example of publicity leading to an aborted operation.[16]

In April 1986, Bush's successor, William Casey, gave a private presentation before the editors of America's leading newspapers. Carefully crafted, his address contained some fascinating insights. He argued that journalists and intelligence officers have 'much in common'. Both professions, he explained, work at the collection and accurate presentation of information that is intended to lead to informed judgements. Journalists and analysts alike spend hours comparing reports from different sources and struggling to put specific events in the context of broader events and issues. He also argued that another key point of commonality was a moral commitment by both journalists and intelligence officers to the protection of their sources. He also accepted that one of the roles of press reporting was to exercise 'an additional check and balance on the US Government'. Nevertheless, his core purpose was to attack the growing culture of accountability through revelation and he went on to argue that:

In recent years, publication of classified information by the media has destroyed or seriously damaged intelligence sources of the highest value. We do not give our adversaries further satisfaction by advertising these disasters, but misuse of or carelessness with intelligence information has cost lives, discouraged sources from dealing with us, complicated liaison relationships, and compromised expensive and complex technical collections systems.

At the same time, Casey accepted that the most effective way of preventing this material reaching the media was persuading officials not to leak material to the press. He confirmed that the executive was considering yet further laws to protect secrecy and to punish those who leaked information.[17]

Opening up in the 1990s

The 1990s saw a relaxation of the attitudes of intelligence agencies towards secrecy. In the United States this was not a direct result of the end of the Cold War in the sense that professional intelligence officers continued to debate the extent to which Russia was an ongoing threat, or else a new partner for some years. It was more a sense that priorities had changed and that the new targets did not require such a high level of anxiety about security since the counter-intelligence threat appeared to be diminished. In the early 1990s James Woolsey was busy telling Congress that the new hot subject for the agencies was economic intelligence. Overall, there was less emphasis on collection from hard targets and closer regulation of the recruitment of problematic agents. Recent historical material continued to be of intense interest to the media and two directors, Robert Gates and James Woolsey made repeated promises about the declassification of records relating to early covert actions in locations such as Iran, Indonesia and Tibet that had long been of intense interest to journalists.[18]

Although not embracing the gleeful predictions made by academics about the 'end of secrecy', the CIA did witness a lessening of secrecy and a change in institutional culture. Greater transparency was visible both inside and outside the organisation. The barriers between the analytical component of the CIA in the Directorate of Intelligence and the super-secret Directorate of Operations that ran agents were gradually broken down. The CIA's Office of Public Information made greater efforts at internal as well as external communications.

There was an energetic drive on the part of CIA's leadership to be more visible and to make a greater effort to explain the nature of the agency to the public. The CIA's efforts at outreach gave concerted attention to academia with repeated sponsorship of conferences dealing with both current and historical subjects. Typically, a major conference to mark the sixtieth anniversary of the CIA's forerunner organisation, OSS, was held at Langley in 2002.[19]

These developments moved in step with a general policy across the Clinton Administration that sought to encourage transparency. This was most clearly signalled in April 1995 by the Clinton Executive Order on declassification that required all government materials older than twenty-five years to be declassified, unless there were overwhelming security objections. In some cases the backlog of documents ran to many millions of documents. The US Army calculated that its declassification 'mountain' totalled some 269 million pages. The CIA was fortunate to have some 90 million pages exempt as especially sensitive, but still had a further 66 million pages to review for possible declassification. The CIA responded by opening its own declassification factory to deal with the weight of material and eventually chose to deposit much of the resulting product on two massive CREST databases at the US National Archives at College Park in Maryland.[20] The first tranches of material tended to be rather tedious and analytical, but gradually operational and organisational material followed. Critics have observed that to some extent this reflected a tendency to conceive of recent history as a component part of public relations, and in most intelligence agencies institutional history tends to be a subset of public relations management. Although the US intelligence agencies were commendably energetic in devoting resources to the preservation of historical materials for use by academics and for use in the writing of their own internal history, there were also subliminal pressures. Veterans were anxious to see history as a process of memorialization, rather than the objective writing of 'warts and all' history.

Increased transparency was not just due to the way in which states reconceptualized their intelligence services after the Cold War. It was also the result of wider developments including the exponential growth of the Internet. Declassified documents that a decade ago were only available through cumbersome microfiche in the vaults of university libraries were suddenly available to all through Internet reading rooms. Alongside official repositories for declassified material, information activists and campaign groups established reading rooms for material that had made its way into the public domain by other means. The best-known of these facilities is John Young's

Cryptome, but there are many others.[21] The more relaxed attitude to declassification in the early to mid-1990s perhaps help to explain the remarkable devolution of state power onto nongovernmental organizations in the realm of the Internet, something which is often commented on but rarely discussed or explained by globalisation specialists. The early Internet was developed by American defence science programmes in the 1980s. However, a decade later, perhaps as a result of the onrush of global optimism, it was clearly mainstream policy in Washington to hand over much of its regulatory authority to a range of nongovernmental organizations and international committees. This trend continued long after the wider political and economic potential of the Internet had become clear. Although counter-intuitive, some of this policy may have reflected a capacity problem, since the exponential growth of the Internet led many state agencies to shrink back from the prospect of responsibly for this burgeoning octopus. It is mostly authoritarian and semi-authoritarian states in Asia that have tried to control it.[22]

Perhaps the most flamboyant sign of the CIA's more relaxed approach to the media was the opening of the CIA's Entertainment Industry Liaison Office in 1997. This was headed by Chase Brandon, who had worked for the CIA's Directorate of Operations for more than twenty years. The CIA's rationale was that the American public drew much of their information about the internal nature of government from film and novels rather than the broadsheet press. In 1999 a Hollywood film was allowed to bring its cameras to the CIA's headquarters at Langley where some fifty staff were allowed to appear as extras. The work of the CIA's liaison office also involves contributions to factual documentaries that typically appear on the History Channel and Discovery, as well as input into fictional material. Arguably the CIA came to the business of entertainment interface rather late, since both the Pentagon and FBI had enjoyed Hollywood liaison officers for half a century.[23]

Operational aspects of the CIA's relations with the media remained a hotly contested topic. In 1996, the controversy over the CIA using journalists as cover for field operations erupted once more, as globalisation seemed to push intelligence agencies towards greater use of non-official cover. In February 1996, Richard Haas, a former senior NSC regional director for President Clinton was chosen to lead an independent task force on intelligence for the Council on Foreign Relations. Many journalists who erroneously presumed that the practice of using journalists had died out in the 1970s were outraged to discover that this was not the case and a public debate ensued. Legislation passed later in 1996 confirmed the long-standing position—that journalistic cover since the 1970s had been used by the CIA only rarely. From 1996, this required presidential approval. More importantly the existing position, that voluntary co-operation with journalists was also permitted, allowed a large loop-hole to continue. On 17 July 1996, Mortimer B. Zuckerman, chairman and editor in chief of *US News and World R*eport and chairman and co-publisher of *The Daily News* testified before the Senate Select Committee on Intelligence. His worry was partly about the safety of journalists overseas who might be mistaken for operatives, typically in the Middle East. He also underlined the potential damage that such operations did to the press as an institution that performed informal oversight in a democracy. Zuckerman added: 'To be the instrument of government rather than a constitutional check on government would undermine the good that independent journalism does for an open society.'[24]

Although, outwardly the CIA seemed to relax its relations with the press in the 1990s and to disclose more information, it was still anxious about the scale of the leaking of top secret material. Professor Fredrick P. Hitz at Princeton University, who was previously Inspector General at the CIA during the 1990s, has confirmed that the CIA held an investigation after *The Washington Post* discussed a classified report on the Aldrich H. Ames espionage case that had been prepared for Congress. Although Hitz and several of his staff were subjected to polygraph tests, the culprit was never found. Many presumed that the leak originated on Capitol Hill.[25] Further counter-intelligence concerns that emerged in 1999, many related to the Wen Ho Lee spy scandal, prompted a secret 'about turn' on transparency by the intelligence agencies during the last year of the Clinton administration. This amounted to a moral panic about what documents they had released during the last five years.[26] In May 1999 the US Congress voted for stringent mandatory penalties for those revealing the names of current or former US intelligence officers and agents.

Accordingly, even before 2001, the tide was turning against transparency in the realm of intelligence. Broadly, the 1990s had not delivered the era of post-Cold War tranquillity that the proponents of democratic peace had predicted. Elsewhere, post-Cold War revelations undoubtedly produced problems for the intelligence agencies and they were now beginning to count the cost of a new culture of *open government* multiplied by the unregulated power of the Internet. For example, the memoirs of a former MI6 officer, Richard Tomlinson appeared on the Internet before the appearance of Russian and then UK editions. During the same time period a disgruntled individual, as yet unidentified, repeatedly posted lists of MI6 operatives on the Internet. The origin and reliability of these lists remains debateable, though the majority of those named appear to have been intelligence officers.[27]

Clamping down after 9/11

The Bush Administration that came into office in January 2001 was already committed to greater official secrecy as a means to improve policy effectiveness. Indeed, aspects of this ebb tide had been visible even during the last months of the previous administration in 2000. While the events of 9/11 accelerated a pre-existing trend, resulting in a marked emphasis on renewed secrecy, the Bush administration's approach to secrecy was more complex and operated at several levels. Most obviously, secrecy was connected to a re-affirmation of presidential power through offering resistance to accountability, either to the public or to Congress. More broadly, it reflected an abstemious interpretation of who might be appropriate persons to receive information and, most importantly, an ideological commitment to a different style of government.[28]

The most fascinating example is the expansion of archival 'reclassification' that was begun in the last year of Clinton's administration, closing down files that had already been released to journalists and researchers. While the reclassification programme of 2000 was limited to a small selection of State Department Lot Files, under Bush the activity became gargantuan. As Matthew Aid has shown, by 2003, the programme had examined no less than 43.4 million pages of documents held by the US National Archives on a sampling basis. It scrutinised 6.1 million pages of documents in the archives on a page-by-page basis. As a result, some 55,500 pages of material that had been open to public inspection for a considerable time were withdrawn from the open shelves at College Park, including, remarkably, mundane material relating to intelligence failures during the approach of the Korean War. It also included material from the Presidential Libraries that had already been published in *Foreign Relations of the United States* and which was available in every major university library in the world. Notwithstanding the absurdity of this 'stable door' activity, the agencies felt they should withdraw such documents 'on principle', underlining the ideological well-spring of this new commitment to secrecy.[29]

There were many other practical examples of the new secrecy. Typically, in December 2001, the US Attorney General, John Ashcroft announced an inter-agency task force to review ways to combat leaks of classified information to the press. Meanwhile, in legal cases government increasingly cited state privilege, refusing to provide information to the court because it simply deemed the matter too secret. This has been especially important in legal cases relating to intelligence activities. Law suits that have sought redress for individuals who have allegedly suffered mistaken extraordinary rendition, or which have sought judicial review of the NSA's warrantless wiretapping activities, have fallen at the first fence because of the assertion of state privilege. The collapse of these cases has the further effect of stemming the flow of information about such cases into the public domain.[30]

The journalist, Ted Gup, has argued that the rise of secrecy since 9/11 has been given insufficient attention by the press. The media, he argues, rarely writes about secrecy *per se*, since it can appear to be an admission of defeat by investigative reporters brought up on stirring tales of Watergate. The press also tends to avoid detailed discussion of increasing secrecy since many regard it as a nerdish subject 'for policy wonks and political scientists'. Gup argues:

In so doing we have tended to overlook one of the more significant stories of our lifetime—an emerging 'secretocracy' that threatens to transform American society and democratic institutions. Systemic or indiscriminate secrecy involves the calculated use of secrecy as a principle instrument of governance, a way to impede scrutiny, obscure process, avoid accountability, suppress dissent, and concentrate power. The tendency to abuse secrecy is as old as power itself, but prior to 9/11 it was usually checked, and even its abuses were cyclical.[31]

While the change of administration in 2001 was important, structural factors have also contributed to secrecy in unexpected ways. The increase of what is termed 'networked governance', through which departments across national governments are able to share information, has resulted in unintentional barriers to transparency, even though it has resulted in better international cooperation. NATO is a good example of a growing international organisation that has emphasised information transfer between partners. Yet the same formulas that allow governments to share information with each other also limit the ability of citizens to access even unclassified information. New Central and East European states joining NATO have in some cases been required to water-down their freedom of information legislation passed after 1989. Moreover, multiple bureaucracies working together rarely have the ability to declassify or release information on their own.[32]

Restrictions on the press since 9/11 have not been all about government. Some have been self-imposed. Insidious financial pressures have born heavily on news organizations leading to substantial cuts in reporters and support staff. Seasoned reporters complain that, compared to the 1990s, news organisations do relatively little investigative reporting and increasingly wait for the news to come to them through wire services and press releases. The most marked change is in the world of television documentaries. The once large research teams of flagship investigative programmes have been replaced by the buying in of programmes put together by freelancers. These programmes are made on tight budgets and often literally edited in someone's living room. As a result, the power of journalistic probes into the executive branch of government in the UK and the US have severely diminished. Alongside these market-based constrictions there has also been a shift in texture and public taste. Media managers now tend to demand documentaries with a stronger human interest focus and less attention to the wider policies of the executive.[33]

Moreover, for approximately two years following 9/11, the American press arguably adopted a war mentality that was largely supportive of government. This is often difficult for external observers to understand, but for those who were in New York or Washington on 11 September 2001, the immediate events certainly felt like a war. Thereafter, during the approach of the invasion of Iraq, the press remained in 'war mode' and was initially reluctant to operate as an overtly critical counter-balance during the public debates that explored the policy options and the arguments about Iraqi WMD. Overall, the American press was remarkably uncritical of the intelligence-based assertions of Bush administration about WMD and the related decision regarding the invasion of Iraq. In retrospect both the *New York Times* and the *Washington Post* reviewed their own activities in 2002 and 2003 and were openly critical of their own stance, admitting that they had failed to probe the intelligence case for war vigorously and act as an independent source of oversight.

With the initiation of the war in Iraq and during the prolonged insurgency that followed, military units and intelligence agencies have been overstretched. This has led to increased out-sourcing and the privatization of services once performed by governments. This in turn has further limited the ability to access information. In Iraq over the period 2003–8, the numbers of contractors reached an estimated highpoint of 25,000. Efforts to 'surge' the intelligence effort against terrorism has resulted in the widespread use of contractors by the intelligence services and one estimate put the CIA's use of private contractors as high as 30% of its total workforce, in many cases the appointees being recent retirees from its own staff. Whereas government agencies need to take some account of freedom of information laws and systems for oversight and accountability, obtaining information from private contractors is harder. In some cases their record-keeping is remarkably poor. Legislatures will need to give attention to this area as more government functions in the security sector are privatized.[34]

Beyond 2003, as more journalists began to recognise the problematic nature of events in Iraq, the media corrective often took the form of more investigative journalists writing books. Indeed, arguably one of the trends that we have seen in journalistic writing about intelligence since 9/11 is the revival of the book format. While many critics of government policy in the UK and the US have been uncomfortable about the notion of their countries being at war, journalists have nevertheless adopted many of the modes of reporting that we have seen in previous wars. Vulnerable to criticism that immediate reporting of security issues might jeopardise intelligence activities or military operations, many have opted for the slower burn full story set out between hard covers. This mimics an approach taken during the Second World War, when journalists found that some of their best stories were censored, or self-censored. If their stories appeared contemporaneously with operations, or even a few days after the event, they were deemed potentially helpful to the enemy. Loathe to discard good material, journalists diverted this material into books and diaries written for publications that often appeared a year or so after the event. The format of the war-diary written for publication was led by William Shirer, the CBS correspondent in Germany until 1941, and the fact that his books proved to be best-sellers lent additional dynamism to the genre.[35] Best-selling accounts of the approach of the Iraq war or else the occupation written by figures such as Seymour Hersh and George Packer have allowed journalists to bring to light torrents of material that would not have made it into the newspapers.[36]

Government was not long in responding to these lengthy exposes of intelligence. Perhaps the most dramatic development since 9/11 has been the active prosecution of American journalists and officials for the breach of state secrecy. The first important example was the case of Valerie Plame Wilson, a CIA operations officer whose covert identity was classified and who was also the wife of former Ambassador Joseph C. Wilson IV. At various times she had operated abroad under non-official cover, typically as an 'energy consultant' for Brewster-Jennings Inc., alleged to be a CIA front-company. She retired in December 2005 after twenty years with the CIA as a result of her classified cover being compromised by an American journalist in the summer of 2003. On 14 July 2003, she was named as a CIA covert operative in a syndicated column in *The Washington Post*. The context was the growing debate over claims that the George W. Bush administration had exaggerated unreliable claims that Iraq intended to purchase uranium yellowcake from Niger to enhance its case for pre-emptive war in Iraq. The public disclosure of the covert CIA identity of 'Valerie Plame' led to what has become known as the *Plame affair*. This prompted a CIA leak grand jury investigation, which resulted in the conviction of Lewis 'Scooter' Libby for perjury, obstruction of justice, and making false statements to federal investigators.[37]

Perhaps even more vexing to the CIA and the Bush administration generally were a series of stories by Dana Priest in *The New York Times* in November 2005 that revealed the CIA's use of secret prisons in Europe. This led to parallel inquiries in Europe by the Council of Europe and the European Parliament and a host of national inquiries by oversight bodies in specific European countries. American intelligence agencies accused European governments of hypocrisy, since they had used the intelligence obtained from the detainees to enhance their own security. Meanwhile, European agencies responded by accusing the CIA of being an unreliable partner who could not keep a secret. Again, internal leak investigations followed. In April 2006, the CIA dismissed intelligence officer Mary O. McCarthy following one of the most extensive leak inquiries in its history. Although the CIA stated that it was not asserting that McCarthy was the person who informed the Pulitzer Prize-winning pieces on secret prisons, the CIA alleged that she had undisclosed contacts with journalists, among them Dana Priest. It is possible that McCarthy was the victim of intra-agency conflict, given the animosity between the DCI General Michael Hayden and the CIA Inspector General, John L. Helgerson, for whom McCarthy worked. The investigation involved the use of the polygraph on dozens of officials who had access to compartmentalised information on the secret prisons. Although McCarthy was close to retirement, the action was widely interpreted as a serious warning to all those within the CIA that their jobs and pensions were in jeopardy if they indulged in further leaks.[38]

In 2008, the government took the unprecedented step of indicting the Pulitzer prize-winning reporter, James Risen of *The New York Times*. Risen was perhaps best known for breaking a controversial story concerning telephone interception by the National Security Agency. Forbidden to tap the communications of Americans without warrant, NSA nevertheless engaged in the warantless tapping of international communications originating or terminating in the United States. Risen won the Pulitzer Prize for this and several other investigations in 2006. No less controversial was his book published in early 2006, entitled *State of War*. This work alleged that in 2000, a

CIA operation conducted jointly with Israel, entitled 'Operation Merlin', backfired badly. The intention was to impede Iran's nuclear weapons program by a deception campaign that would provide flawed plans for nuclear weapons. Risen asserts that the mistakes were identified and corrected by the Iranians and also alleges that the CIA lost a number of agents in Iran as a result. The Israeli intelligence service, Mossad, is thought to have complained bitterly about the leakage of this information. During March and April 2008, former government officials were confronted with phone records revealing conversations with Risen. This turn of events was not without irony since his 2006 Pulitzer Prize was for articles that exposed eavesdropping. Professional journalist organisations have asserted that the Bush administration was trying to limit press freedoms by intimidating reporters and their sources and was now advising journalists that they should stop using their home and office phones to communicate with sources on sensitive topics.[39]

The numerous lengthy books on recent intelligence matter by journalists have been fantastically revealing. They have also been important in proving that news managers are wrong in deciding that there is no public appetite for traditional in-depth investigative reporting. Bob Drogin's study of the case of *Curveball*, the phoney Iraqi defector who informed the case for war put to the UN by Secretary of State Colin Powell, is a powerful example.[40] The public's appetite for both detailed books and their willingness to devour huge amounts of official documentation have surprised news editors. Indeed, Stephen Aftergood has argued that the Internet is gradually changing the nature of national security reporting by the press. Now, newspapers not only cover national security issues but also use their web-based versions to offer direct access to source documents. They have discovered that, rather like policy-makers who have increasing access to online-databases and so have developed a taste for assessing raw intelligence themselves, newspaper readers also want to become their own DIY analysts. 'They don't merely want to be told what some new official document says, they want to see the document for themselves.' Aftergood argues that this is resulting in a virtuous circle, since direct access to government documents creates a new culture of expectation and therefore a subsequent demand for greater availability.[41]

Equally revealing is the nascent universe of blogs where citizens, officials and retired officials mingle and discuss current affairs and national policy. While they allow active citizens to confer with other individuals, those inside the loop often drop in titbits of information or seek to correct misunderstandings. The blog is the security officer's nightmare and the US government has recently moved to restrict access by serving military personnel to blogs, citing concerns about current operations. All parties recognise that regulation through untrammelled revelation is problematic. Stephen Aftergood, director of the Federation of American Scientists (FAS) Project on Secrecy claims that he is regularly in receipt of government instruction manuals from open sources that he chooses not to put on his FAS website. Subjects for judicious self-censorship by Aftergood have included manuals on subjects such as the preparation and use of improvised explosives, the training of snipers and the operation of shoulder-fired missiles.[42]

While journalists and bloggers often try to use their discretion about 'revelations', in reality those outside the loop have no practical reference point from which to identify what is sensitive and what is not sensitive. Moreover, their amateur efforts to self-censor or redact sensitive material can prove ineffective. In April 2000, *The New York Times* acquired an illicit copy of the classified internal history of the CIA/MI6 coup carried out in Iran in 1953. This coup removed Prime Minister Mossadeq and installed the Shah, a rather craven figure whom the intelligence services had nicknamed 'Boy Scout'. The lengthy document entitled 'Clandestine Service History—Overthrow of Premier Mosaddeq of Iran—November 1952–August 1953' was judged relatively non-sensitive, but *The New York Times* decided to redact the names of local Iranian collaborators, correctly surmising that the Iranian security agencies have long memories and might take action against the family members and descendants of the Iranians named as CIA/MI6 footsoldiers. The document was duly redacted with blacked out sections before it was placed on *The New York Times* website. Unfortunately, the blacking out was undertaken electronically, over the top of the document, and not on the original scanned into the system. Accordingly, if the CIA internal history was accessed on an old computer that ran slowly, it would download a page of the CIA history and then add the redactions some seconds later. In other words the full text was available for a few tantalising seconds and by freezing the document at sequential points all was revealed. Predictably, the full text was soon in the public domain.[43] Fortunately, no reverberations from the full release of the CIA history of the Iran coup have been reported.

Regulation by revelation?

Despite their frequent moments of friction, intelligence agencies and the media have many similarities. As William Casey pointed out in 1986, they not only have similar overall functions, namely to inform and enlighten, but they also employ similar methodologies, not least the central role of secret informants. They interact at many more points than we realise and their mutual influences are complex. What is also striking is that all the various parties simultaneously believe that they are losing the battle for dominance in this rapidly changing arena. Investigative journalists write long essays bemoaning the fact that their activity is a dying art form. Meanwhile, intelligence agencies in European and the United States are seemingly anxious about figures like Seymour Hersh and sometimes reject options simply because they do not believe that they can keep the operations secret for very long.

Moreover, despite a sustained campaign by the Bush administration to tighten up secrecy and to punish indiscreet officials, the White House seems resigned to leaks. In October 2003, President Bush responded to tongue in cheek questions from the press corps about the latest leak inquiry and was inclined to admit defeat on secrecy:

Randy, you tell me, how many sources have you had that's leaked information that you've exposed or have been exposed? Probably none. I mean this town is a—is a town full of people who like to leak information. And I don't know if we're going to find out the senior administration official. Now, this is a large administration, and there's a lot of senior officials … I have no idea whether we'll find out who the leaker is-partially because, in all due respect to your profession, you do a very good job of protecting the leakers. [44]

Yet those who hanker after transparency as a route to good government simultaneously despair of achieving real transparency. They argue that reporters mis-represent their rate of success by writing about the small number of secrets that they have uncovered. The way in which they write them up tends to cover up all the things they have failed to find out about. The citizen may feel the press is able to place before them the majority of the facts but they are probably wrong.

The field is rendered more complex because the media in heavily engaged in battles over the way that intelligence is represented in the recent past, as well as the present. Journalists are no less interested in the intelligence operations of the last few decades than contemporary historians. Moreover, there is a growing recognition that the 'history' of the CIA filters into the public consciousness as much through film and fiction as it does through factual accounts. This in turn has led to a broader conception of the points at which intelligence agencies, the media and public perceptions intersect. As we have seen, in the 1990s, the CIA began to take an interest in how the agency was represented in film and fiction, opening its Entertainment Industry Liaison Office in Hollywood in 1997. A decade later, its nemesis, the America Civil Libraries Union appointed its own Entertainment Industry Liaison, staffed by Allison Walker, who successfully launched a 'Close Guantanamo' campaign to coincide with the 2008 Oscars. She persuaded many of the stars attending the ceremony to wear orange ribbons. What is clear is that the battle over the visualisation of intelligence in the media spread far beyond the pages of *The New York Times* and *The Washington Post*. The various adversaries now pay no less attention to film, fiction and the Internet.

The revelation of misdeeds at Guantanamo and Abu Ghraib have, inevitably, led to a further swing of the pendulum. In April 2008, Senator Barack Obama sponsored a new Free Flow of Information Act. This effectively constitutes a proposed 'shield' law that would increase the legal protection extended to reporters who were revealing abuses and would also protect them against any compulsion to disclose their sources. Interestingly, this Bill received support not only from Senator Hilary Clinton, but also from Senator John McCain. On 15 April 2008, McCain addressed the Associated Press and explained that, after a lot of thought, he had narrowly decided to support the shield legislation. He was concerned that it was a licence to do harm, but accepted that it was outweighed by the fact that it was also 'a licence to do good, to disclose injustice and unlawfulness and inequities, and to encourage their swift correction.' McCain specifically cited the revelations about the events at Abu Ghraib through the illegal disclosure of classified Army material as evidence for why regulation through revelation was needed. Predictably perhaps, the Attorney General Michael Mukasey, the Homeland Security Secretary Michael Chertoff and the Director of National Intelligence Mike McConnell all declared their opposition, denouncing it as a leaker's charter. However, there are unlikely to prevail against what appears to be a united political front.[45]

Accordingly, the future points towards a more nuanced legal regime for the reporting of intelligence matters that would provide, not only for disclosure when reporters consider it to be in the public interest, but also a formula for non-disclosure by the press that would try to prevent obvious harm. The development of legislation that might seek such common ground would be a novel departure for the United States, but would arguably reflect a new realism. As George Bush observed, the leakers rarely get caught and are already raising their game to avoid surveillance. The sight of Pulitzer Prize winners heading for jail is unlikely to be considered edifying. In the long-term, the executive seems to have accepted that their only hope of preventing really damaging leaks is to secure the co-operation of the press themselves. This in turn will require some acceptance by the executive of a degree of 'regulation by revelation'. This does not herald the apocalyptic 'end of secrecy' or indeed the 'death of privacy' that has been gleefully forecast by some academics. It does suggest an increasing sensitivity to what Stephen Aftergood has called the tensions between secrecy and citizenship. Accordingly, we are likely to see the continued empowerment of the dissident individual in partnership with the press and formal oversight mechanisms as a source of constraint on the activities of the intelligence services.

2

INTELLIGENCE SECRETS AND MEDIA SPOTLIGHTS
BALANCING ILLUMINATION AND DARK CORNERS

David Omand

Editors' Notes: In a career that included being director of the Government Commun-ications Headquarters (GCHQ), a seat on the Joint Intelligence Committee (JIC) and becoming the first UK Security and Intelligence Coordinator, Sir David Omand had ample opportunity to reflect on the challenging relationship between intelligence agencies and media outlets. In this chapter he highlights the symbiosis in the two fields, in terms of methods and ethos, and the power to influence the political canvas. He also highlights the challenge for agencies of being held to account by the media, while also providing a useful tool for government to inform the citizenry about the threats posed to national interests and how they are being confronted.

Journalists and spooks have more in common these days than they may like to admit. Both professions seek to uncover what is hidden. Both professions work to deadlines and have sources which they guard with care. The relation-ship between journalist and spook is never more tangled than when the former writes about the latter, and adopts their investigative practices, or the latter tries to exploit the access of the former.

Journalists can make a living out of exposing secrets, using all the tools learned from the secret world—informants, bugging, sting operations and the rest. Over the Cold War period an increasingly confident media, not least through the investigations of Chapman Pincher, scarred the UK Intelligence Agencies by publicising their very existence and exposing the nature of their activity as well bringing to light their scandals such as the penetrations by the 'Cambridge spies'.[1] Intelligence failures were publicised, while inevitably most successes remained hidden.[2] Popular authors found that they could live off writing about the tragedies and triumphs, not to speak of the occasional hero- ism, of those working in the secret world. The intelligence agencies for their part drew tame journalists into their orbit as unwitting channels for informa- tion operations or simply in the hope of having their work portrayed in a bet- ter light. The natural cover of the international correspondent proved ideally suited for information-gathering (the 1976 Church Committee report, pre- pared by the US Senate Select Committee on Intelligence, revealed that more than fifty journalists served clandestinely as agents during the early part of the Cold War, a practice that now requires Presidential authority).[3] The Cold War archives are now revealing the many instances where the intelligence Agencies of the West sought to use the media to further anti-Communist information operations, such as the stories planted overseas by the UK Foreign Office Information Research Department.[4]

Like charges repel like, in this case I hope positive to positive rather than negative to negative. The worlds of secret intelligence and journalism have thus often been forced to interact but have never co-existed without strain. Today the Fourth Estate of the traditional media, and we might add the Fifth Estate of the Internet bloggers, finds itself once again in a tense relationship with the counter-terrorism security and intelligence community (what we might construe as the $9\frac{3}{4}^{th}$ Estate?).[5] A *modus vivendi* is needed. The public cannot be adequately protected from terrorism without pre-emptive secret intelligence. Public confidence in the integrity of those who gather, assess and use such information matters. How those processes and results are reported by the media bears directly on the necessary level of trust that the public must have in the good faith, professionalism and common sense of the work of the security authorities, as well as on their continuing ability to use secret sources and methods. Yet much of the media remains institutionally suspicious of the value of intelligence work while being over-fascinated by its trade-craft. The use, and many would say misuse, of secret intelligence by government in justi- fying their case for pre-emptive actions and for counter-terrorism measures is a natural and justified target for investigative reporting. This chapter addresses the interacting dilemmas faced respectively by governments, their secret intelligence agencies and the media over the reporting and analysis of activities that are based on secret intelligence.

In order to bring the issues more vividly to mind, imagine a live television current affairs interview in front of a studio audience as well as the cameras. On stage, sweating under the studio lights, are an experienced and forceful media interviewer and a government Minister. The cross-examination might be part of a programme examining the justification for a recent controversial police counter-terrorism raid, or perhaps new security measures to be imposed on air travellers, or the introduction of controversial counter-terrorist legislation. All topical subjects. Let us also add into our mental picture senior officers from the intelligence community and their police colleagues watching the broadcast anxiously from their homes or offices. And for a moment consider what might be the layers of conscious and unconscious motives influencing these characters in what is after all an everyday encounter in these times.

We may suppose first that the interviewer is looking to enhance the reputation of the programme for fearless reporting and exposure of the real stories behind the news. The programme's researchers may well have revealed that the public is confused or sceptical following excited newspaper headlines about whatever is the latest security issue on which the Government's statements to date have not been entirely convincing (recent ESRC research highlights the extent of British public perception that the government exaggerates and the media magnify the terrorist threat).[6] The public does not want the Government Minister let off lightly. In the words of Jeremy Paxman,

that we ask the questions the average reasonably intelligent member of the public would like to see asked. And if you ask a question, you owe it to the audience to get an answer. Even if you have to ask the question more than once. Or more than a dozen times.[7]

The interviewer will be very conscious therefore that the wider public looks to the interview as a holding to account of the government over a matter that has already been dramatised by the media as of crucial interest. Paxman again,

News is the most important element in the overall ecology of television. It is the canary in the miner's cage.

It may also be that at the back of the interviewer's mind is the fear that ratings are being scrutinised and, given the huge increase in competition in the media, commercial decisions affecting programmes and channels may be pending. Such considerations are hard to separate out too from natural concerns over personal repute and the inevitable peer pressure on the interviewer following each performance. In some cases there may well be back history of previous encounters, won and lost, with this 'here today, gone tomorrow' Minister.[8]

To achieve his desired result, the interviewer has to generate passion based on bringing an emotional charge to the issue. As ex-Prime Minister Tony Blair concluded:

Impact is what matters. It is all that can distinguish, can rise above the clamour, can get noticed. Impact gives competitive edge.[9]

The interviewer knows too that the presence of the live audience enhances this sense of theatre. That may have been assisted by the use earlier in the programme of dramatic or shocking footage (quite possibly these days shot by a member of the public with a videophone) from some scene of terrorism or of security forces action. The issue may have been deliberately framed in terms of recalling past controversies/bungles, well illustrated with appropriate library film clips and over-dramatic music. Perhaps retired police and security officers will have been interviewed as 'shadow expertise' giving their (quite possibly uninformed or dated) opinions. The programme editors may indeed have spiced up the introduction by recalling, if only to dismiss, parallels with past conspiracy theories or scandals so as to create the impression that there is more to be uncovered, and this is the programme that will do just that. The editorial function is key here since 'to edit is to choose'.

The audience will be expecting gladiatorial entertainment as much as enlightenment from the interview itself. The experienced interviewer knows how to generate that interest given the short modern attention span by ruthlessly homing in on repeated simple statements of the issue and cutting short complicated explanations. In the words of the apocryphal editorial guidance of the *Economist* magazine, 'simplify then exaggerate'[10] or as Paxman concludes

All television is artifice to some degree. Let's not pretend it isn't. Even the news: when we see a reporter in waders broadcasting live from a flooded street, do we honestly think the whole town is underwater, and with it the OB truck? Every time you stick a noddy into an interview, that's artifice. Even the live television interview itself is artifice. The key thing is that the audience have to be able to have confidence in us to show them something which, while being manufactured, is a fair representation of the true state of affairs.[11]

The Government Minister will have a similar mix of institutional and personal objectives. This may be the best opportunity to put over the Government's argument and deny the circling sharks further blood in the water (or at least make it more likely that it will be the blood of another). The Minister will be uneasily aware that his answers have to convey the Government's case on counter-terrorism with different emphasis to two very different segments of a British audience, quite apart from any international dimension which is usually present with terrorism. Towards the majority domestic audience, the intention will be to provide encouragement that public security remains the top priority and that the Government is not shirking taking tough measures against those responsible. The minority audiences of the UK's Muslim communities, however, need to be able to hear reassurance in these words, for example that the Government's policies and actions will be non-discriminatory in their application and that the Government continues to safeguard civil liberties for all. Demotic messages therefore, simultaneously tough and tender, firm yet fair.

At the back of the Government's thinking, which the hapless Minister has to represent, may even be the hope that the very robustness of the approach being advocated wrong-foots the political Opposition by painting them as weak on terror, and may at least help keep backbenchers in line. Such accusations of politicisation of the debate are often levelled in the media.[12] As Matthew d'Ancona has complained,

We have looked through the wrong end of a telescope and refracted a worldwide phenomenon through the prism of everyday politics.[13]

Unlike the position over policy towards violence in Northern Ireland over the last thirty years the Minister has to speak knowing that there is no current UK cross-Party consensus on the correct responses to international terrorism.

The public discourse also has to convey potentially contradictory messages about the terrorist threat itself. On the one hand, in order to justify Government policies and the actions of the security authorities, the Minister will need to leave the audience in no doubt about the gravity of the security threat facing the nation. To heighten that message, the possibility of even more widespread or serious terrorist outrages may be put forward, including the literally awful prospects should neo-jihadist extremists obtain weapons of mass effect.[14] It will be tempting to cite in support of this line statements from the intelligence community, such as the periodic speeches by the Director General of the Security Service. Such excursions of senior intelligence officials into the public domain have as a result provoked from British columnists regular if unjust complaints that their timing is stage-managed to fit political calculations, and that there is exaggeration of the threat, such as from Simon Jenkins in *The Guardian*:

I strongly suspect Britain's secret service is doing a good job and has more than enough money already. There have been only two bombing incidents, in London and Glasgow, since 9/11. But, while being freed of bombs, we have not been freed of fear. Scaremongering by ministers, the police and security officials has bordered on the hysterical.[15]

Nevertheless, the Minister needs to convince the public that the course the Government is following will generate more security. Further, he needs at all times to reassure the public, and the international audience, that the UK is still a safe place in which to live, work and invest (the official strategic aim of UK policy in that respect is 'to reduce the risk from international terrorism, so that people can go about their daily lives freely, and with confidence').[16] There is no inherent contradiction between the Minister maintaining that the personal likelihood of an individual being caught up in a terrorist attack remains tiny, much lower than the everyday risks we manage such as driving on a motorway, and yet pointing out that, even if the individual likelihood is small, the national risk is large if vulnerability and impact, including economic confidence, social cohesion and political consequences, remain high. But pity the poor Minister who is trying in his interview to find the words to reassure the public that it is safe to get on with normal life, while at the same time helping the public understand that for the whole of government there has to be a compelling priority to reduce the overall level of national risk. This dynamic in public information between individual and national risks is important and difficult.

The Minister will know much more about the true nature of the threat from secret intelligence than he or she has been advised can be revealed. The Minister knows at least in general terms the basis of the secret intelligence on which police and security authorities have been taking operational decisions day in day out and will have seen the intelligence assessments on which the Departmental policy advice to Government relies. The Minister may well have had to adjudicate in arguments between his lawyers and security advisers where, as often is the case, issues of subjudice rules arise in order not to risk prejudice to forthcoming terrorist trials, or arguments with the intelligence agencies and police over how much of the intelligence assessment can be revealed. A dramatic case in point was the furore over the deployment of a large Army and police presence to Heathrow airport in February 2004. It was through unofficial briefing rather than an on the record statement that it became known that the threat concerning the authorities (never subsequently confirmed) was of a surface to air missile attack:

Confirming that Mr Blair had personally authorised the Heathrow deployment, the Prime Minister's official spokesman said the decision to draft in troops and armoured vehicles was 'an ongoing operation in relation to a specific threat'...Mr Blair's spokesman would not disclose details of the threat at Heathrow, but did not deny reports that it involved a possible missile attack on an aircraft 'There are good operational and security reasons why we are not commenting in detail on this' he said.

The following day's newspapers were critical of this reticence:

Police and the Army yesterday mounted the biggest security operation seen in Britain, amid confusing signals from ministers over the scale of the threat from international terrorism.[17]

That accusation, of confusion in government, is one that the media will be quick to level whenever there is less than complete and immediate disclosure of the reasons for the steps being taken. That, however, is a degree of transparency that often the police in briefing the media cannot safely authorize. What then may result, in well-meaning attempts to ease this conflict, are unauthorised and partial briefings, but these may well just add to the sense of confusion.

The main concern of the watching intelligence and police officers is therefore likely to be over what the Minister may be led on to say during the interview. Under pressure will he or she fall back on the counter-argument that 'if you could see the intelligence I see' or go as far as 'Let me spell it out. We know from our intelligence of the risk that....' Such formulae have the effect of highlighting the role of the intelligence community and indeed publicly placing the primary responsibility for precipitating action on the intelligence agencies. Such debate then opens up a further line of questioning about how the intelligence community can know what it claims to know, and what it had to do to obtain it. How far does a society that believes in individual liberty and the rule of law turn a blind eye to alleged abuses by security authorities pursuing 'a war on terror'. The interviewer may attack here on at least three distinct flanks. The first might be to explore how information was obtained from human sources, for example in presenting allegations of ill-treatment of suspects during interrogation or coercion during recruitment of agents. The second is to pursue allegations of invasion of personal privacy that may be potentially involved in the techniques of modern electronic surveillance and data mining. A third approach might be to probe the extent to which British authorities are taking action on the basis of intelligence obtained by cooperating countries overseas that may use methods that would be prohibited for use by British authorities. The effect of such questioning is to highlight the extent to which it is now essential for the intelligence agencies to gain public and legislative support for the continued collection of secret intelligence for public security. All three tracks involve public discussion of what should be the acceptable ethical limits on the sources and methods of secret intelligence, a hard debate to have when those sources and methods must inevitably remain largely secret.

It may well be (usually is) the case that the television interview is dealing with security events that did not go entirely according to plan. In which case what I call 'the Rififi factor' comes into play. The media have been exposed to too many heist and secret agent movies in which all goes according to meticulous planning (relying on impossibly perfect information, literally 'Mission Impossible'). The presence of Clausewitz's 'friction' is not a failure but a demonstration of his profound truth that no plan survives the shock of contact with reality. The interviewer may well then lead the discussion back to Iraq on the lines of 'their intelligence was deficient then, what makes you so sure, Minister, that they are right now...?'. And will the Minister under such further pressure imply a distancing of the Government from its professional advisers ('but this was information that we/the police were assured by the intelligence authorities was reliable' or 'but we can only act on the basis of the assessment of the threat we are given and that had not highlighted this problem')? If so, the result is to push the intelligence community further forward into the public consciousness, and to heighten the need for public confidence.

As if all that was not enough, we can add deeper agendas of hidden meaning to our analysis of the television studio discourse. The intelligence officers will be very conscious that among the viewers will very likely be a few terrorist supporters themselves, who have every interest in tracking the development of the work of the security authorities, and in pursuing information operations of their own exploiting any incautious Government statements. In an Internet age with modern search engines of course any indiscretion can easily picked up by the opponent, and can prejudice operations (or the prospect of a conviction in Court).

Perhaps the Minister will let slip innocent sounding detail that may nevertheless provide valuable hints that can be exploited for counter-intelligence purposes, as when Prime Minister Baldwin in the House of Commons under pressure to justify the 1927 raid on the offices of the Russian trade company ARCOS, revealed enough for Moscow to deduce that their ciphers were being read.

Or worse perhaps, there will be fear that one of the aides or special advisers in government privy to Ministerial briefing might already have given a backgrounder to the producer or researcher for the programme in which, strictly off the record of course, sensitive details of the case may have been revealed to establish the adviser's credibility or to spice up the account. A well-known US example was the sudden loss in 1998 of the ability of the signals intelligence agencies to intercept Bin Laden's satellite communications, a loss that followed revealing articles in the US newspapers, and there are several more recent examples. Such material may then be deployed to trip up the Minister and make him look out of touch or unduly evasive.

These are justified fears, as it turns out, since there is unfortunately a history of such briefing—that is, leaking—for tactical political gain or to acquire media leverage. In relation to intelligence and security issues damaging disclosures can come from the reciprocal favours that fuel the intense relationship between the media and the political class, for example when made privy to intelligence successes. Neither side is well placed to be able to assess the true sensitivity of the information being passed. As Metropolitan Police deputy commissioner Peter Clarke said of one incident:

What I am talking about is the deliberate leaking of highly sensitive operational intelligence, often classified, and the unauthorised release of which can be a criminal offence. What is clear is that there are a number, a small number I am sure, of misguided individuals who betray confidences. Perhaps they look to curry favour with certain journalists, or to squeeze out some short-term presentational advantage—I do not know what motivates them...The people who do this either do not know or do not care what damage they do. If they do know, then they are beneath contempt. If they do not know, then let me tell them. They compromise investigations. They reveal sources of life-saving intelligence. In the worst cases they put lives at risk. I wonder if they simply do not care.

An encounter in a television studio is just one small very local skirmish in a global battle of information. As General Rupert Smith has put the point:

If you are fighting for the will of the people, however many tactical successes you achieve they will be as naught if the people do not think you are winning. It is by communicating through the media that this understanding is in large measure achieved.[18]

The security authorities will be very conscious that terrorism is only possible because of the power of modern media to broadcast and amplify the violent communications of the terrorists. The neo-jihadists know this, and have proved themselves adept at using the Internet:

I say to you: that we are in a battle, and that more than half of this battle is taking place in the battlefield of the media. And that we are in a media battle in a race for the hearts and minds of our Ummah[19]

on which US Defense Secretary Donald Rumsfeld commented:

If I were grading I would say we probably deserve a 'D' or a 'D-plus' as a country as to how well we're doing in the battle of ideas that's taking place in the world today.[20]

Often it is the exploitation of unforced errors by the security forces that causes problems (Abu Ghraib comes to mind) rather than the capacity of the neo-jihadists to entrap the Western media into falling victim to a deliberate propaganda operation. But the extremists know that the very objectivity of the Western media allows their actions to be reported widely, even when those actions are engineered deliberately to come to such attention. In many cases the key target audience the extremists wishes to reach through the international media is the domestic Muslim communities from whom the terrorists hope to gain support and recruits by demonstrating their capability to inspire such sacrifice. What words can the government Minister find in those circumstances that will sound the right note after a screening of the 'video will' of a suicide bomber?

Returning to the studio debate, the stakes from such televised encounters are high. Being seen to be tested in combat by interview—and prevailing—will add credibility both to the case and to the reputation of the Minister as a safe pair of hands. Downing Street will be watching. But the Minister is likely to be as conscious of the risks of failure, not least the operational or legal consequences from revealing too much.

And finally, the audience too are participating unconsciously in the discourse by bringing their own experiences, perceptions and prejudices to their interpretation of the programme. How people think about security and intelligence matters will be coloured by experience of popular media portrayals of the secret world. We might reflect in that context on the enduring fascination of the UK media—and the UK public—with anything that seems to open a window on the world of spies and secret agents. The part that the secret world plays in contemporary British popular culture cannot help but crucially colour the meaning attributed to Government statements and media analysis alike. For example, as recent UK research illuminates,

drama series like *Spooks* have a disproportionate effect on viewers' perceptions of how the intelligence services operate. Such series also circulate and reproduce discourses on Islamic [sic] terrorism.[21]

The same UK research concludes that

More well scripted, but less stereotypical drama serials may assist security policy makers in explaining and communicating the policy dilemmas they face. This can be more effective than a thousand earnest documentaries.

After recent programmes in the *Spooks* series there must be large numbers of British viewers who have absorbed a subliminal message that the Security Service has no compunction about beating up terrorist suspects in the basement of Thames House, and that those at the top of the intelligence community (including a portrayal of my own old post of Security and Intelligence Coordinator) are amoral spin merchants pandering to political agendas. An even starker conclusion would be justified in relation to the highly popular US television series *24* in which there is frequent recourse to torture and violent intimidation to secure timely information on terrorist plots.

The commercial realities for editors and their headline writers, and the career realities for journalists, leave little room for self-restraint when an intelligence story surfaces. Intelligence sells, as shown by the remarkable post-imperial prominence of secret intelligence in British popular culture (it has been estimated that half of the world's population has seen a James Bond film).[22] Popular depictions of the British secret intelligence world have been in circulation for over a century. The tone has changed over the years signifying changes in underlying national self-perceptions. This spy story transition has taken us from the anti-German nationalism of Erskine Childer's *Riddle of the Sands*, and the early novels of John Buchan, through the intrigues and conspiracies of the international arms manufacturers and cosmopolitan secret agents of Eric Ambler's adventures, the realism of Alan Judd to the increasingly fantastic later novels of Ian Fleming, the betrayals and post-Imperial disillusion of Le Carré (noting that Graham Green may be said in that respect to have got to the depressive position first) and finally the send-ups of *Austin Powers*.

Spies and secret intelligence may be to popular British culture what the frontier has been to American culture in reflecting the emotions associated with the end of an era. The sheriff, sitting tall in his saddle, making and enforcing his own law, galvanising the townsfolk to run the trouble-makers out of town, is an enduring national image for the United States long after the disappearance of the internal frontier. Such self-reliance and distrust of the enemy outside is an important concept in the self-definition of what made America, and Americans, and we see it still in the way the 'global war on terror' has evoked unconscious resonance with that self-image. The British frontier became the external Empire, and as the nation was forced to retreat from the great game so the tone of the spy novelists chronicled the impact of its loss on national self-belief. Why is it so compelling a narrative to our public? Perhaps some of the enduring fascination stems from the unconscious feeling that although Britain had lost an empire and could no longer during the Cold War afford the old overt global military and economic power, we could cling to the (largely true) assumption that, at least in the shadows, the UK still counted.

To this brew we might add the simplifying role that conspiracy theory can play in easing private explanation of what seems a hostile and complicated world. And we should add the attraction of the peep under the skirts of the world of secret intelligence for those who have not digested what Freudians might call their fascination with the primal scene. Prurient curiosity still sells newspapers in large numbers, and as every sub-editor knows, the word 'secret' acts as an accelerant on a breaking story.

In considering public views of intelligence and security we are dealing with a magical reality, a psychological construct, not direct portrayals of the real world. But it is one that sells cinema tickets and newspapers. It is hard for journalists to write about this subject, however serious and well informed they are, without these harmonies being evoked in the reader or viewer. And sub-editors and editors of course play on this, since the economics of journalism is harsh, competition is fierce, and people have a living to make. So deconstruction of the layers of evoked meaning is essential when reading what is written about secret intelligence. As a result, for Governments to comment on intelligence matters or to deploy intelligence in the public domain in support of their policies is a highly hazardous business in any circumstance. Is it really necessary for them to do so?

As a general rule in the past, the point of having secret agencies was that they and their work could be kept secret. As Austen Chamberlain informed the House of Commons in 1924,

It is of the essence of a Secret Service that it must be secret, and if you once begin disclosure it is perfectly obvious to me as to honourable members opposite that there is no longer any Secret Service and you must do without it.[23]

Nevertheless, a combination of factors—disclosures of the crucial role of intelligence in the Second World War as well as of alleged intelligence failures and scandals; growth in the size, technical complexity and cost of secret agencies; and the demands human rights legislation places on accountability and openness—has led to a gradual disclosure of much of the workings of the UK and allied intelligence communities.[24] The specific inquiries launched after 9/11 and Iraq in particular have led to unparalleled openness about matters that would previously been shrouded in mystery. One of the consequences of counter-terrorist intelligence work is that, in the words of the US Director of Central Intelligence (DCI) Mike McConnell

Most important, the long-standing policy of only allowing officials access to intelligence on a 'need to know' basis should be abandoned and replaced by a 'responsibility to provide' to state and local officials and the private sector, whilst 'still reasonably protecting sources and methods.'[25]

The inevitable result is that general knowledge of the national intelligence community becomes much more widespread in society, and that has to extend to the media. It is now in practice as well as in law impossible to envisage reversing this trend and for the secret agencies to retreat back into the shadows.

Public and Parliamentary support is needed for the legitimisation of the activities of the intelligence community. That matters more than ever given the primary responsibility of government, central to the contract with the citizen, to take anticipatory action to enable terrorism and other major threats facing society to be managed. The ability to take such pre-emptive action in the interests of public security depends crucially on obtaining secret intelligence and on the ability to use that secret intelligence effectively. We see transatlantic flights having to be cancelled for fear they have been targeted for attack; concrete bollards appearing outside public buildings to deter vehicle bombs; armoured vehicles surrounding the UK's main airport to counter a possible surface to air missile attack; and armed police storming a house in a residential area looking for a chemical explosive device. The common factor behind these (real) UK examples of counter-terrorist action is that they rest on pre-emptive intelligence that may or may not have been accurate, but was in each case sufficiently well sourced that it could not be ignored. The intelligence forced the security authorities to act, to act quickly, and to act publicly.

It is common for such cases to be followed by media stories questioning the quality of the intelligence behind the warnings, with commentators claiming that the threat is being talked up for political motives or questioning the morality of methods alleged to have been used to obtain the intelligence.[26] The use of accurate pre-emptive secret intelligence has the huge benefit of enabling the security authorities to act selectively to remove the trouble-makers from the community without the need for 'the bludgeon of state power'[27] to be deployed (mass arrests and house to house searches, detention without trial, coercive interrogation and so on) thus helping to maintain community confidence. But intelligence is by its nature incomplete, fragmentary and sometimes wrong. The importance of anticipatory action will thus inevitably at times mean that the agencies and their role are forced to the surface in the debate.

As already noted in describing the imaginary interview with a Government Minister, long shadows were cast over many such debates by the controversy over the use of intelligence on Iraqi weapons of mass destruction before the invasion of Iraq. Even when the issue is not cited directly, the public's trust in 'intelligence' as a basis for pre-emptive action has been damaged, and this will take a long time to ebb. How best, therefore, can Government safely convey to the media and public the arguments for its public safety policies, and defend the operational decisions of the security authorities, where these are based on secret intelligence? There are two general lessons here for how governments present and justify the use of secret intelligence for public protection.

Firstly, that the inherently uncertain nature of secret intelligence needs to be explained and that any warnings on the limitations of intelligence need to be spelt out for a lay audience, and clear and effective dividing lines between assessment and advocacy need to be maintained. Secondly, that it is preferable for Government to take responsibility for justifying its own conclusions in its own words (albeit cleared for accuracy by the intelligence authorities), and not fall back on exploiting the 'branding' of the name and authority of the intelligence authorities such as the Joint Intelligence Committee (JIC). What the Butler Committee, and its witnesses, saw as a wholly exceptional event—the problem of how to publish an unclassified JIC intelligence 'assessment' on Iraq—becomes an everyday dilemma in the case of the justification for counter-terrorist action. As our opening example illustrated, CT intelligence is being thrust into unaccustomed and uncomfortable public role front of house rather than backstage.

The golden rule is not to wait until crisis hits before trying to communicate with the public.[28] It may help to anticipate three different sets of circumstances in which government may feel it necessary to draw on at least the headlines of intelligence derived from secret sources in their interactions with the media. These circumstances are, respectively, helping to maintain a knowledgeable and supportive public opinion, informing and alerting public services and private sector organisations to potential future threats against which they should plan, and finally, in emergency, warning the public of impending danger and advising on what to do to minimise the risk.

Under the first heading I would place the necessity for Government to seek to sustain a supportive public opinion and proper understanding of the role of the intelligence community and its constituent parts (and importantly what it is not) and to understand how the work of that community is regulated and overseen, both through Statute law and as a matter of practice. I have suggested elsewhere the value of having an explicit code of ethical principles for the intelligence community to bring together the principles, such as proportionality and right authority, by which they carry out their day to day work and according to which standards they are overseen.[29]

Additionally, there needs to be in the public domain authoritative accounts of how the government views the threat from terrorism, and how it sees the progress of its strategy. Such information—with the message of 'alert not alarmed'—needs to be provided to Parliament and the public in ways and at times that distance it from the pressures of the introduction of legislation or the need to justify some new security measure. Some commentators have suggested annual threat assessments or that the UK should follow recent US practice of publishing unclassified versions of National Intelligence Assessments as was done for US intelligence of the Iranian nuclear weapons programme (although that might be held to run counter to the thrust of the Butler approach).[30]

Media correspondents need to be properly informed but there is also much that government can do to make information directly available without having to rely on the filtering and interpretation of the media. A start has been made on terrorism with the websites of MI5 and the Home Office describing their assessments of the threat and with the Cabinet Office website proving basic description of the workings of the UK intelligence community. However it is done, there is a real necessity for greater public understanding of the nature of secret intelligence, and its limitations. And a need for understanding of the mechanisms of political and legal accountability that apply to the more intrusive methods that are essential if secret intelligence is to be collected on a target such as neo-jihadist terrorism.

Such general public awareness needs to be distinguished from the more focused information required by those charged with implementing counter-terrorist and public security measures. The UK emergency services and health services and the operators, mostly in the private sector, of the key critical national infrastructure need authoritative planning assumptions about what to prepare for. Similar considerations must apply to the way that government describes its exercises and training, without raising public anxiety. The risk is that by even mentioning the need to plan for, say, decontamination services capable of dealing with a 'dirty bomb' the government is read by the more excitable sections of Parliament and the media as predicting such catastrophe. In relation to enhanced security it is the effectiveness of pre-emptive measures that may actually reduce the threat. When the British Government in 2002 invested £32m in smallpox vaccine, the BBC rightly reported:

Millions of doses of the smallpox vaccine are to be stockpiled by the government to prepare for mass vaccination in the event of a bio-terrorist attack. The Department of Health said that while there was no evidence of a specific threat, it was carrying out intensive planning

but the *Daily Mail* still managed the headline: 'New smallpox terror alert'. There is now on Home Office and MI5 websites a welcome increase in information about contingency planning, and encouragement to industry to invest in innovation and scientific research, against the more extreme developments that terrorism may take. The media and the public need to be educated to distinguish such planning information from the issue of specific warnings of current threats.

The final category of public information covers what should be said when an emergency arises and when it is necessary to seize the attention of the affected public—and reassure those not affected that they can get on with normal life. Systems are now in place in the UK for the Government to request the broadcast media, including local radio, to alert sections of the public to heightened potential risk whether arising from natural disasters or man-made causes. Government and media (especially the BBC with its 'Connecting in a Crisis' arrangements) have worked closely together on these arrangements through the joint national Media Emergency Forum and the Regional Media Emergency Fora that operate under the Civil Contingencies Act 2000.[31]

We can see Government beginning to use the web to communicate directly with the public to reassure where risks are being managed or to explain the introduction of measures such as bag searches at public venues and events. We can also get advice on changed threats when travelling to certain regions overseas or an explanation of specific airline and other security measures. When necessary, the police must continue to be able, on their own responsibility, to take the initiative to warn the affected public in the event of impending or actual attack or other emergency. In such circumstances government and police need to communicate clear advice on how individuals should act, including cooperating with measures such as evacuation so as to reduce the risk to themselves and their families. In the case of terrorist incidents, where the risk of follow-on attacks is always present, it becomes even more important to avoid unauthorised disclosures of intelligence-related information that may lie behind the warnings. Experience is that the traditional British media is capable of showing responsibility, for example over not broadcasting details relating to current hostage or hijacking operations or revealing obviously sensitive operational techniques. Government too needs to recognise that at such times it must be trusted to provide factual and neutral briefings, a level of trust that is harder to achieve given the prevalence in recent years of the general practice of politicised and unattributable briefings by Ministerial advisers.

Problems can arise when the nature of the sensitivity is not obvious, or the journalist has only got hold of part of the story. Over the years, the UK has evolved a much misunderstood voluntary mechanism, the 'DA Notice' system, bringing together senior print and broadcast news editors with senior government officials in the belief that there is a state of affairs that both media and government wish to arrive at, whereby a free press takes its own decisions, within the law, as to what to publish but does so in the light of up to date advice from those who ought to know in order to prevent unintentional damage to national security.[32] The logic is that of 'the prisoner's dilemma': if both parties are allowed to communicate in confidence then the outcome with be far better for the public interest than that obtained if the parties have to act in ignorance of each others' position and intentions. Any recommended approach to these issues must be capable of being followed in the world of the new media as well as the old. With the inexorable rise of the blogosphere, and with cameras ubiquitous on mobile phones, everyone becomes their own news correspondent, which carries significant risks for the viability of traditional journalism, with opinion increasingly crowding out factual reporting. As Tony Blair has observed of the reporting of politicians,

In the interpretation, what matters is not what they mean; but what they could be taken to mean.[33]

We should be aware of the changes taking place in the studios and editorial offices in which the media confronts government. The 24/7 media age has brought the rolling news broadcast, which in turn has led to profound shifts in the grammar of news reporting. The use of multiple windows, graphics and stock footage (including clichés of the intelligence world such as the modern MI6 HQ). Availability of images governs the editorial and production decisions over the story dominating newsroom and production decision-making. I have already alluded to the commercial pressures on both print and broadcast media, with increasingly fragmented and segmented audiences and channels.

Highly portable recording and transmission equipment is now standard for the media with on location live-feeds. These developments carry obvious real risks for compromise of operations. Screening of amateur footage of the police raid in Forest Gate, East London, helped foster the impression of an excessively heavy-handed operation (an impression the police may have mistakenly fostered from the outset by briefing the media on the scale of the operation, over-estimating perhaps the precision of the intelligence behind the raid). Whereas in the military sphere 'embedding' of journalists with deployed forces has led, for the most part, to sensitising a generation of war correspondents to the realities of combat and its dangers, no such opportunity is obvious for the front-line work of the secret agencies and the level of general knowledge of operational sensitivities remains low.

In recent years the media has increasingly assumed to itself the role, in part usurping that traditionally held by Parliament, of holding government to public account, even—or perhaps especially—for those activities government would wish to hide from public gaze. To that end the media have developed their own effective capabilities to acquire information by covert means, whether by the investigative reporter, the undercover or sting operation, or the recruiting of networks of 'agents' willing to provide unauthorised disclosures whether out of public spiritedness, sheer devilry, or for personal gain. What for the editor is public interest reporting may well for the Intelligence Agency represent a fatal breach of trust. We may note that newspaper editors and journalists are themselves not held accountable and have no requirement to make evidence accessible to readers.[34] Nevertheless, the intelligence agencies have no option but to accept this 24/7 media news and entertainment reality and learn to operate as safely as they can in it. To accept, as Jeremy Paxman has put it, that they are dealing with

an entity in its own right, a collective being with its own distinct nervous system. It eats, it breathes, it excretes. It has distinct pleasure centres in its brain and it has an awful lot of problems with its eyesight.

There is much to be said therefore for modern avowed intelligence agencies having declared and transparent press briefing arrangements through press offices staffed by professional information officers, so that attributable statements can be made on the record. According to John Lloyd, director of journalism at the Reuters Institute at Oxford, the arguments for this have become stronger as the agencies have shifted roles.

During the Cold War, their main concerns were remote from most people's lives... Now, when they're concentrating on domestic terrorism and subversion ... their public exposure is much greater. This kind of secrecy becomes more objectionable the more they become part of daily life. It will always be difficult for reporters to verify or refute secret intelligence, but we should at least be able to state openly what the source of a story is. Increasing their accountability will also increase the confidence the public has in the agencies.[35]

The US National Security Agency recently released under Freedom of Information (FOI) legislation the arrangements they have used for bringing prominent media correspondents into the secret US National Sigint Operations Centre in Fort Meade so that they can learn which the really sensitive parts of a story are. The journalists were, we are told, given real examples of damaging disclosures in media stories and shown how they could have been rewritten in ways that left an exciting story but did not damage national security (I cannot quote an example since the NSA has redacted that part of the released document).

There are always going to be areas of particular operational sensitivity for the Agencies and security authorities arising from traditional intelligence gathering in support of military operations policy and foreign policy, and from secret action where media intrusion would be damaging. For such subjects the 'neither confirm nor deny policy' will continue to make sense. As US DCI Mike McConnell explained to an audience of journalists

I have been in this community now either as an inside professional or as a consultant providing some level of support for 40 years, and there are numerous times when we had sources and methods compromised that either cost us lives or the source, or the method, or the ability to do our job...my view is that you [journalists] have a job that is vital for this country and for those of us in the intelligence business who work with secrets have a job which is protecting the nation. And we have to find that balance that accommodates both.[36]

For the media there will always be the role of verifying that which government asserts to be the case, critically testing the value of its actions, and thus setting the agenda for government. McConnell again:

in the morning when I'm up at 4:00...and I'm going to the White House...what is it I look at first...its the same thing everybody in this town looks at first, particularly if you are more senior, and that is what is in the press...I'm looking for what you all found out and what you have said because that is going to frame the debate.

In the future that concern will increasingly spill over from the traditional print and broadcast media into the wider world of web-based communications, formal and informal.

One basic conclusion that seems unavoidable—and I believe should be welcomed—is that the intelligence community has to work for greater public understanding of its role, purpose and ethics, and greater public confidence in the effective oversight of its secret work, in return for greater understanding of why sources and methods must remain secret. The first step must be to secure this objective with the networks of serious journalists and editors who are still the primary means of communication with the public. It is simply too important for public safety for the development of the relationship with the media to be left to chance. We must indeed hope that the intelligence agencies will be able to retain the necessary dark corners in which their secret operations can continue while building public confidence in the value of their role and their necessary intrusions into the privacy of the public, the paradox that is the existence of secret intelligence in an open society.

3

TERRORISM AND THE MEDIA

THE INFORMATION WAR

Gordon Corera

Editors' Notes: As the BBC's Security Editor Gordon Corera has considerable experience in the frontline of what he describes as 'the information war'. In this chapter he seeks to explain why he believes this 'information war' is now an important and vital aspect of the war against jihadist terrorism. The ethical considerations for journalists reporting on intelligence—brought out by Chapman Pincher in his chapter—are rehearsed here in a contemporary context by Corera, with a discussion of what western media outlets should report on, and how far they should go to counter jihadist propaganda. The advantages Al Qaeda has over western governments in the media fight are also discussed, suggesting that the asymmetric underdog actually holds a dominant position.

We are in a battle, and more than half of this battle is taking place in the battlefield of the media...we are in a media battle for the hearts and minds of our umma.[1]

According to its ideological architect, more than half of Al Qaeda's war is taking place in the battlefield of the media—a war for the hearts and minds of Muslims—and a war in which Al Qaeda has been showing increasing signs of sophistication. This 'information war' has posed real challenges for western governments trying to counter Al Qaeda but also for the media whose position in the information war is increasingly challenging and contested.

In the immediate aftermath of 9/11, almost the entire focus of western efforts against Al Qaeda was on the hard, physical, 'kinetic' side of the conflict—whether in terms of coping with terrorist attacks, arresting suspects or rooting out terrorist sanctuaries. It took a long time—many critics believe much too long—for those opposing Al Qaeda to engage and ask hard questions about the battle which Al Qaeda *itself* says is more important—the information war conducted via the media.

It is now widely recognised that the struggle by and against Al Qaeda is as much an ideological struggle as a military and policing one. And by virtue of that, it is played out in the realm of information and the media, placing journalists in a tricky position. This has been heightened by changes in the media landscape on which the information war is fought, providing if not advantages then at least an equalising force for Al Qaeda and the jihadist ideology. The Internet, in particular, has become crucial to Al Qaeda's strategy and has proved to be a battlefield on which Al Qaeda can match and even outgun its opponents.

One of the most challenging questions is conceptualising how the 'hard physical' conflict relates to the information war and whether it is possible to win the kinetic battles but lose the information war. Information operations are at the heart of what Al Qaeda does but that has not necessarily always been the case with those fighting against it. One former British army officer, John Mackinlay, has argued that not all of his former colleagues in the military have grasped that the media effect of a military act is now more important than its tactical value.[2]

Terrorism has always been an inherently public act. It has always, in the words of the RAND Corporation terrorism expert Michael Jenkins, been about 'theatre'. Terrorists have long sought to exploit the media but recent years have seen the media landscape changing rapidly due to the proliferation and democratisation of media production and distribution—developments which Al Qaeda and related groups have been adept at exploiting. The democratisation of media production means that now anyone—including terrorists—can create their own media outlets easily, cheaply and anonymously with little chance of detection. Terrorist groups and even lone individuals can use technology in terms of cameras and the Internet to put out messages even if the mainstream media will not necessarily show them. This means that in order to fight the information war and spread propaganda they are less reliant on mainstream mass media, which is discriminating, as they can bypass it using their own media which has no such filters. Al Qaeda and jihadist groups have understood how to exploit these trends. In Iraq, they take their own 'reporters' out on attacks—effectively mimicking the US process of embedding journalists to cover the action from their point of view. They can film attacks from all the best possible angles. Footage of attacks is uploaded onto the Internet often within thirty minutes of the attack taking place, ready for a world-wide audience for whom jihadist videos have become mainstream.

Al Qaeda has been highly active in its video and TV usage. According to those who monitor Al Qaeda's activity, 2007 saw an all time high in terms of video releases with an average of one every three days from *Al-Sahab*, a noticeably higher tempo than in the previous year.[3] The scale of the output reflects a resilient, sophisticated and hard-working media operation. This is a sign of the resurgent organisation of core Al Qaeda and its ability to once again run communication, logistics and command and control from its base in Pakistan. The speed of release and ability to react to news events has increased, as has the sophistication, with feature length documentaries interspersed with archive footage and new commentary, as well as the use of graphics more commonly seen on news bulletins. 2007 also saw the return of Osama Bin Laden as a primary spokesperson. Other groups who have affiliated themselves, like Al Qaeda in the Islamic Maghreb, considerably boosted their media operations following their declarations of allegiance to the Al Qaeda core and began mimicking the Al Qaeda style by filming attacks and uploading videos.

The proliferation of media has also had its impact by changing the patterns of consumption. The media landscape is increasingly segmented so that people can get what they want—whether on satellite TV or the Internet. About a quarter of Americans currently use the Internet as their primary news source. This means people often consume the media that reinforces their existing views. There has been a decline in what is known as 'appointment news' and a rise in low budget, local and specialist media with people free to go to content that matches their own interests. This leads to the audience splintering—a major challenge for big broadcasters and to those who seek to communicate through them. The costs of entry to being a broadcaster are now much lower, allowing even jihadists to set up their own TV news programme: *Voice of the Caliphate*, which mimicked the standard news format and was produced by the Global Islamic Media Front. The mainstream media faces growing criticism from a range of different perspectives to the effect that it is biased and ignores stories. Such segmentation opens the way for Al Qaeda and other groups to present their own narrative through their own media, or sympathetic outlets, in a way that was previously denied.

The content of jihadist media is complex, ranging from the stories of martyrs (and increasingly their videos) to long theological tracts justifying particular actions. But much of it serves to support the so-called 'single narrative' that Al Qaeda espouses—the notion that the West is engaged in a war against Islam and that it is the duty of individual Muslims to wage a jihad to resist this.

Terrorist groups have also proved creative in their use of media, expanding beyond simply straight 'news'. For instance, a video was produced called *Lee's Life for Lies*—which, it was claimed, is based on a USB drive captured off a soldier in Iraq. It uses real material in it such as letters and pictures to present a faked audio and visual diary of his time in Iraq expressing frustration and anger at what's going on:

Until when will I stay in this hell? Why are we even here? The people hate us and they still don't want our presence.

The voice says on the video, which can still be watched on YouTube.[4]

The most effective propaganda is often embedded within entertainment. A programme called *Hidden Camera Jihad* involves a slick video compilation of attacks on US forces in Iraq which is a pastiche of western shows, even to the extent of having a laughter track. It originally appeared on message boards in September 2006 but was shown repeatedly on Al-Zawraa TV, a channel that was banned by the Iraqi government in November 2006 for inciting 'violence and murder' but which resumed broadcasting almost immediately via a satellite uplink thought to be outside Iraqi borders. It can be viewed in Middle East, North Africa and also in Europe and is improving in its quality—for instance with fewer repeats and more announcements. Video compilations of the so-called Baghdad Sniper attacking coalition targets in Iraq also are viewed as much as entertainment as anything else.

Jihadist groups have also proved adept at using new and unconventional media, for instance video games. The Global Islamic Media Front created a game called *Night of Bush Capturing* which involves shooting American troops as well as President Bush and actually seems to be an adaptation of a game produced in America called *The Quest for Saddam*. Arguably the video is no more violent (or ideological in its content) than many produced by western companies but the importance is that they allow jihadist groups to reach an audience of young people and children. There are even claims that terrorists and organised criminals have spotted the potential utility of online virtual worlds like Second Life as a means to move money and organise.[5] The anonymity involved in financial transfers may be of value.[6]

The Internet is the key to the global reach of Al Qaeda and the propagation of its ideology because it has allowed jihadists to break what Ayman Al-Zawahiri called the 'siege' by bypassing traditional media. The Internet performs a number of functions for Al Qaeda. It is used to publish propaganda, to recruit, indoctrinate, train, gather information and raise money. The Internet has been described as a 'virtual sanctuary' and training ground in the years after 2001 when the physical sanctuary and training ground of Afghanistan was lost.

There was a period after 9/11 when the idea took hold that Al Qaeda was no longer an organisation but more an ideology.[7] Al Qaeda was seen as an ideology which could survive and grow through the Internet even when the organisation's leadership was under pressure and operating under severe constraints. During these years, the Internet became particularly important for training, with a huge volume of manuals and information being put on line and the Internet acting as a virtual training camp, lowering the threshold for home-grown jihadists to acquire the capability to move from intent to actually being able to carry out attacks and to be able to do so without leaving their bedroom and travelling to Afghanistan. Many of the details on how to set up a terrorist cell, how to ensure operational security, how to make explosives and conduct reconnaissance can now be found on-line. It would be wrong though to suggest that this kind of on-line training is an equal substitute for attending a camp in Pakistan and Afghanistan (and the evidence from the UK is that many of the leaders of cells did attend training camps in person to learn skills rather than over the Internet).

The Internet has huge advantages for this type of activity because of the ease of producing content, the relative anonymity and the potentially massive audience meaning that for very little money, one individual can reach thousands of others around the world, competing with global media organisations. High end websites present themselves as news providers and are actually used on Google News as such. Web 2.0 or the democratisation of production means that it is as easy to contribute as it is to consume. To that end there are estimated to be around 4–5,000 jihadist websites in all and jihadists have even launched their own technical magazines on the web—one called the *Technical Mujahid* contains guidance on setting up a website and how to make it look professional.

More generally, the Internet is also the place where radicalised Muslims or those who simply feel un-rooted in western society and who reject the traditional Islam of their parents' generation can find their identity in the global *umma*—the Muslim community—by connecting with like-minded individuals and finding a new vision of a globalised Islam. One of the paradoxes of this approach is the use of western media and media techniques while rejecting the west and globalisation as part of this strange hybrid of neo-fundamentalism.

Al Qaeda has also grasped the important lesson of audience participation and interactivity in modern media. For instance, Ayman Al-Zawahiri took the unusual step of inviting questions to be sent to him over the Internet in December 2007. One of the most illuminating aspects is the nature of the questions sent in. Most focus on two areas—questions on why certain geographic areas received more attention from Al Qaeda than others in its calls for jihad and secondly, a call for the clarification of theological points relating to jihad. Questions included:

Will Islamic armies join in Palestine?

Is there a branch of Al Qaeda in Kashmir? Have you ordered them to suspend operations?

Is Yemen suited for jihadist operations? And, if yes, why are we hearing that an order has been given that action should not be taken there?

Should women be allowed to carry out suicide operations?[8]

Zawahiri's responses which came a few months later were equally illuminating, if also lengthy and dense, a sign that while Al Qaeda is trying to embrace new media trends, its concerns over security and controlling its message still can occasionally make its responses look cumbersome.

Jihadist groups have even been conducting on-line polls, much beloved of Western media organisations. In February 2008, a participant on a webforum asked members to vote on whether or not they agreed that Al Qaeda should attack Denmark after cartoons of the Prophet were published there. More than 95% voted yes.[9] Some of the discussions in Al Qaeda sites and on webforums can be interesting. For instance, there has been considerable debate and division over what the approach should be to Hamas and Hezbollah and their political rise in the Middle East. There has also been a very strong reaction and debate to the serialisation in late 2007 of writings by Sayyid Imam, an Egyptian Islamist, who turned away from violent jihad. Al-Zawahiri has even gone so far as to write a book to rebut his arguments, a sign of how seriously they are being taken and an example of how debates within the Muslim community are far more important to them than what is said by Western governments.

Al Qaeda's highly organised media division currently runs a small number of password-protected websites which put out statements and communiqués from leaders, guaranteeing their authenticity and allowing a plethora of other groups around the world to pick them up and distribute them. At the centre of Al Qaeda's media operations is *Al-Sahab*, part of core element of Al Qaeda, which produces a regular stream of relatively high production videos, which are also usually distributed through websites.

Along with *Al-Sahab*, the two other main entities are *Dawn* (or *Al-Fajr*) and the *Global Islamic Media Front*. According to an in-depth study by Daniel Kimmage, these three organisations provide the bulk of all Al Qaeda related content, mimicking traditional media in order to gain credibility.[10] In another echo of mainstream media, their output is also consistently and systematically branded with logos to try and control authenticity and credibility and maintain discipline. Al Qaeda in Iraq's military statements consciously mimic those of the Pentagon in an attempt to establish the organisation's reputation as a serious military force, Kimmage argues and in some cases, these distributors have expressed their annoyance at 'media exuberance' when others distribute jihadist material without permission.[11] On the web there are signs of increased co-ordination among jihadist websites but also more evidence of disruption with some of the open access sites being taken off line and content being forced onto more closed sites like *Al-Ikhlas*, sites which have proved to be generally more resilient. In 2008, *Dawn* began producing regular Urdu translations of Al Qaeda speeches and material more regularly than before, a reflection of the importance of Pakistan as a battleground.

Jihadists are quick to claim that their operations are censored by others. One statement appeared on the website announcing that:

The campaign—Exposing the Media Censorship—begins. This will be done by gathering all the videos that were censored by the global media. In doing so, we are striving to lift the doubt and uncertainty that the devils of men and jinn have cloaked over the people to discourage them.[12]

The statement went on to refer to an operation destroying a bridge and took an excerpt from a BBC report and then criticised its language arguing that it had implied that those killed were innocent people when in fact they were Americans, it claimed. Their plea is for the viewers to judge the materials for themselves, rather than through western lenses.[13]

One of the best examples of the role the Internet can play is in the story of the rise and fall of Younes Tsouli—or to use his preferred title *Irhabi 007* (Irhabi meaning terrorist in Arabic).[14] Tsouli was a loner who came to London and studied information technology. He quickly began using his computer skills to surf the web for propaganda and became radicalised by what he saw, including videos from Iraq which he believed showed the US attacking innocent Muslims. In effect, he became a subscriber to the single jihadist narrative. But then from his bedroom in West London, Tsouli moved from being a passive consumer of this material to playing a more active role, posting manuals on computer hacking and then transmitting the propaganda itself. *Al Qaeda in Iraq* then spotted his potential as a means to disseminate their material to a much wider audience. Tsouli was emailed links that allowed him to download videos from a server. He then converted the material into various formats, including one that allowed the videos to be watched on mobile phones, thereby reaching a much wider audience. The videos were also uploaded to unsuspecting external web pages, often done by hacking into and 'hijacking' websites, whose creators did not realise that they were hosting terrorist propaganda. Evan Kohlmann, an expert on cyber-terrorism who gave evidence at Tsouli's trial, explains:

007 came at this with a Western perspective. He had a flair for marketing, and he had the technical knowledge and skills to be able to place this stuff in areas on the net where it wouldn't be easily erased, where lots of people could download it, view it and save it.

Representatives of Abu Musab al-Zarqawi, Al Qaeda's leader in Iraq until his death in 2006, issued messages of support for Irhabi 007, including the telling message of 'May Allah protect you'.

Tsouli's websites were being shut down either when hosts realised they had been hijacked or when cyber-trackers or officials spotted one of Tsouli's own sites and shut it down. This meant that Tsouli had to continually setup new websites to host the material. This required money and here he was helped by two other associates, also arrested in October 2005. They were Waseem Mughal and Tariq Al-Daour. Al Daour was the money man, on his computer drives police would find 37,000 credit card details, including security codes. These had been stolen in phishing attacks or purchased in on-line forums where stolen information circulates. Innocent people who thought they were simply following a link to verify their account information were unwittingly helping the group fund their terrorist activities. Police identified over 2.5 million euros worth of fraudulent transactions carried out by him. The money had been laundered through the labyrinthine world of e-banking systems—accounts ranging from the UK to the US to as far a field as Russia and Panama. Much of the money went to a site based in Florida in which gold is bought which can then be easily transferred. In online chat in December 2003, Al Daour was asked what he would do with four million pounds. 'Sponsor terrorist attacks—become the new Osama' was his reply. Detectives are still unsure where all the money went but are sure that Al Daour was not spending it himself. Another remarkable aspect of this case is that there is no evidence Tsouli and Al Daour ever met in person—they were connected through cyberspace, as were so many others in the broader network.

As well as distributing videos to a wider audience, Tsouli also played a crucial role in the other major plank of Al Qaeda's online presence, the web-forums. The interactive nature of web-forums and chat rooms is especially important because of the opportunities it allows for contact, recruitment and encouragement in the way that the passive reading of terrorist literature does not. In 2005, he became administrator of the *al-Ansar forum* which was used by around 4,500 extremists to communicate and share practical information, including how to make explosives and how to get into Iraq to become a suicide bomber. One message read:

I'm ready to run off but I'm under 18. Am I too young?

The reply was:

They have no objection to age.

These webforums are vital in facilitating contact around the world for those who cannot easily meet in person and allow for social networking. Akin to the popular website Facebook, people would post updates as to what activities they were involved in. One Sudanese man said he was off to fight in Fallujah, others later informed members that he had died. Marc Sageman argues that:

The new forums have the same influence that…radical mosques played in the previous generations of terrorists.[15]

Tsouli's case is also interesting because he made the transition from viewing material to publishing it to running websites to becoming involved in planning actual attacks. It was Tsouli's links to a planned attack in the Balkans that led to his arrest in October 2005. In an echo of 9/11, a group calling itself *Al Qaeda in Northern Europe* posted a declaration on *al-Ansar* at 8.46 am on September 11, 2005. One of the men behind the declaration was 18–year-old Mirsad Bektasevic, who called himself *Maximus*. After publishing the declaration he went from his home in Sweden to Bosnia and with an accomplice filmed a suicide video in which the two were surrounded by weapons and explosives, including a suicide vest, and in which they claim they were preparing for attacks against those who have troops in Iraq and Afghanistan. The men were under surveillance and when arrested their phone records led British police to Tsouli. When officers raided his home they found his computer still running revealing that had had been working on creating a website called *YOUBOMBIT* although it took them weeks of painstaking computer forensic work to realise the man they had caught was the famous *Irhabi 007*. Peter Clarke, the head of the Metropolitan Police Counter-Terrorism Command said:

What it did show us was the extent to which they could conduct operational planning on the Internet. It was the first virtual conspiracy to murder that we had seen.

If one benefit of the Internet is its ability to put like-minded people in touch from every corner of the world, then one advantage for counter-terrorist officers is that it can also allow them to trace contacts electronically and try and roll up a network in a way that was often impossible with more old-fashioned tightly compartmentalized terrorist cells. Since his departure, no single individual has taken Tsouli's place or matched his influence on the web. In practice, he has been replaced by a plethora of similar, less high-profile figures, making the structure more resilient to disruption. *Al-Ikhlas* now seems to have taken over from *Al-Ansar*. These twenty something cyber-jihadists pose a serious problem for intelligence and law-enforcement agencies, not least because the government agencies often lack the understanding of the web that the new generation of jihadists has. Tsouli is an example of how the new generation of post-9/11 jihadists may lack the military training provided in Afghan camps in the 1990s in area but can effectively wield their new weapon of information war.

The issue of youth is also important for our understanding of the sophistication of Al Qaeda's media operations. All too often Al Qaeda can outpace western governments in the information war simply because its supporters and activists come from a generation well-versed with the latest technology and the advantages it has to offer. Many of those at a senior level in the military or police or intelligence agencies are unlikely to have as good a grasp of the new world of global communications. In addition, a dispersed Al Qaeda network often finds it easier to adopt technology faster and utilise it more effectively than governments encumbered by bureaucracy and slower decision making cycles.

The Internet can be effective for propaganda, radicalisation and recruit-ment—there is very little contradiction or censorship of the professional material clearly targeted at the vulnerable and the young. Youth is a real con-cern with lots of cases of teenagers becoming involved in jihad in the UK. As MI5 director General Jonathan Evans said in 2007:

As I speak, terrorists are methodically and intentionally targeting young people and children in this country. They are radicalising, indoctrinating and grooming young, vulnerable people to carry out acts of terrorism.

There is also growing concern over what is known as self-radicalisation or self-ignition. The evidence from the UK is that active recruitment person-to-person by people scouting for the more vulnerable is still important but so is a more mixed, interactive model of people going to recruiters and being encouraged, often over the Internet, a process of volunteering, encouragement and vetting. Individuals are often seen asking for advice on how to do jihad or how to get Iraq and be tested.

One Saudi official claimed that the Internet is responsible for 80% of the Jihadi recruitment in his country and is the hardest to control. The process here seems to be people going to websites for information, engaging in com-munication with the websites, proving their loyalty by some action and being vetted before being exposed to more incendiary material to complete the process. One interesting question is how many people who go to the sites are radicalised or do they come to the sites already radicalised? And are surfing habits really an indication of extremist proclivities or just curiosity? Relatively few of those convicted of terrorism in the UK appear to have been radicalised initially by the Internet. Instead social interaction seems more important, although the watching of radical videos in a group may play a role in reinforc-ing views. Participating and interacting on web-forums may be a better indica-tion of intent than say simply watching videos of beheadings.

Observers like Stephen Ulph, at the Jamestown Foundation, argue that the key material on the Internet is not the news or comment but the doctrine and guidance which provides the underpinnings for the ideology of jihad, justify-ing through religious interpretation what is and is not acceptable. This is perhaps the crucial area of debate. It is also one that Western governments cannot become directly involved in (although they can clearly overtly and perhaps more usefully covertly) support those who are. Fighting the informa-tion war on the battlefield of the Internet poses some difficult challenges for authorities. Simply taking down websites is not that effective. They often simply re-appear somewhere else. There are also questions of whether it is more useful to keep them up and monitor activity or to close them down, a process complicated by the work of some private cyber-trackers who spend their time shutting the sites down. The US has also employed people to blog and post on various websites to influence opinion and the debates, but the numbers doing this are so small they end up being totally outgunned.

Covering terrorism as a journalist has always raised difficult practical and moral questions, but these are increasing all the time. The media has long been accused of providing the oxygen of publicity for terrorists leading to intense scrutiny and criticism. Notions of impartiality are also being challenged—partly by the segmenting of the media. The polarisation of 'you are either with us or against us', which is encouraged by many participants in the information war, leaves little room for the impartial journalist. Journalists are increasingly becoming targets—one reason is that terrorists no longer need the mainstream media in the way they used to get their message out. In the 1970s terrorists brought journalists along for the hostage-taking, now the terrorists shoot and publish the footage themselves. The uncomfortable problem for the media is that in an information war it is no longer a passive observer, but an actor in its own right.

The centrality of the media in the new information war poses serious challenges for journalists. Should it broadcast hostage videos? Doing so clearly serves the interests of those who seek to 'terrorise' but is ignoring this footage a realistic option? Similar issues apply to most Al Qaeda videos and other propaganda. Who should the media use as commentators on terrorism and which voices from the Muslim community should be given one of the limited chances to discuss the issues? If what Al Qaeda does is propaganda, are western activities also propaganda or 'strategic communications'? How far should intelligence on terrorism and government pronouncements about 'the threat' be trusted and how should they be communicated? To some extent these challenges have always been there but the changing environment with multiple competing 24 hour news channels as well as the Internet and alternative media (often highly critical of the mainstream media) has greatly complicated this task and made the debates more stark.

In a world of segmented, politicised and competing media, credibility becomes increasingly important. Credibility is hard to gain but easy to lose. This goes for both the media itself as well as those seeking to communicate through it, as governments have found. Government officials have found themselves increasingly frustrated by their inability to communicate to their own publics about the issue of terrorism, a reflection of the difficulties since 9/11 that governments have had in fighting the information war.

Western government have often lacked the ability to exploit new trends in media production and dissemination. They also struggle because they are expected to tell the truth, unlike Al Qaeda, in their communication and any attempts to lie to the media are quickly picked up on and examined. For instance, after an incident in Afghanistan, the Taliban may claim there have been many civilian casualties. The number may well be exaggerated wildly but NATO or coalition communicators have to be careful before saying there have been none or getting their facts wrong. This means a slower response while facts are collected creating an information vacuum which opponents will greedily fill.

Governments have had to learn quickly that global communications means that it's no longer possible to communicate discretely with one audience and hope that other audiences do not hear. There have even been problems of what is known as 'information fratricide' between allies with alternative explanations given for events under the pressure of the fast news cycles. Overall, the changes in media production and distribution mean that it is much harder for governments to deliver their message amidst all the noise and different media platforms and voices that now exist in abundance. And missteps are quickly transmitted around the world. Even tactical military victories can quickly be turned into strategic defeats by Al Qaeda leveraging its media operations to portray an American attack on military targets as being responsible for the death of civilians.

Western governments have also suffered from a lack of clarity on who within government is responsible for leading the information and ideological war from their side, especially since it crosses so many boundaries. In the UK, there have been institutional developments, for instance in the formation of RICU—the Research Information Communications Unit—to co-ordinate information operations across UK government departments reaching target audiences of Muslims both in the UK and overseas.

Military commanders have also had to adapt to the importance of the information war. John Mackinlay, a former Army officer turned academic has written:

Conceptually, the lessons emerging from the propaganda of the deed were so radical, so confrontational to our military orthodoxy that it is hardly surprising in the 1980s and 90s that analysts, doctrine writers and military staff were reluctant to embrace them. The idea that the media effect of a military act was now more important than its tactical value threatened to stand our entire concept of operations on its head. It meant that unless we began to operate ourselves in this manner we would be responding to an adversary whose intent and strategic centre of gravity lay in a different operational domain to our own. It meant that our tangible orthodox objectives (to stabilize, to secure and so forth) were going to be constantly eroded by a campaign which took place on a completely different plane, a plane on which we scarcely had a foothold and in a campaign where every military act would have to be part of a larger strategic information plan.[16]

Joining up military operations to a wider communications strategy remains an important task as does ensuring that the strategies employed by all the different governments trying to confront Al Qaeda at the very least do not conflict, and at best complement each other. The democratisation of media production and distribution as well as changing consumption patterns have also greatly complicated the ability of governments to communicate coherently.

The challenges in finding effective ways of communicating to those audiences and finding credible voices to whom they will listen remain enormous, with much work needed to overcome the lack of strategic thought in the years immediately after 9/11. These challenges have meant that western governments have all too often been outpaced by jihadists putting out their information. And if Al Qaeda prioritises the information war over the physical kinetic war, thus playing to its strengths, western governments are in danger of fighting tactical military battles to defeat an enemy who is fighting a completely different war with different rules and objectives and leveraging the actions of western governments against them, using their own actions (whether military or not) as ammunition.

4

GOOD ANTHROPOLOGY, BAD HISTORY

AMERICA'S CULTURAL TURN IN THE WAR ON TERROR

Patrick Porter [1]

Editors' Notes: A core element of western intelligence analysis is discerning the intentions of the enemy. Patrick Porter explores that utility of culture as a driver of conflict and a means to understand the adversary. While not tackling the means by which these cultural messages are transmitted this chapter suggests the ways in which cultural and historical lessons inform the many conflicts of our time. The problems surrounding 'culture' are brought to the fore and lessons are drawn for strategists and analysts to consider.

...we're an army of strangers in the midst of strangers. [2]

To wage war, become an anthropologist. Lose the fetish for Clausewitz, and embrace culture as the way to understand conflict. Or so argue strategists, intelligence analysts, historians, and officers on both sides of the Atlantic. From academia to the Pentagon, fresh attention is being focussed on the value of knowing the enemy. Those who take this view assume that different ways of life produce different ways of war. They see the differences between civilisations reflected in the profound contrast between the opposing sides in today's 'war on terror', between American-led forces on one hand, and *jihadist* warriors or tribal warlords on the other. To make sense of recent military failures in exotic places, they have turned back to cultural knowledge of the adversary. This also often influences their reading of history. They project the same themes back into the distant past. Today's military and counter-terrorism confrontations of 'the west vs. the rest', they argue, replays ancient differences between strategic cultures.

This new anthropology has good intentions. It aims to foster greater cultural awareness and sophistication among military officers, intelligence officers and governments. And cultural agility is surely important. It matters at every level—strategic, operational, and tactical. It matters particularly in a time of volatile occupations of foreign soil, when soldiers are also being asked to act as policemen, nation-builders and peace brokers and similarly in a time of home grown radicalisation. And today's Iraq war demonstrates the strategic costs of misunderstanding the enemy at the grand strategic level. Both President Bush and Saddam Hussein were victims of their own misperceptions. Declaring 'mission accomplished' in May 2003, the Bush administration was misguided by its narrow conception of war. It assumed that its opponents shared its view that hostilities were terminated by the defeat of Iraq's field army. It neglected post-invasion strategy as a second-order administrative task separate to war. And it refused for too long to admit the existence of an insurgency. For his part, Saddam Hussein wrongly calculated that America would never risk a full-scale ground invasion of Iraq, as the rich enemy was too casualty averse and timid. He saw this strategic worldview confirmed in America's retreat from Mogadishu in 1993, and distributed the film *Black Hawk Down* to his generals.[3] Overthrown, tried and executed, he had underestimated American political will, the same error that misled the ideologues of Nazi Germany and Imperial Japan.[4] Both Bush and Hussein failed, in Clausewitz's words, to grasp 'the kind of war on which they are embarking.'[5]

But when it comes to writing history and interpreting today's crises, the 'cultural turn' also has a down side. It comes often with an overly determinist view of the tangled relationship between war and culture. Paradoxically, while it aims to encourage greater sensitivity to the nuances that differentiate cultures, it actually encourages a crude view of ancient and fixed 'ways of war.' It risks replacing strategy with stereotypes. The theory of strategic culture in its many forms has much to offer, but particularly at critical moments in wartime, it becomes unsatisfactory as an interpretation. Instead of arguing that we need to abandon culture as an analytical tool, it is hoped this chapter will show

how a more circumscribed approach, tempered by sober political awareness and a little creative scepticism, can enable us to refine it, and grasp the relationship between war and culture more effectively.

The argument

This chapter makes five key arguments that are relevant to the way that western powers are conducting the war on terror. First, it shows that there has been a 'cultural turn' towards an anthropological approach to war—in all its guises—and that this often entails a particular view of both strategic texts and historical behaviour. Second, it argues that this drive to discover the cultural essence of the enemy, or to find intrinsic differences in the core texts of the 'east' and 'west', is mistaken. It rests on a flawed concept of culture, and in its 'metacultural' form, oversimplifies the 'western' strategic tradition and overstates its differences with 'eastern' conceptions of war. Thirdly, when it comes to understanding the actual behaviour of cultures at war, it is empirically unviable. There are too many exceptions and qualifications that must be made to the supposed picture of two conflicting eastern and western 'ways of war.' Fourth, by depicting culture as the driver of military history, it risks being politically naïve, overlooking the many moments where strategic cultures do not control actors, but where actors control and instrumentalise their cultures, and where the differences between conflicting approaches to war are dictated less by traditions and more by the hard realities of power, weakness and pragmatism. Finally, the chapter argues for a rethinking of the definition of culture in the strategic context and its relationship with war.

'Culture' in the strategic context can be defined as 'a distinct and lasting set of beliefs [and] values' and preferences regarding the use of force, its role and effectiveness in political affairs.[6] This includes an array of factors, such as prevailing attitudes, habits and values of the military and in their parent societies, geopolitical position, historical experience and collective memory of war, and the professional ethos of the military and security agencies. But this definition itself is problematic. As we shall see, culture in its relationship to war turns out to be contested, highly politicised, and malleable.

The latest 'culturalism', like its former versions, is a moving target. It has been articulated at different levels of magnitude and with varying sophistication. It has been given many alternative meanings. It varies from more nuanced attempts to isolate and define cultural traits and their impact on strategy, to overarching views of exotic warfare placed into 'metacultural' categories of east versus west, to cruder approaches, which treat culture in a deterministic manner. The argument should be met at its most sophisticated, but also in its most widespread and dogmatic form. To question crude culturalism is not to attack a convenient 'straw man.' In the UK and US, a zealous form of culturalism has taken hold within and outside security circles.

Any discussion of culture therefore risks degenerating into a sterile 'definition debate.' To avoid this, here I question the core assumptions that these different culturalist approaches share. This is the simple but powerful idea that people fight as they do mainly because of the assumptions, memories and values they have inherited, and that national strategies are primarily shaped or determined by geography, ethnicity, political development and a heritage of received wisdom and historical narrative. Or in more crude versions, they fight as they do because they are Orientals, Muslims, or Americans.

The cultural turn

Do 'non-westerners' approach war and conflict in fundamentally different ways? The question is more than academic. According to traditional wisdom both ancient and modern, one must know the enemy to succeed in war. Chinese philosopher Sun Tzu advised strategists to 'Know your enemy and know yourself.'[7] Mastering war would require self-knowledge and an accurate reading of the enemy, a dialectical exercise that would reward the strategist with victory upon victory. And cultural illiteracy, the 'anthropology deficit' within the national-security establishment, is being blamed for current failures. America and its allies are confronted with the difficulties of negotiating cultural differences in alien environments. They face the implosion of Iraq, where a bloody insurgency mutates into a civil war, while NATO struggles to navigate the tribal world of Afghanistan and a resurgent Taliban.

American military—and indeed intelligence—strategy of the 1990 was marked by the technology-driven quest for a 'Revolution in Military Affairs' (RMA). The RMA envisaged a future in which the American colossus would prevail against armies in the field by exploiting its strengths, such as information and knowledge of the battlespace, precision munitions, rapid mobility and decision-making.[8] But the world's dominant superpower now faces a very different world. Neither the doctrine, training and tools designed to counter the Soviet threat, nor the revolution of the 1990 seemed capable of dealing with 'low-intensity' counterinsurgency. America's advantages have been offset by the indirect methods its enemies employ, who refuse to play to these strengths and fight as America would like them to; by the complex terrain and gangland of urban warfare, in which industrial might or superior firepower do not guarantee success; and by their enemies' different organisation, more a shadowy network than a traditional command structure. Prepared for conventional battles, surgical invasion and withdrawal, and swift, overwhelming strikes, America's military was unprepared for the post-invasion disorder in Iraq, and for the intimacy of prolonged contact with a complex foreign society.

Given the shortcomings of the revolution in military technology, strategists argue now for a cultural counter-revolution.[9] They claim that we should cultivate understanding of the intricacies of tribes, clans, customs and traditions. We need a better grasp of the relationship between how people fight and their traditions, identities, religion, collective memory, preconceptions, and sheer force of habit. A return to an anthropological approach to war, it is hoped, 'will shed light on the grammar and logic of tribal warfare', and create the 'conceptual weapons necessary to return fire.'[10] To some, culture now seems the essence of strategy, even the key to strategic salvation.

This 'cultural turn' is driven by a number of forces. As well as a reaction to the failures of recent American military interventions, it is also part of a larger debate about whether the nature of war is fundamentally changing, in ways that make it obsolete to talk about universal principles of strategy. And it is inspired by a wider backlash against the universalism of Bush administration, its attempt to remake the world in America's image, a vision which some argue has caused all the trouble.

There are many signs of this cultural turn. Within the military, cultural competence is a central value in America's new Counterinsurgency Field Manual (FM 3–24), which mentions 'culture' 88 times and 'cultural' 90 times in 282 pages. It calls for 'agile, well-informed, culturally astute leaders.'[11] Likewise, soldiers distressed by the failures they have seen in Iraq and Afghanistan are drawn to culture as the missing answer. Senior leaders such as retired Major General Robert H. Scales call for 'culture-centric warfare', arguing that the Iraq crisis requires 'an exceptional ability to understand people, their culture, and their motivation.'[12] Returning from Afghanistan, British ex-soldier Leo Docherty claimed that a large conventional force should be replaced by small numbers of 'Afghan experts', immersed in the country with a 'profound knowledge of local culture, language and politics.'[13] Donald Rumsfeld in 2004 noted the military's need for 'foreign language skill and regional and cultural expertise.'[14] The US State Department's new Chief Strategist for counter-terrorism has a doctorate in political anthropology.[15] Deterministic culturalism is preached by Montgomery McFate, an influential cultural anthropologist working with the Pentagon. She argues that the Iraqi insurgents' and al Qaeda's 'form of warfare, organizational structure, and motivations are determined by the society and the culture from which they come.'[16] McFate defends the use of Raphael Patai's *The Arab Mind*, a work that cast Arabs from Algeria to Saudi Arabia as a monolithic people, loveable but infantile, drawn to fantasy and aggression by their language and music, and acting out a role scripted by their Bedouin origins and climate.[17] The most recent edition of this book is approvingly introduced by Colonel Norvelle Atkine, who used to prescribe the text to the American military personnel he briefed.

Culturalism has also found appeal outside of the core military and security services. Campaigning for President, Senator John McCain claims that 'understanding foreign cultures is not a luxury but a strategic necessity.' As president, he would create an 'Office of Strategic Services' and launch a new acculturation programme of language training and anthropological study.[18] In Britain, sales have surged of T.E. Lawrence's classic account of the Arab revolt against the Ottoman Empire, *The Seven Pillars of Wisdom*, which has also been commended by counter-insurgency experts in Iraq.[19] The *Economist* asserts an essentialist view of the timeless cultural flaw of Iraqi national character, quoting a retired British diplomat to show that Iraqis are bright but disputatious people and only governable by strong men.[20] Robert Kaplan, veteran chronicler of American military expeditions, argues that Herodotus' ethnographic stories about foreign cultures are a better guide to the present than Thucydides' attempts to discover the norms of war, statecraft or human nature.[21]

The 'cultural turn' has also left is mark on history. Several recent military histories and prescriptive guides to counter-insurgency are drawn to culture as an explanatory device. They are premised upon an idea that there has long existed a culture-bound 'eastern' way of war, a set of concepts and behaviour that differentiate east from west. At its most ambitious, it is treated as an unbroken strategic and military tradition, uniting cultures as dispersed as ancient China, medieval Arabia and modern Turkey, stretching from the writings of Sun Tzu through to the Arab and Islamic[MD1] insurgencies of today.

This concept is a moving target, as different historians give it different inflections. John Keegan argued that war is culture by other means, and that Oriental warfare is 'different and apart from European warfare', its peculiarities including 'evasion, delay and indirectness.'[22] After 9/11, Keegan turned this analysis into a sweeping and insensitive judgment about non-westerners. The war launched on 9/11 between deceitful easterners and direct westerners was only the latest round in an 'older conflict between settled, creative productive Westerners and predatory, destructive Orientals.'[23] Cultures in this view are hermetically sealed boxes, separate and distinct. It is an analysis based on erroneous contrasts between nomadic and sedentary peoples. What is China to make of this, for centuries a productive, settled and creative culture? But Keegan was articulating cultural war to find a vision of future victory, reducing military history to a morality play, where war showcased the unchanging merits and failures of whole cultures. Keegan deployed this reading of history to embolden the west in its new conflict.

Others have argued for the same east/west duality. The concept of a western way of war is the organising principle behind the recent *Cambridge History of Warfare*.[24] Political scientist Paul Bracken claims Eastern war was 'embodied by the stealthy archer', unlike the archetypal western swordsman 'charging forward, seeking a decisive showdown, eager to administer the blow that will obliterate the enemy.'[25] Victor Davis Hanson makes perhaps the most eloquent and sustained case for this grand narrative. Hanson judges the western tradition superior, crediting its military dominance to its culture's strengths. Western culture from the Greek city states onwards spawns shock infantry that seeks decisive battle, and draws its lethality from its political freedom, capitalism, self-criticism, scientific inquiry, and civic militarism.[26] In these works, western culture is the ultimate 'force multiplier.'

But in light of recent difficulties encountered by the American model of warmaking, another version of similar ideas is gathering strength. Military officers such as John Poole have used concepts of 'Asian' or 'Islamic' ways of war didactically to highlight the defects of their own nations' strategic cultures. Poole identifies an 'Eastern thought process' stretching from ancient China to modern Turkey, which generates effective light infantry, and fights indirectly with loose encirclements, probes, dispersal, and trickery.[27] This has been endorsed by William Lind himself, the prophet of 'fourth generation warfare' who urged the military planners and intelligence agencies to re-imagine the nature of future conflict and recognise its own deficiencies:

The Oriental way of war is far more sophisticated. It plays across the full spectrum of conflict—the moral and mental levels as well as the physical. Even at the physical level, it relies on the indirect approach, on stratagem and deception, far more than on simple bombardment. Seldom do Asians fall into mindless *Materialschlacht* or 'body counts'; and while Oriental armies often can (and have) taken many casualties, their tactics at the small-unit infantry level are often cleverly designed to spare their own men's lives in the face of massive Western firepower.[28]

Others share Lind's assumption that different 'ways of war' are fixed. Robert Cassidy, another officer, argues that the 'Eastern way of war' is rooted in the philosophies of Sun Tzu and Mao Tse-Tung. It is marked by 'reliance on indirectness, perfidy, attrition and protraction', and is 'inherently more irregular, unorthodox, and asymmetric than our traditional conception of war.'[29] 'Inherently' is a very strong word. How helpful is this view of an almost hereditary tradition spanning millennia?

What's wrong with culturalism?

Before questioning it, the hypothesis of the cultural turn should be credited with some important insights. Culture is an influential variable among a range of negotiated interests. It can shape war aims, incentivise a population's will to fight, define victory and conflict termination, rank preferences and create geostrategic priorities, which are all important elements in intelligence estimates or assessments.

To some extent, the new culturalism represents a healthy corrective to the overconfidence and technological determinism that marked aspects of recent strategic thinking, even if it threatens to replace one determinism with another. Technology cannot ultimately replace human judgement, as the anthropological approach cautions. And geography, custom, collective memory, institutions and traditions are undoubtedly influential variables in shaping mentalities and behaviour. In terms of the present, the ability to map out the labyrinth of power structures, networks, and confessional or ethnic perspectives in a foreign society is a vital part of intelligence activity. And it also promotes the healthy practice of overcoming ethnocentrism to imagine others' perspectives.

That said, the 'culturalist' interpretation has a number of weaknesses. First there is in some of its versions an implicit self-contradiction. It asserts that there are enduring and ancient patterns in the way cultures approach war. Yet its exponents also often argue that western military and security structures must adapt to deal better with their adversaries, even to become more like them. Against a historical model of continuity in which strategy is rooted in timeless traditions, it assumes that its own institutions and doctrines are open to transformation. It is unclear how we can have it both ways. It might rest on an unspoken assumption that non-western peoples, tribes or warring communities are primarily cultural actors while westerners are primarily rational actors. Where 'we' have rationality, politics and calculated strategy, 'they' have custom, tradition and warrior culture.[30] Non-westerners, in other words, are astrategic.

Much of this Atlantic 'culture talk' revolves around the legacy of British colonial wisdom. America's debate hovers around Britain's record of counter-insurgency, particularly its success in Malaya, set against its own failures in Vietnam. Some argue that in policing its new frontiers, Britain's example should play sophisticated Greece to America's mighty but uncouth Rome. In his testimony before Congress, Major General Robert Scales urged the US military to follow the footsteps of British soldier-adventurers such as 'China' Gordon and T.E. Lawrence, and that Britain's relative success in Basra was due considerably 'to the self-assurance and comfort with foreign culture derived from centuries of practicing the art of soldier diplomacy and liaison.'[31]

But these are not necessarily desirable examples of successful cross-cultural statecraft. Gordon was a gifted diplomat and soldier, but was unable to quell a prolonged uprising in the Sudan and allowed himself to be besieged and defeated. T.E. Lawrence developed contempt for Arabs, judging them 'a limited, narrow-minded people, whose inert intellect lay fallow in incurious resignation.'[32] This is a reminder of the closeness of cultural awareness and colonial condescension. Lawrence's role in the Arab revolt, like the role of modern-day occupiers, was as a strategic actor rather than a disinterested observer. This is a power relationship as well as a cultural exchange. Where 'the people are the prize', the goal is not just to 'know' the culture but to persuade it or coerce it into identifying its interests with the occupier.[33] So the culturally aware military figure can grow quickly disillusioned when the same host population does not behave as desired. Because the relationship happens in this context, it is a fine line between knowing a culture and despising it.

And this colonial mindset often leaves chaos in its wake. It is doubtful whether Basra province demonstrates the occupier's cultural expertise. Confidence in one's capacity to master local knowledge can lead to error, leaving chaos in its wake. Since entering southern Iraq, British narratives of the account praised their own role in making Basra peaceful and stable with a lighter footprint, wearing berets not helmets, upholding their urban peace-keeping 'as the tactical antithesis to the brutal and aggressive Yanks.'[34] Scales' testimony echoed this theme. But now that UK forces have withdrawn, the new Iraqi police chief reports the legacy he inherits under British 'overwatch': 'They left me militia, they left me gangsters, and they left me all the troubles in the world.'[35] Scales was wrong about Basra partly because he was wrong about the colonial past. Because it rests on a foundation of bad history, the new culturalism is a poor guide to the present and helps to account for some of the military and intelligence failures in the war on terror.

It also rests on other suspect assumptions. The primal scene of the 'cultural turn' is the interpretation of the classic texts on strategy, such as Sun Tzu and Clausewitz. Whereas Clausewitz was fashionable in the circles of military intellectuals around the time of the 1991 Gulf War, the Chinese sage is now in the ascendancy. But just how peculiar to eastern traditions are Sun Tzu's ideas? Sun Tzu may have stressed the value of intelligence and deception, praised the ideal of the bloodless victory, and stressed the economical logic of finding non-military ways to prevail. However, so did the Florentine diplomat and philosopher Niccolo Machiavelli, whose *Art of War* was one of the most prominent authorities on strategy before Clausewitz.[36] Like Sun Tzu in the 'Warring States' period, Machiavelli lived in a fragile, multi-polar and predatory political environment, of competing city-states, ever-shifting alliances and meddling foreign powers. Costly mercenary armies and multiple fronts of conflict made war a particularly risky and expensive business. His environment, more than cultural stereotypes, may explain why he asserted that 'He who overcomes the enemy by fraud is as much to be praised as he who does so by force.'[37] Moreover, Machiavelli argued for a synthesis of the 'sledgehammer' power of Roman citizen-armies and the 'sneaky' gambits of manoeuvre, surprise and deception, practised by the Parthian horsemen of antiquity, an antecedent of the asymmetric military actor, so in vogue in contemporary security commentaries.[38] He resolved the opposition between eastern and western modes of warfare pragmatically: depending on the circumstances and the terrain, sometimes the caution and indirectness of the Parthians worked better, at other times the bold Roman approach made sense. Machiavelli bridged principles often thought to be opposite, and saw past the limitations of narrow traditions.

So Sun Tzu's concepts were not so culturally-specific. What of the Prussian general Clausewitz? Proponents of a new generation of war, such as Martin van Creveld, claim he is losing his relevance in an age of post-modern 'non-trinitarian' war, with a shift of initiative to non-state actors (from terrorist networks to organised crime), the rise of 'low-intensity' war and the blurring of boundaries between citizen and soldiers, war and peace, which reframes and upsets the received view.[39] Clausewitz may have lived in an era of intense wars and decisive battles between great powers. But he cannot be totally confined to the horizons of his generation. He recognised the phenomena of 'people's armies' and 'small wars'. Stateless forces were part of his world too, from Spain's guerrillas to Russia's Tartars, just as international piracy prefigured today's global black market.[40] He also stated that war is rarely final, and that popular uprisings may arise after the defeat of state militaries. Echoing his critics, Clausewitz also argued that such uprisings were a symptom of the 'breaking down of barriers', which had been 'swept away in our lifetime by the elemental violence of war.'[41]

As well as emptying strategic texts of their richness, the cultural turn might be slightly naïve when it comes to the issue of reception, or understanding how those texts are read and used. Like sacred texts, the great strategic works have been invoked in very different ways to justify different and conflicting policies. And this is not just a problem of interpretation. Rather than just being influenced by these texts, military commanders and rulers at times have selected the parts that fitted their own interests, in other words, have used these texts instrumentally, in common parlance fixing around a policy end. The Clausewitz of the nineteenth century was invoked by Prussian generals to justify the pursuit of decisive battles to destroy the enemy's forces, to preach the inevitability of heavy casualties and the central value of morale, even to urge civilian government to stand aside as they prosecuted the war. By contrast, decision-makers in the twentieth century appealed to Clausewitz to argue different and even opposite principles, such as the assertion that the military should be subordinate to political direction and political ends. Such concepts inspired the US Weinberger-Powell doctrine, which codified the principles of prudent statecraft, the controlled application of force for achievable goals, concrete national interests and a clear exit strategy.[42] Clausewitz as an authority has been ransacked to justify conflicting outlooks and policies.

A similar pattern of opportunism in the relationship between actors and texts can be found in medieval Chinese history. As Alistair Johnston has shown in his study of the Ming dynasty (1368–1644), Chinese rulers over centuries were happy to appeal to their supposed strategic culture selectively when it suited them.[43] As Alistair Johnson showed, China's official version of its own strategic culture claims that historically, it was inspired by the Confucian-Mencian disparagement of the utility of force, and that it was non-expansionist, non-aggressive, and preoccupied with internal anarchy. Chinese rulers often appealed to this supposed tradition of prudent conciliation and compromise, claiming that they were in tune with ancestral wisdom. But this they happily abandoned when they saw opportunities to go on the offensive. Ming rulers did so with great frequency, externally against Vietnamese, Koreans, Uighers, Mongols, and Tibetans.

To justify a more aggressive posture, they could appeal to an alternative tradition that was also to be found in their strategic texts—a philosophy of watchful aggressiveness. In this tradition, offensive force was desirable and preferred, to be mediated by sensitivity to the enemy's relative capabilities. Force could be used when the time was ripe. Supposed strategic traditions did matter, but often only so far as they accorded with the hard-headed calculations of elites. Culture may exist as an influential factor in decision-making, but culture does not always drive decision-makers—decision-makers often exploit culture, which poses an enormous challenge to analysts trying to make sense of their enemies' intentions.

Strength and weakness

So much for the use, and abuse, of strategic texts. The cultural turn is also arguably a dubious account of actual historical behaviour. Too often, it falls prey to a crude and false polarity. In one corner, there are the children of Clausewitz, blundering and guileless Western forces obsessed with decisive combat and wielding the blunt instrument of overwhelming force. In the other corner, there are Sun Tzu's oriental acolytes, weaker but more sophisticated foes, who prefer deception and the 'indirect approach,' and who avoid the excessive slaughters on display at Verdun and Stalingrad.

At least as it has been articulated so far, the hypothesis of culturally determined 'ways of war' ignores too many awkward contrary cases that cut across its neat frontiers. The longest conventional war of the twentieth century was fought between Arabs and Persians, the Iraq-Iran war of 1980–1988. It featured ruinous economic and human costs, and the fighting was reminiscent of the western front: positional combat over entrenched positions and the use of poison gas, and continual waves of young men charging to their deaths, driven by ideologies of martyrdom. Conversely, one of the most elaborate pieces of deception in history, using key intelligence assets, was executed by a western alliance in 1944, 'Operation Bodyguard' to mask the D-Day Normandy Landings. The Allies misled German spies, built dummies, broadcast false radio transmissions, published false newspaper reports and used double bluff, to such effect that the Germans continued to believe the Normandy landings were a feint. This illustrated also that deception and overwhelming force are not mutually exclusive absolutes, but relative parts of a spectrum.

The 'cultural turn' might also neglect the dynamism of culture, of how strategic cultures can change in the course of wars, so that in order to find tactics and strategies that work, cultural norms are violated and remade to fit utility. There is evidence that insurgents and other stateless actors, rather than being determined and constrained by culture, actually violate norms and remake their culture for reasons of pragmatic calculation. Islamist insurgent groups, from Hamas to Al Qaeda, have recently broken with patriarchal values by employing women in increasing numbers as suicide bombers. And this despite religious taboos among male-dominated movements about employing women in war.[44] Women offer a range of benefits as jihadists. Their profile defies stereotypes and is below the radar; they are stealthier and harder to detect; they are overlooked by governments and officials thinking in terms of the typical male 'profile' of a suicide bomber; they inflict greater psychological impact because of perceptions that they are atypical; and even shame men into participation.[45] Recall the changing attitude of Sheikh Ahmed Yassin, spiritual leader of Hamas, who initially 'categorically renounced the use of women as suicide bombers' in January 2002. Two years later, after Hamas struck with its first female suicide attack, he justified it on grounds of utility. 'The male fighters face many obstacles, so women can more easily reach the targets...Women are like the reserve army—when there is a necessity, we use them.'[46] Female suicide bombing, once abhorrent, became a compelling method. Hamas and others doubly violated tradition in strongly felt forms—attitudes to suicide and to women—and remade it to fit strategic circumstances.

To justify this switch, those in favour went back to the Qur'an. If cultures are repertoires with diverse and clashing ideas, what better instance than sacred texts, where messages, guides to action and symbols can be found to justify almost any act? Within Islam, there was a heritage of women fighting in jihad. The Qur'an recognized women's participation in jihad, and contains passages that recognize women's equal status. Women as fighters appear in the early precedents of the prophet's own wife and granddaughter fighting in battles, to the legendary Nusayba bint K'ab, who fought in the Battle of Uhud in 625, as well as other women who supported jihad through nursing the wounded, donating jewellery, and encouraging their male family members. The heroism of these women, icons for modern-day imitators, is celebrated in the Muslim world.[47] Islamic traditions, like all cultural traditions, can be instrumentalised. The suicide bomber, stereotyped as a young man in a state of religious exaltation, turns out to be an overlooked woman. Here is a case where assumptions about the culturally static profile of the enemy could prove not only misguided but deadly.

'Know thyself' is also one of Sun Tzu's commands, yet the cultural turn also offers a misleading portrayal of the west. It overlooks patterns of behaviour that upset the clean narrative of a 'western' tradition. Metacultural analysis draws stark contrasts. It uses the polarizing notions of Orient and Occident, eastern and western strategic traditions. It often springs from a desire to distinguish not only the warfare and conflict of east and west, but their cultural life. War becomes a commentary on the worth and value of different civilizations. Combat in particular becomes a kind of value judgement on the societies that wage it. Hence the portrayal of 'Oriental cunning', evasion or subtlety, against western 'openness', or naivety.

As a matter of self-definition, westerners have often thought of their desire for pitched battle as a reflection of their integrity. As Col. Harry Summers said to Col. Tu in Hanoi as North Vietnam's guerrilla strategy was paying dividends in 1975, 'you never defeated us on the battlefield'.[48] If war is the ultimate political act, it is also tempting to see it as the ultimate expression of one's political values. And it may be that because they have relied for evidence partly on westerners' statements about themselves, culturalists have reproduced this self-image. We might also have a nostalgia for set-piece battles in open fields, in a world when such battles with such clarity are denied to conventional forces, and where war is dominated by a 'dismal globalised continuum' of urban terror, long-range bombing and massacres of unarmed civilians. Americans, Israelis or Britons might yearn for a time when their enemies shared their preference for a fair fight.[49]

But if we examine the record of actual behaviour, a more mixed picture emerges. In fact, strategies of avoidance and indirection have a rich pedigree in western military practice. The more formidable the enemy and the more undesirable a decisive showdown, the more acceptable indirect methods seem, whether against a determined Japan in the Burma jungles, a Hannibal emerging from the slaughter at Cannae, or the northern Union with its industrial might, during the American civil war. Duplicitous moves including pretending to be friendly, pretending to be done for the day, sending false information, or making a misleading agreement are timeless lessons of warfare. The 'Odysseus' stratagem of ancient Greece competed with the 'Achilles' ethos with its thirst for battle, and what might be derided as the enemy's dishonesty could be reconfigured as one's own artfulness.[50]

The western fixation with a 'fair and open' fight—as opposed to the duplicity of terrorists—should not overshadow a frequent practice in European medieval war, also presumably part of the western tradition: of battle avoidance. Regardless of their elite warrior cultures, medieval commanders were often wary of the dangers of pitched battle, and were constrained by problems of supply, hygiene, and of survival itself in expeditionary wars. Defenders also had an advantage. Defensive strongholds enabled one side to refuse battle. Between 1071 and 1328 in Flanders, often invaded, there were only eleven battles of note.[51] And the weak did not have to be reared in eastern traditions to find alternative ways to combat the strong. When they calculated that they could not resist English invasion through direct combat, Welsh and Scots defenders chose defensive strategies that eastern guerrillas would be proud of, such as scorched earth retreats, cutting off supply lines, punitive raids and the exploitation of terrain.

In terms of norms and codes of honour, the western tradition has in fact not always bound itself to the 'hoplite' ideal of upright, direct warfare of stand-up battles on level terms within strict protocols. Western forces, like any others with the same means, have indiscriminately bombed civilians, launched surprise attacks, used chemical and nuclear weapons, and today embrace risk-aversion through unmanned aerial vehicles, taking their individuals out of the battlespace, but which contributes to the paucity of available human intelligence.

One does not have to be 'eastern' to practise indirect methods. At the risk of stating the obvious, weaker sides of any culture, whether secular or religious, nationalist or Marxist, Arab or Asian, have had to find effective ways to get around their enemies' strengths and exploit their vulnerabilities. When on the wrong end of a disparity in 'hard' power, weaker sides have historically faced the grim arithmetic that they must be resourceful and flexible and avoid or postpone massed confrontation. No culture enjoys a monopoly over this logic. Being Vietnamese, Islamic, eastern or 'oriental' was probably not the main driving force behind the 'asymmetric' strategies of the Viet Cong or Al Qaeda, any more than being Spanish or American was the main driving force behind the indirect methods of those who took on Napoleon or the British Empire.[52]

Because it is so tied to a quest for western cultural identity, it is no accident that the overarching thesis of a 'western way of war' is often selective and historically problematic. The desire to contrast one's own form of war with Orientals, and to think of the world as a set of homogenous cultural traditions, creates a pre-existing bias. Advocates of a western way of war bypass the history of western strategies of deception, evasion, and indirectness, in their desire to present combat and strategic cultures as symptomatic of core societal values. Treating war as the manifestation of a society's pathologies rather than a shifting response to changing circumstances, culturalism divorces war from external political context. It is also dangerously permissive. As Jonathan Mirsky argues, 'If we have "curious rules of honour" on one side, and deceit, ambush, treachery and surprise on the other, we give ourselves permission to do horrible things.'[53] A prescient warning for practices such as rendition and 'special interrogation techniques'.

The cultural turn misses out the pragmatism and wiliness of both states and non-state actors at war. To cut it to its proper size without dismissing it altogether, it should be tempered by a less fashionable concept: power and weakness. The size, wealth, resources and technology of the adversary is a major driver of behaviour in war. Rather than being necessarily determinative, a war culture can be an epiphenomenal adaptation to a material environment. Codes of morality and honour can also be reactions to the distribution of power. Unable to compete in pitched battle, the French Resistance and Hezbollah were scorned by their opponents for hiding among the civilian population, while the frustrations of the powerful were summarised by an American military observer in Southeast Asia in 1964: 'If only the little bastards would come out of the jungle and fight like men, we'd cream them.'[54]

Furthermore, the claim that 'easterners' are distinctive for avoiding 'excess' or mindless loss of life misunderstands the strategic vision of weaker, 'nonwestern' opponents. From Ho Chi Minh to Osama Bin Laden, weaker protagonists have announced their will to make sacrifice without limit. It is precisely this which they reckon advantages them against the stronger enemy, with its nervous politicians reluctant to spend endless bloody and treasure. As demonstrated by more than a million dead Communists in the North's ultimate victory in Vietnam, or in the wave after wave of attacks made by Vietnamese or Chinese armies at Dien Bien Phu or throughout the Korean War. Bloodless methods and being economical with casualties were emphatically not always their war-winning strategies.

As well as oversimplifying the nature of different traditions, the assumptions of the 'culturalists' also paint a misleading picture of moments where 'eastern' and 'western' cultures clash. Consider John Poole's account of the failed amphibious Gallipoli campaign of 1915, when the British and French empires tried and failed to storm the Dardanelles straits against Ottoman mobile artillery, on a boundary between Europe and Asia. Poole shows, with some force, that Turkish light infantry lured the British 1/5th Norfolk battalion into a trap, by withdrawing into the interior and surrounding and ambushing terrified Tommies. This trap, he argues, was an example of the military heritage of Asia Minor.

Apart from the problem that the Turks were being advised by the Germans, Poole's account does not tell the whole story about the nature of the western invaders. The most striking exercise of deception was carried out not by the Turks, but by the British four months later, who pulled off one of the most difficult tasks in war: a large-scale retreat. British estimates reckoned that the withdrawal from Suvla Bay and Anzac Cove would cost casualties of forty thousand. But Sir Charles Monro devised ruses, such as the appearance of routine, fires left burning and rifles rigged to fire themselves. Eighty thousand men with their vehicles, guns and animals were evacuated. Only five men were wounded.[55]

The dogma of cultural determinism, then, often fails to deal with many of the complexities of militarised performance. And its empirical and conceptual shortcomings reflect a more fundamental problem. It sees what it wants to see in history, making facts fit a theory to confirm its urgent contemporary agenda, which is to alert today's military and security decision-makers to the profound differences between cultural traditions. But however seductive and well-intentioned the theory, competing 'ways of war' are hammered out in a matrix in which culture was one element that interacts with others, such as material circumstances, power imbalances, and individuals. It would be ironic if the many war cultures of the past were forced into simplistic categories in order to encourage cultural sensitivity in the present.

Culture: rethinking the definition

There are different versions of what culture is, and how it relates to war and conflict. These vary in sophistication. Here I have argued that we should abandon any idea of culture as a central or even determining force, or a clear 'script' of traditions and meanings that drives behaviour. With the help of more insightful anthropological models, we can develop a better definition. In a recent report of November 2007, the American Anthropological Association cautioned against simplistic structural-functionalist models of culture being employed within the military, and by inference in the intelligence community. Culture, it argues, is the encoding of meaning. But it is not so much a system of eternal values as a process and phenomenon constantly remade and changing. There is the 'idea of culture as an historically contingent, power-laden, dynamic and emerging property of human relations, and the theoretical and methodological entanglements that such a view implies', as opposed to the idea of culture as 'a set of discrete and static elements that can be neatly catalogued, captured, stored, and pulled out to support decision making.'[56]

As argued here, the pressures of war are particularly potent when they force strategic imperatives to clash with ideas of cultural tradition.

We are concerned here with the relationship between cultural context and action. Even if culture is an inescapable context, it is only part of the context in which strategic decisions are made, but one variable in a matrix of negotiated interests.[57] Culture is part of the process of decision-making and behaviour, but not exhaustive of it. In times of pressure and the quest for survival, actors can behave despite their culture.

Rather than seeing culture as a clear script for action, a better view is that culture is more a loose repertoire. It supplies a set of memories, values, symbols, metaphors, interpreted experience, principles and 'lessons'. Crucially, culture can be an ambiguous heritage, with contradictory ideas that are open to conflicting interpretations. And rather than viewing states, tribes or insurgents as passive bi-products of their cultures, we should also see them as strategic users of culture. People invoke culture, instrumentalise it, and recast it in order to support policy choices and options. Thus the war/culture relationship is highly politicised.

In our own time, we have seen this process at work. Consider the debate within Hamas or al Qaeda over two taboos, the adoption of suicide bombing and recruiting female *jihadists*. This shows movements internally debating their norms of war, and changing their mind in order to find a method that would be effective against the overwhelming military force of its enemies, and then justifying it by reworking interpretations of a sacred text.

On the other side of the hill, Britain and America also have an ambiguous heritage of strategic ideas, as shown in academic and public argument. Debating military choices, they have disagreed over whether to apply the analogies of World War One, World War Two or Vietnam. Supporters of the Iraq war in 2003 often invoked Chamberlain, Hitler and Munich in 1938, arguing that against dangerous tyrants, an aggressive strategy was a winning strategy. Those against it raised Vietnam or even the July Crisis of 1914, warning that an uncompromising stance would lead to disastrous war with unanticipated consequences.[58] Where some warned against appeasement, others spoke of quagmire. Culture did not supply a clear grid for action, but threw up clashing lessons and analogies.

Conclusion

So what? Why does the history of war and culture matter beyond fireside conversation? As I have argued, those advocating the 'cultural turn' often appeal to a reading of history that is in some respects flawed. By falling prey to cultural determinism, or 'national character' analysis, or lumping disparate 'non-western' cultures together, this misreading of history may also have strategic costs.

The United States and Israel, are paying the price for misreading history through misconceived metacultural analysis. After the rout of Saddam's forces, Sunni Arabs did not behave as people easily cowed by the 'Shock and Awe' of a stronger force, but proved to be resilient guerrillas.[59] Once the insurgency was underway, the United States also treated the Iraqi insurgency through the lens of Vietnam. The classic Maoist insurgencies in Vietnam, Malaya and the Philippines during the 1960's were homogenous, top-down and unified. Thus they were differently structured from the fragmented and networked insurgency of disparate groups in Iraq, and the wider battlefront against Al Qaeda.[60] Though there are certain dynamics that unite insurgencies and 'non-western' war down the ages, it is misleading to infer giant 'non-western' paradigms. And today, Iraq illustrates the problems of culture-centric approaches that are divorced from the dynamic political context of war. Although some argue that Iraq can be trisected into three permanent parts, like Caesar's Gaul its internal divisions are proving more manifold, more subtle and more unstable. Sunni insurgents, for example, have realigned against their former allies Al Qaeda in Iraq, for the moment cooperating with the US in the 'Anbar awakening.' Misreading history has also cost the Israeli Defence Force. It is reeling still from its discovery that fighting guerrillas in the West Bank made it overconfident in combating the small-unit, agile, media-savvy fighters of Lebanon's Hezbollah in the July war of 2006.[61] By misconceiving the past and overlooking this kind of fluidity, the 'cultural turn' runs the risk of mischaracterising the nature of conflict and the enemies of the west.

If the technology-driven revolution of the 1990s failed to deliver on all of its promises, we should also be cautious about the culture-driven revolution. A more careful reading of history will help to guard against seeing culture as the new magic bullet. Today's strategists and intelligence analysts cannot afford to presume that East is always East.

5

OPEN SOURCE INTELLIGENCE AND NUCLEAR SAFEGUARDS

Wyn Q. Bowen

Editors' Notes: Open source intelligence has been hailed by many as the most cost-effective and efficient way to gather knowledge in the information revolution of the twenty-first century. In this chapter, a former UN weapons inspector in Iraq discusses the role of 'new media' in intelligence work. Specifically the chapter focuses on clandestine nuclear weapons programmes and the state's desires to evade international safeguards obligations. Bowen addresses the role that open source can and has played, but also warns against complacency and relying too heavily on open source intelligence.

Generating accurate, timely and actionable intelligence for national and international decision-makers in the nuclear field involves creating knowledge and further understanding of both the 'capability' and 'intentions' underlying state level nuclear programmes. These programmes are located in various regions across the globe within an increasingly transnational security environment and present a diverse array of intelligence challenges. From the perspective of open source intelligence (OSINT), individual states may be characterized as either an open society, with straightforward access guaranteed to pertinent and locally generated open source materials; conversely, some states like North

Korea are relatively closed societies and as a consequence tend to be somewhat opaque when it comes to open source research. There are states that sit somewhere in the middle, such as Iran, which are characterized by relatively open societies but where publishing in print and electronic forms is still subjected to state sanction.

While it is important not to oversell the role of open source intelligence in the context of nuclear safeguards, there can be little doubt that the systematic exploitation of open source research can make a very real contribution to governments, and particularly to international organizations, that have a requirement to track, to understand and to respond to the challenges posed in this area. Open source research can often provide the essential context required by governments and international organizations to better understand secret intelligence or UN classified information; it can provide a quick and easy means to meet unexpected and urgent information requirements; open sources can sometimes provide a 'tip-off' capability; it can be used to protect, or to avoid having to share, classified information; and, occasionally, open sources can provide the information that solves the intelligence puzzle or flags up a problem that had hitherto been overlooked.

The value of open sources in the context of assessing proliferation challenges was highlighted by *The Commission on the Intelligence Capabilities of the United States Regarding Weapons of Mass Destruction* (WMD) in its report of March 2005. Established following the failure of WMD intelligence in the run up to the Iraq war in 2002–3, a significant recommendation of the Commission was that the US intelligence community needed to establish 'an Open Source Directorate in the CIA to use the Internet and modern information processing tools to greatly enhance the availability of open source information analysts, collectors, and users of intelligence'.[1] This recommendation was duly acted upon with the launch in November 2005 of the Director of National Intelligence's (DNI) Open Source Center (OSC). Administered by the Director of the CIA (DCIA) on behalf of the DNI, the OSC was described by DCIA Porter Goss as representing 'a major strategic initiative and commitment to the value we place on openly available information'.[2] The establishment of the OSC is certainly indicative of the growing significance that has been accorded in recent years by US and other intelligence communities to the exploitation of open sources as part of the all-source intelligence process.

Against this backdrop the chapter will seek to do several things. First, consideration is given to what the IAEA means by '*safeguards*' and the various sources of information available to the Agency to evaluate the compliance of individual states with their safeguards agreements. Similar to other agencies of the United Nations, the IAEA lacks an official intelligence arm so the exploitation of open sources offers a highly cost-effective means of generating relevant safeguards information. The Agency's use of open sources will be explained and some real world examples will be provided regarding how this has contributed to the safeguards process. The chapter also examines some of the limitations, drawbacks and challenges associated with OSINT in order to provide some necessary balance.

Safeguards and the state evaluation process

The IAEA describes safeguards as 'measures through which the IAEA seeks to verify that nuclear material is not diverted from peaceful uses. States accept the application of such measures through the conclusion of safeguards agreements with the IAEA'. As the IAEA notes, 'the vast majority of States have undertaken not to produce or otherwise acquire nuclear weapons and to place *all* of their nuclear material and activities under safeguards to allow the IAEA to verify that undertaking'.[3]

There are various types of safeguards agreements but the most pertinent in the context of preventing nuclear proliferation, and the role of OSINT therein, are 'Comprehensive Safeguards Agreements' (CSA) and 'Additional Protocols'. 'All non-nuclear-weapon States [NNWS] party to the Treaty on the Non-Proliferation of Nuclear Weapons (NPT), as well as States party to the regional nuclear weapon-free zone treaties' are required to negotiate CSAs with the IAEA. In line with these agreements a NNWS commits 'to accept safeguards on all nuclear material in all peaceful nuclear activities, within its territory, under its jurisdiction or carried out under its control anywhere for the purpose of verifying that such material is not diverted to nuclear weapons or other nuclear explosive devices'. The IAEA 'has the right and obligation' under these agreements 'to ensure that safeguards are applied on all such nuclear material'.[4]

'Additional protocols' are 'designed for states having a safeguards agreement with the IAEA, in order to strengthen the effectiveness and improve the efficiency of the safeguards system as a contribution to global non-proliferation objectives'.[5] Strengthened safeguards were required following the nuclear proliferation shocks provided by Iraq and North Korea during the 1990s which, despite being NNWS parties to the NPT, had conducted extensive clandestine nuclear weapons programmes beyond the view of IAEA inspectors.

Additional protocols require additional types of measures to be implemented including the following:

State provision of information about, and IAEA inspector access to, all parts of a State's nuclear fuel cycle, from uranium mines to nuclear waste and any other location where nuclear material intended for non-nuclear use is present;

State provision of information on, and IAEA short notice access to, all buildings on a site;

State provision of information about, and IAEA inspector access to, a State's nuclear fuel cycle R&D activities not involving nuclear material. State provision of information on the manufacture and export of sensitive nuclear related equipment and material, and IAEA inspector access to manufacturing and import locations in the State;

IAEA collection of environmental samples at locations beyond those provided under safeguards agreements;

State acceptance of streamlined procedures for IAEA inspector designation and requirement for multiple entry visas (valid for at least one year) for inspectors;

IAEA's right to use internationally established communications systems, including satellite systems and other forms of telecommunication; Wide area environmental sampling, after Board of Governors approval of such sampling and consultations with the State concerned.[6]

While the significantly expanded mandate provided by Additional Protocols has certainly strengthened the IAEA's ability to safeguard nuclear technology for peaceful purposes in those states that have negotiated one with the Agency, it has also brought with it a much greater requirement for safeguards-related information because of the broader array of locations and activities covered. This, in turn, has fuelled the requirement for open source research to assist with the safeguards process.

As part of its safeguards mandate the IAEA performs evaluations of state party compliance with the NPT and periodically produces State Evaluation Reports (SER) for internal review. The SERs will include relevant information and analysis of the political and economic status of the state in question, as well as detailed coverage of those nuclear fuel cycle elements present in the country and related research, development and industrial capabilities. The state evaluation process leads to conclusions being made about compliance and it is central to planning and conducting safeguards related activities including inspections on the ground. Within the Agency a 'dedicated, high-level interdepartmental committee reviews the content of the SERs in detail' and takes 'the final decision regarding the conclusion for each State that will be reported in the annual Safeguards Implementation Report (SIR)'.[7]

To inform the evaluation process the IAEA has four main sources of information available to it. First, there is the information provided by a state party (primarily in the form of state declarations) under the terms of its safeguards agreements and, if one is in place, an additional protocol. Second, information is generated as a result of in-country verification activities including site visits. Third, the IAEA actively acquires and assesses open source information.[8] Finally, information is also provided by third parties (other member states) and this is actually an obligation under Article VIII of the IAEA Statute which states that all members 'should make available such information as would, in the judgment of the member, be helpful to the Agency'.[9] However, the provision of information by third parties is not without its challenges, primarily due to concerns about the UN maintaining its impartiality and sensitivities over whether intelligence has been provided selectively to influence an issue in a particular direction.

Open sources and IAEA safeguards

Where, then, does open source intelligence fit in, what is its utility and are there any drawbacks? The IAEA's systematic exploitation of open source information began during the mid-1990s. Over the past decade or so the acquisition and analysis of open source materials has become a 'core component of the information analysis process' within the Agency.[10] In a very basic sense there are two types of open source information that the IAEA draws upon: (1) information derived from documentation in both electronic and hard-copy formats; and (2) information derived from commercially available satellite imagery.

The vast majority of safeguards—relevant, open source information comes in text document format, either electronically (via the Internet, on-line databases, etc) or in hard copy, and it can come in many different languages. This material is accessed in various ways including 'from databases that contain non-restricted information and that have been developed by institutes specialized in the field of nuclear nonproliferation'. Other approaches include web searches for pertinent material produced by governments, NGOs, the specialized and non-specialized media, science and technology journals and the academic community.[11] While some of this material will be freely available, accessing much of the open source information relevant to safeguards will require allocating resources to subscriptions.

In very broad terms then, research of open source documentation can make a contribution in two main areas. First, it can be used to generate an understanding of the political and economic status of the country in question. This can contribute to the development of the necessary political-strategic and economic awareness required to make sense of narrower developments that take place or potentially might occur in the nuclear field. Research of open sources can illuminate how a country, or more specifically how political factions and elites within a country, perceive the prevailing and evolving strategic environment, and how they have done so in the past. This can provide insights into national threat perception and the nature of a country's strategic relations with neighbours and countries further afield. All of this is directly relevant to identifying potential indicators of nuclear intent. Open sources can also cast valuable light on the economic rationale of a given county for developing nuclear power. This is a particularly relevant issue if, for instance, a country possesses major hydrocarbon reserves and there are doubts about a stated nuclear requirement. In terms of the economic context for understanding nuclear issues, for example, the US Energy Information Administration[12] and the Economist Intelligence Unit provide very informative assessments.[13]

A good example of how open sources can be applied to assess political context might be their role in monitoring the risk of a nuclear 'cascade' in the Middle East following the announcements by several Arab states in recent years of new, or renewed, interest in setting up nuclear power programmes. Many analysts perceive these to be part of a 'hedging' strategy *vis-à-vis* a nuclearising Iran. Monitoring English and Arabic language reports on local websites (official government sites, news sites, think tanks, and so on) can provide rapid and up-to-date information on the current state of play on nuclear policies and debates in countries such as the UAE, Egypt and Turkey. Moreover, the relative openness of the Iranian polity has meant that monitoring newspapers and websites known to be affiliated with different parts of the political establishment can provide pertinent and informative insights into the 'nuclear debate' in that country. For example, reading the *Keyhan* newspaper associated with the Intelligence Ministry and the reformist *Shargh* newspaper will provide very different perspectives of the nuclear and other security issues. More recently blogs have become an increasingly valuable open source of information in this and other respects.

At the more technical and tactical (if you will) level, open source research can provide pertinent information on a country's nuclear research programme and specific facilities either directly or indirectly related to the fuel cycle. This can provide some very specific insights into a country's existing nuclear capabilities and potential for expansion and change. At one level this might involve assessments of the various aspects of the fuel cycle itself, such as the mining, milling, conversion and enrichment of uranium, fuel fabrication, research and power reactors, reprocessing, and waste disposal. However, as Bevaart *et al.* note, generating useful information in these areas

...poses the greatest challenge [for the IAEA, for] while general information on a State is usually readily available, more specific information on facilities, research and nuclear materials requires a more specialized effort and the focused collection and evaluation of materials.[14]

Moreover, it should be recognized that open sources have their general limits in the technical area, notably with regard to generating specific information and insights into the really sensitive elements of the fuel cycle such as enrichment, reprocessing/separation and weaponisation. Obviously, such activities will be the focus of the utmost secrecy in all countries where they are being pursued. At another level open source research can be used to evaluate a country's critical supporting infrastructure including local industries, research centres, university departments and other educational and training establishments.

As Joanna Kidd and I have noted elsewhere:

relevant technical and scientific information can be accessed via a range of different sources including international scientific databases, national educational and scientific databases, university websites, company publications and websites, and material and websites associated with professional societies.

For example, ISI Web of Science[15] contains 'references for approximately 8,700 journals' and Elsevier Science Direct[16] 'claims to have more than 25% of the world's science, technology and medical full-text and bibliographic information'.[17] Moreover, the websites of national nuclear authorities in the Middle East and North Africa can also be a useful source of information in part because they tend to change over time. Such alterations can often be quite significant and in recent years some countries have been making much less detailed information available, at least on their English language versions, and frequently also on their original language versions. One can speculate about the rationale for certain countries reducing the level of detail provided on these websites. To track such changes one relevant open source research tool is the free-to-use Internet Archive. This not-for-profit website was established 'to build an Internet library, with the purpose of offering permanent access for researchers, historians, and scholars to historical collections that exist in digital format'.[18] Internet Archive allows the user to look at previous versions of web-pages for specific organizations that may not exist anymore or which have been modified. An informative example here is the website of Saudi Arabia's Atomic Energy Research Institute (AERI). The current (as of 17 August 2008) version of the webpage describing AERI makes no mention of its laboratories for chemical separation, while the 15 August 2005 version accessed using Internet Archive certainly did.

The second main type of open source information utilized by the IAEA as part of evaluating states' compliance with their safeguards obligations is commercially available satellite imagery. According to the IAEA, commercial satellite imagery

has become a key tool that is now used routinely to evaluate information provided by States on their nuclear activities and to plan inspections, visits to facilities to verify design information and complementary access.

Satellite images can help the Agency in utilizing its resources more efficiently by assisting with the choice of sites to be inspected and occasionally eliminating the need to conduct visits to facilities on the ground. It also 'increases the possibility of detecting proscribed nuclear activities', such as preparations for nuclear tests, or activities that should have, but have not, been declared.[19] At an operational level the IAEA has its own Satellite Imagery Analysis Unit.[20] The Agency purchases commercially available imagery from several companies in the form of optical, thermal or radar data. IAEA contracts with the providers mean that images can be provided in a timely fashion and the Agency can also access relevant imagery archives as and when necessary.[21]

Open sources in practice

Having established, in relatively generic terms, the main types of open sources used by the IAEA and how these are applied as part of the safeguards process, it is informative to provide some concrete examples of how useful open sources can actually be in practice. The first two examples (Iran/AQ Khan and Egypt) are ones which the IAEA itself has flagged up in terms of highlighting the utility of open source intelligence. The third example of Libya has not specifically been highlighted by the IAEA but it does provide a fascinating insight into how monitoring OSINT for insights into the evolving intentions and capabilities of a particular state can provide contradictory indicators.

OSINT searches triggered by inspections: Iran and the AQ Khan network

The first example relates to the use of open sources to address very specific questions raised by unexplained indicators picked up as a result of IAEA investigations. In an evident reference to the AQ Khan proliferation network and its provision of gas centrifuge enrichment technology to Iran, some of which, the IAEA discovered, had traces of enriched uranium as a result of previous use in the Pakistani enrichment programme[22], a recent conference paper by several IAEA officials highlights the utility of open source research in investigating proscribed nuclear activities. Specifically, the authors noted that:

...the analysis of proliferation often requires investigating less obvious and subtle indicators. Small amounts of uranium hexafluoride, even in gram amounts, in a State without a declared uranium enrichment capacity could raise a question as to why the location has such material. What is manufactured in the State or imported? If manufactured domestically, then why? Was it for conversion experiments? Checks of nuclear material accounting reports would also be performed to confirm if the material had been imported, when and from where. Were any enrichment activities (or conversion activities) included in the additional protocol declarations? *Questions such as these could trigger extensive searches in open sources for enrichment research or nuclear cooperation with another State that has mastered enrichment technology. If the material was imported, open sources would be searched to determine the past and present nature of any nuclear cooperation, including the technical capabilities of the exporter* [emphasis added].[23]

OSINT as 'tip-off': Egyptian non-compliance

The second example highlights the utility of open source research as a means of generating specific questions that need to be addressed by the IAEA as part of its safeguards-related investigation for a particular country because of the possibility that certain activities might have taken place that should have been declared in line with its safeguards agreements; a 'tip off' capability if you will.

The example involves Egypt and the IAEA's updating of its state evaluation report for that country in 2004. During the evaluation process the Agency's consultation of open source, scientific and technical documents raised questions over whether some of those published by Egyptian authors indicated that the country had failed to declare some very specific and sensitive nuclear activities relevant to weapons development. Specifically, as noted by the IAEA:

the Agency concluded that it was necessary to follow up with Egypt indications derived from a number of open source documents published by the Egyptian Atomic Energy Authority (AEA) and by former and current staff of the AEA suggesting the possibility of nuclear material, activities and facilities in Egypt relating to uranium extraction and conversion, irradiation of uranium targets and reprocessing that had not been reported to the Agency.[24]

The questions raised by the review of open source literature prompted a meeting between the IAEA Deputy Director General for Safeguards, the Chairman of Egypt's Atomic Energy Authority, and other senior Egyptian officials. Examples of the relevant open source documents were presented to the Egyptians in order to illustrate the concerns that some nuclear activities had gone unreported. The main outcome of the meeting was an agreement by the Egyptian side to allow the IAEA to visit the Inshas nuclear research centre to 'assess the situation'.[25] The IAEA subsequently confirmed that Egypt had indeed failed to report various things to the Agency 'in accordance with its obligations under its Safeguards Agreement' including: (1) its initial inventory of imported UF_4, imported and domestically produced uranium metal, imported thorium compounds, small quantities of domestically produced UO_2, UO_3 and UF_4, and a number of unirradiated low enriched and natural uranium fuel rods; (2) its uranyl nitrate and scrap UO_2 pellets, and their use for acceptance testing of the Hydrometallurgy Pilot Plant; (3) its irradiation of small amounts of natural uranium and thorium and their subsequent dissolution in the Nuclear Chemistry Building laboratories, including the production and transfer of waste; and (4) its failure to provide initial design information for its Hydrometallurgy Pilot Plant and Radioisotope Production Facility, and modified design information for the two reactors.[26]

OSINT and contradictory indicators: the case of Libya

While the example of Libya has not specifically been highlighted by the IAEA, it is informative because it illuminates the role of open sources in the context of responding to unexpected developments in the safeguards field. As I noted with Joanna Kidd,

On occasions when information is required urgently to inform a situation that has not been expected or predicted, open sources may offer the only solution to meet such a requirement at least in the short term.. The suddenness of Libya's announcement on its nuclear programme in December 2003 is probably a good example of such a situation because it took by surprise all parties outside of a small group of Libyan, British and American officials.[27]

The information on Libya in the following paragraphs is drawn from a longer study by the author published as part of an edited volume in 2006.[28] This earlier study compared what was known in available open sources about Libya's nuclear programme and intentions prior to December 2003, with what has since become publicly known as a result of IAEA and other investigations.

An examination of some of the political indicators retrospectively derived from available open sources prior to late 2003 suggested that the regime of Colonel Qadhafi had evidently been moderating its ways since the late 1990s at the regional and international levels. This had involved the regime moving significantly away from its past involvement in sponsoring terrorism, attempts to undermine other governments in the region and traditional bellicosity towards Israel. Specifically on the question of nuclear and other WMD, open sources certainly carried much fewer reports of Qadhafi making statements on nuclear weapons, which he had a penchant for doing from the 1970s and right into the 1990s. The regime also made some positive moves to demonstrate that Libya may be changing its views on developing and possessing unconventional weapons capabilities. In November 2002 Libya became the only traditional state of 'proliferation concern' to sign up to the Hague Code of Conduct Against Ballistic Missile Proliferation (ICOC). In August 2003, the Libyan leader even called for inspectors from international organizations such as the IAEA to visit sites in his country that could potentially be used in the development of chemical and biological weapons.[29]

At one level, of course, these indicators proved to be highly accurate in that Libya did give up its nuclear and other programmes following negotiations with the British and American governments, culminating in the public announcement by the regime in December 2003 that it was giving up these projects and capabilities. At another level, however, relying solely on such open source indicators without significant insights into the technical dimension of the programme would have been problematic. This is because information that has since emerged into the public domain as a result of IAEA and other investigations has shown that while Libya was politically moving in the right direction, it had secretly reinvigorated its nuclear weapons programme, principally by procuring relevant equipment, materials and knowledge from the AQ Khan proliferation network.[30]

So, while Libya was making positive progress politically, including its public statements and actions on WMD related issues, it was rapidly developing its nuclear weapons and beginning to make far more significant progress than at any other time over the preceding three decades. The IAEA evidently did not pick up on any open source or other indicators related to this activity at the technical level. Indeed, it took a major secret intelligence effort by the British and American governments to uncover the nature and scale of the network's activities and customers from the late 1990s onwards.[31] The case of Libya, then, is a good example of how open sources can provide contradictory indicators in the field of nuclear proliferation and safeguards.

Limitations, drawbacks and challenges

Having highlighted the role and utility of open source research in the field of nuclear safeguards, it is important to end by adding some balance by addressing some of the limitations, drawbacks and challenges associated with OSINT. The first and possibly most obvious limitation is that proscribed nuclear activities are usually deeply and carefully concealed by proliferators, so open sources will have their natural limits. If the society in question is relatively closed in nature then the challenge of generating relevant open source information is going to be even greater. The failure of the IAEA to pick up open source indicators, or any other for that matter, *vis-à-vis* Libyan and Iranian violations of their safeguards agreements prior to 2003 and 2002, respectively, is a testament to the fact that proliferators take great care to conceal their illicit activities.

A second challenge confronted by the IAEA and other organizations is how to derive 'safeguards relevant knowledge from an ever increasing volume of information' in open sources.[32] As Baute notes,

Open sources can be overwhelming [due to the] vast quantity of information, multiple languages, information origins from news media to scientific and technical literature.[33]

The huge expansion of web-based sources in recent years has been primarily responsible for this challenge. Moreover, the process of identifying, assessing and validating relevant open source information is very time consuming. It is of no surprise, then, that the Agency's open-source information technology infrastructure 'is continually being upgraded to incorporate new search and organizational capabilities', and 'the introduction of new, analytical skills and tools' is considered to be 'essential' by the IAEA.[34] Beyond database management and innovation, a more mundane approach to minimizing the effect of information overload involves building and maintaining lists of open sources that have a proven track record in terms of their credibility.

A further issue worth highlighting is that of language. A significant amount of safeguards relevant information will only be available in original language sources and not in the two most widely used UN languages of English and French. This presents the challenge of having to identify and then translate source materials that are only available in the original language. While machine translation may present a partial solution, the technical nature of much of the relevant language in the safeguards field generates some not insignificant complications in this respect. The upshot from this is that there may not currently be a credible option other than relying on professional translators, however costly they may be. Another particularly expensive dimension of open source exploitation, of course, involves the purchase of commercial satellite imagery.

Finally, as Bevaart *et al.* note, relevant open sources in the safeguards field can be of 'varying quality, reliability, and credibility'.[35] Baute also warns that much open source information can be 'unreliable', for instance, because it might be 'based on pure political agendas and not on factual reporting'.[36] These are observations from IAEA officials with direct experience of the contribution that open sources can make to nuclear safeguards. Indeed, recognizing and accounting for bias, inaccuracy and even disinformation is of the upmost importance to effectively harnessing the full potential of OSINT.

Conclusion

Researching open source material can make a significant contribution to both governments and international organizations that have a requirement to track and assess nuclear proliferation. For the IAEA in particular, OSINT makes a very real contribution to the state evaluation process and without it the Agency's ability to fulfil its safeguards mandate would be significantly undermined. The principal contribution of OSINT is the provision of context for better understanding secret or UN classified information. In this respect open sources can provide a cost effective means for organizations working on limited budgets. As this chapter has demonstrated, open sources can also have a much more direct role in the safeguards process by providing the IAEA with a 'tip-off' capability about the questions that it should be asking of certain states in the nuclear area as part of the evaluation process. Although open sources will always have to be read with an eye on the potential for bias, inaccuracy and even disinformation, their contribution only looks set to grow in the future as the information technology revolution continues to present new data storage, search and information retrieval options.

6

ALL THE SECRETS THAT ARE FIT TO PRINT?

THE MEDIA AND US INTELLIGENCE SERVICES BEFORE AND AFTER 9/11

Steve Hewitt and Scott Lucas[1]

Editors' Notes: In this chapter two leading academics investigate the evolution of the US intelligence community's relationship with the media, concentrating on the informal links that have shaped its contours. Initially the media served to support American actions, yet with several early failures—including the infamous inability to predict North Korea's invasion of the South in 1950—this balance began to sway in favour of outright criticism. Relations once more shifted with the US-led war in Iraq. In the wake of 9/11 the media initially suppressed negative stories before the invasion, yet once it was clear that weapons of mass destruction would not be found, widespread discontent in the press ensued. The authors conclude that national security is dependent on the insecurity of the people, as portrayed through the media, for if the 'threat' disappears, what is the future for intelligence agencies?

At the end of the 1976 film, *Three Days of the Condor*, a disaffected analyst, played by Robert Redford, tells a senior CIA officer that he has given details of an illegal and murderous Agency operation to the *New York Times*. The officer, unperturbed, replies, 'How do you know they'll print it?'[2] The fictional jibe points to the very real complexity of the relationship(s) between media and intelligence agencies. There is the adversarial relationship; there is the dependent relationship; there is the manipulative relationship; there is the laudatory relationship; there is the supportive relationship. From the onset of the Cold War to the era after the dissolution of the Soviet Union, these relationships have shifted, overlapped, and varied in the United States and Britain, yet they still await examination and critique by scholars.

Consider, for example, the projection of the leaders of US intelligence agencies. FBI Director J. Edgar Hoover was a pervasive figure with frequent (ghost-written) books, films, and television programmes carrying the FBI label and Hoover's approval, capped by a long-running crime drama that ran from 1965 to 1974 on American primetime television.[3] Allen Dulles, the Director of Central Intelligence, building on his Second World War reputation as a key Office of Strategic Services' operative in Switzerland and his Wall Street and legal connections, established a near-legendary profile including a display on the front cover of *Time* magazine in August 1953.[4]

This presentation of 'leaders' of the intelligence community contrasts sharply, for example, with the lack of attention that such figures in the United Kingdom received until recently. The identities of the heads of the Security Service (MI5) and the Secret Intelligence Service (MI6) were concealed until the 1990s. Even now, little is known about these figures. Stella Rimington broke ground not only as the first woman to head MI5 but also as the first to be publicly declared and the first to write a post-retirement memoir. The current director, Jonathan Evans, has escaped attention apart from a media reference to his previous involvement in running informers in Northern Ireland.[5]

This emphasis on personality in the United States points to, even as it obscures, the media's subservient position. Dependent on the provision of information from those whom they are supposedly monitoring—displease the intelligence services and assistance will end—the media are channelled into certain narratives and projections.[6] Structures, bureaucracies, and operations are neglected except when attention to them serves the aims of the agencies or their political masters. The CIA's celebrated Berlin Tunnel, codenamed 'Operation Gold' and initiated in 1953 to facilitate American interception of Soviet communications, offers a dramatic example. Soon after the Soviets announced in 1956 that they had 'discovered' the tunnel, the apparent setback was presented instead as a testament to the technical achievement of the CIA in implementing and sustaining an ambitious operation in the mid-1950s.[7] Even that success could have been challenged, however: it later emerged that thanks to George Blake, a British spy working for the Soviets, Moscow knew of the tunnel's existence even before it was completed and had fed useless and misleading information to the Western spies.[8]

Even more striking is the use of celebration to obscure broader failings and tensions between operations, intelligence, and analysis. Bob Woodward's heralded trilogy on the Bush Administration's wars in Afghanistan and Iraq has lengthy passages on the brave exploits of CIA squads supporting local paramilitaries and encouraging defectors through the distribution of millions of dollars.[9] Such *Boys' Own* tales offer an exciting read but they are a division from operational complexities—Woodward never mentions, for example, the most serious failing of covert intervention in Afghanistan, the capture and execution of the allegedly CIA-supported Abdul Haq[10]—and the long-term consequence of aid to particular individuals and factions. Most importantly, Woodward's personality-driven exaltation of the operational warriors risks an eclipse of the more important bureaucratic battle, the politicisation of the CIA's functions of intelligence-gathering and analysis.[11]

Yet, more than fifty years after Allen Dulles graced *Time*'s cover, it is an unhelpful simplification to assert that the media faithfully follow a path set down by the intelligence services, even though individual journalists and news' executives have been co-opted at times by the same such agencies.[12] Instead, the media's coverage is defined in a fundamental way by discourses of power such as 'national security' or, in its current, more aggressive, incarnation, 'the War on Terror.' When these concepts come under strain, usually because of political, economic, and paramilitary complications, then a space emerges in which the media may operate as critic rather than cheerleader.

Projections of fear, projections of security

Looking back, there is an almost whimsical naiveté about the depiction of the birth of the post-World War II intelligence system in the United States. At the launch of the Central Intelligence Group, the forerunner of the CIA, President Harry Truman sported a cloak and wielded a dagger in order to announce the creation of the 'Cloak and Dagger Group of Snoopers.'[13] Within two years, the CIA found itself cast publicly not as energetic protector but as bumbling villain. The Agency was widely and unfairly perceived as having failed to predict unrest in Bogotá, Colombia during the Ninth International Conference of American States and faced a congressional investigation as a result.[14] Its image took a further battering with North Korea's surprise

June 1950 invasion of its southern neighbour, an occurrence that the CIA had failed to predict. Although a low point in its history, the invasion led to the arrival of a new director in the form of Walter Bedell Smith, along with greater resources and a renewed emphasis on the part of the American state on the covert capabilities that a secret intelligence agency could bring to bear.[15] Through the 1950s the status of the CIA would only grow, with the arrival of Allen Dulles as Director in 1953 and the perception of a period as a 'Golden Age' in the history of American foreign intelligence.[16]

This apparently far-from-consistent representation established some long-term guidelines. From its inception in 1947, the CIA was part of an unprecedented 'national security state'. This re-conception of the US Government, which also included the creation of the National Security Council and the formation of the Department of Defense, rested upon the assurance to the American public that their welfare depended upon the promotion and development of such agencies. However, in a conflict with the Soviet Union defined as a protracted if not perpetual 'Cold War', rather than a direct confrontation between the two superpowers, the projection of security paradoxically relied upon the mobilisation of a 'climate of fear'. If the populace ever believed that it was secure, the rationale for protectors such as the CIA might disappear. The Agency's development was thus finely balanced: its expansion might be sanctioned by the outbreak of the Korean War but it could also be blamed for the intelligence lapse which failed to anticipate the North Korean invasion of the South. It could be hailed as America's defence against Communist expansion abroad but might be assailed at home—as it was by Joseph McCarthy in 1953—for harbouring the 'enemy within'.[17]

This tension in turn pointed to an even more important maxim: lacking a secure power base within the American state, the image and well-being of the Agency was always dependent on the support of the executive branch. Far from being a maverick, the CIA's Golden Age of 1950s covert operations stemmed from the mandate of President Dwight Eisenhower. Conversely, when that Golden Age suddenly ended in April 1961 with the Bay of Pigs debacle, the CIA would be stripped of its operational authority, finding the direction of its future at the mercy of politicians.[18] These lessons—beyond traumas such as Vietnam and Watergate, beyond the 'Reagan Revival' of covert operations, and beyond the supposed end of the Cold War—are still relevant today. In the post-9/11 War on Terror, the CIA could be presented as a vital unit, one which had found a role after the loss of its Soviet foe in 1991. At the same time, the Agency was always vulnerable to the charge that its failures—in collection of intelligence, in analysis, and in operations against Middle Eastern threats to the United States—had contributed to the tragedies of 11 September 2001 and to the decision to invade Iraq in 2003.[19]

The new international conflict thus presented an opportunity for the CIA, which had struggled in the 1990s to find new roles, to project its importance, one eagerly supported in print and on the airwaves. George Tenet, the Director of Central Intelligence from 1997 to 2004, was exalted in Annie Liebowitz's photography as the Protector of the Bush Administration,[20] and the Agency once more became the 'can do' covert warriors offering the key to victory in Afghanistan. Bob Woodward wrote of the Agency's success at 'winning' Afghanistan through its Jawbreaker team which bribed key tribal chiefs undermining support for the Taliban prior to the arrival of American troops in October 2001. There was also a fascination that the CIA now seemed to have a James-Bond-like 'licence to kill', beginning when an Agency-operated Predator drone killed five Al Qaeda suspects, including an American citizen, in Yemen in November 2002.[21]

At the same time, with the prospect of commissions investigating the American intelligence failure on 9/11, Administration rivals could keep the CIA as a hostage for blame; indeed, this vulnerability was exploited by the White House to ensure support for its overseas ventures. As the Bush Administration shifted its attention to Iraq, Vice President Dick Cheney and his office pressed Agency analysts to provide the 'right' information on Baghdad's threat.[22] From 11 September 2001, newspapers, magazines, and broadcasting outlets offered lurid tales—often based on information from alleged Iraqi defectors—of Iraq's weapons programmes. The Iraqi National Congress, the opposition group based in London and Washington with strong ties to the Bush Administration, alone was the source for 108 English-language news stories that were published between October 2001 and May 2002.[23] This was not a simple case of co-optation. Reporters such as Walter Pincus of the *Washington Post* offered some scrutiny of purported intelligence and the quest to link Iraq to the War on Terror was paralleled by the ongoing queries over intelligence services' responsibility for 9/11. The essential point was that, within the framework of security and fear, the media's consideration and portrayal was inherently incomplete while serving at times as a propaganda tool for those pushing for the invasion of Iraq.[24]

Notable in this partial display was the failure to acknowledge a vital bureaucratic shift. The key agency providing intelligence was not the CIA but the Pentagon. In November 2001, Secretary of Defense Donald Rumsfeld's assistants, notably Wolfowitz and Douglas Feith, had established the Policy Coun-terterrorism Evaluation Group (PCTEG) as an alternative location for assessment of raw intelligence.[25] It was this office, rather than the CIA, that arranged for the tales of the Iraqi National Congress—the head of the group, Ahmed Chalabi, was a long-time contact and friend of Wolfowitz, Feith, and Pentagon consultant Richard Perle. Moreover, Feith went further by linking intelligence and analysis to planning and operations: with the support of Wol-fowitz and Rumsfeld, he established the Office of Special Projects in the fall of 2002 in an effort to discover evidence connecting the regime of Saddam Hussein to Al Qaeda and Weapons of Mass Destruction programmes.[26]

Although there were very public clues to this inter-agency conflict and consolidation of power in the Pentagon, such as Donald Rumsfeld's public castigation of Tenet for providing misleading information to Congress,[27] most of the US media preferred to follow and present the Administration's line of an integrated assessment of the Iraqi threat. The focus on personality was exemplified by the presence of Tenet directly behind Secretary of State Colin Powell during the latter's presentation of 5 February 2003 at the United Nations.[28] None of the stories noted that Powell had demanded Tenet's attendance not because the intelligence was so strong but rather because he did not want to take sole responsibility for the material being presented.[29] None of those stories noted that much of the contentious material came from a single source, an Iraqi codenamed 'Curveball' who had defected to Germany.[30]

The US media's position—'independent' yet, in its failure to offer a signifi-cant critique, effectively serving as a conduit for the Government's construc-tions and projections of threat and security—was complemented by its British counterpart, which often served the Blair government's effort to convince a sceptical British public of Iraq's menace. In September 2002 and February 2003, dossiers, seemingly with the stamp of approval of British intelligence, were released to the public. Originally criticism focused on the February dos-sier, which Foreign Secretary Jack Straw later called an 'embarrassment' and a 'complete Horlicks',[31] after a British academic revealed that parts of the dossier were plagiarized from a PhD dissertation with changes having been made to exaggerate the threat posed by the Saddam Hussein government.

For a longer period of time the September 2002 dossier, signed off on by John Scarlett, the then chairman of the Joint Intelligence Committee, went unchallenged. Contained within it was a claim, poorly sourced, that Iraq could deploy WMDs within 45 minutes. This purported threat received great play in the British media, including alarming headlines in a number of British newspapers. Leading the way was the country's highest-selling daily newspaper, *The Sun*, which warned of the threat posed by Iraq to British troops in Cyprus under the heading of 'Brits 45 Mins From Doom'.[32] In that sense the media served as a messenger for the government, only too happy to relay what was portrayed as the latest intelligence. This role continued after the invasion when a fraudulent letter, allegedly created by the CIA at the behest of the Bush Administration, linking Saddam Hussein's regime to the 9/11 attacks, ended up being pushed as a legitimate document in a story written by journalist Con Coughlin for the *Daily Telegraph*.[33]

Still, despite the widespread complicity of the British media in Downing Street's presentation of intelligence, the most significant signs of dissent before the March 2003 invasion came from the United Kingdom. On the day Colin Powell was to make his presentation at the United Nations, someone from within the British government or intelligence community leaked a classified military intelligence assessment written the previous month, which indicated that there were no links between Saddam Hussein's regime and Al Qaeda.[34] In the same month, the *Observer* newspaper ran a front-page exclusive of an American request to Britain's signals intelligence agency, Government Communications Headquarters (GCHQ), based on a document leaked by GCHQ analyst Katherine Gun. The National Security Agency (NSA) sought a 'surge' in monitoring of the conversations of non-permanent members of the United Nations Security Council, both to ascertain how they might vote on a second resolution against Iraq and to obtain information to ensure their compliance with American wishes.[35]

In the US, Knight Ridder pursued an often solitary journalistic quest with a series of articles questioning the case for war.[36] Other media accounts were held back or spiked, however, on both sides of the Atlantic. From autumn 2002, Ed Vulliamy of the *Observer* was reliably informed that CIA analysts were reporting that the Iraqis did not have weapons of mass destruction; on seven occasions up to March 2003, the story was spiked by his editors.[37] At the *Washington Post*, both Bob Woodward and Walter Pincus did not protest when their stories, based on high-level sources who cast doubt on the Bush Administration's official claims, were relegated well inside the front section of the paper. Woodward later admitted, 'I blame myself for not pushing harder.'[38]

The impetus for a critique of 'intelligence' in its fullest sense—not just the raw information but the manipulation and presentation of that information by persons and agencies beyond the CIA—would have to come from the breakdown of the notion of security, specifically, through the inability to present victory in the War on Terror with a secure and stable Iraq. The failure to find Saddam Hussein's weapons of mass destruction was, of course, a blow to the US and British Government's control of a well-defined narrative, but equally important was the descent of the country into disorder and insurgency. Formally the critique would be inscribed—and at the same time circumscribed—by the Hutton and Butler inquiries in Britain and by the 9/11 and Silberman-Robb (WMD) Commissions in the United States. Beyond this, there would be a belated unravelling of the pretexts for war through revelations such as the July 2002 'Downing Street Memorandum', which recorded the impressions of British officials—including MI6 Chief Sir Richard Dearlove—that the Bush Administration had already decided upon war with Iraq.

The space opened up first by disquiet in the lead-up to the invasion of Iraq, and then by the post-liberation failure in Iraq, was so great that it brought a re-alignment in which members of the intelligence services worked with the media *against* their Governments. Many of these were by officials who had had qualms about the Iraqi invasion and, beyond this, who resisted the seizure of operational authority by the Pentagon or advisors to Prime Minister Tony Blair. Repeated stories in 2003 by Seymour Hersh, who admitted that he himself was initially cowed in the aftermath of 9/11, relied heavily on inside information and revealed the turmoil within the Bush administration between the CIA and the Pentagon, and the CIA and the office of the vice president.[39]

This would not be a triumph for an independent media—allied with dissenting officials—over the Executive Branch in the United States. On the contrary, as in the Bay of Pigs episode in 1961, the critique would both be accepted and constrained through the laying of blame upon the CIA. In that sense the media would aid both Downing Street and the White House as all problems related to Iraq (the exaggerated WMD threat, the lack of ties between Saddam's government and Al Qaeda, the decision to invade, the failure to find WMDs) became in the official discourse an 'intelligence failure', with the blame squarely laid at the feet of the CIA. When confronted about the failure to discover WMDs, politicians through the media would retort that the intelligence community had believed that they existed. In this castigation of the Agency and, to a lesser extent, MI6, the Pentagon escaped largely unscathed by the revelations; ad hoc structures such as the PCTEG and the OSP had been dismantled with little publicity, and Rumsfeld would carry on as Secretary of Defense until 2006. Cheney also escaped censure. His assistant Lewis Libby, in a spin-off from the manufacture of intelligence, would be convicted of perjury in the Joseph Wilson/Valerie Plame case, but the acquisition by the Vice President's office of power over intelligence and analysis would not be addressed.

In contrast, the Director of Central Intelligence saw his power and influence reduced in a restructuring, recommended by the 9/11 Commission, which established a Director of National Intelligence to supervise all intelligence agencies. The curbing of George Tenet's authority was accompanied by the laying of blame for faulty assessment of Iraq upon the CIA, notably through the leaked claim to author Bob Woodward that Tenet had assured President Bush of a 'slam dunk' case on Iraq's WMDs. As Tenet recalled in April 2007, 'I remember picking up the phone and calling [Bush's Chief of Staff] Andy Card... "What's happened here is you've gone out and made me look stupid. It's the most despicable thing I've ever heard in my life. Men of honor don't do this".[40] Ultimately, for the Bush administration it was a case of 'heads you lose, tails we win'. If the WMDs turned up the decision to go to war would be validated, if they did not, it would be the fault of Tenet and the CIA.

Meanwhile, in Britain the narrative of Iraq was not to be one of an ill-conceived, ill-executed foreign policy but one of failed intelligence. Thus any consideration of the political manipulation and/or distortion of intelligence were off-limits. In Britain, Lord Hutton declared in his report on the death of Dr David Kelly:

There has been a great deal of controversy and debate whether the intelligence in relation to weapons of mass destruction set out in the dossier published by the Government on 24 September 2002 was of sufficient strength and reliability to justify the Government in deciding that Iraq under Saddam Hussein posed such a threat to the safety and interests of the United Kingdom that military action should be taken against that country...I concluded that a question of such wide import, which would involve the consideration of a wide range of evidence, is not one which falls within my terms of reference.[41]

Thus the only casualties of the inquiry were the Chairman and the Director General of the British Broadcasting Corporation. In the United States, despite extensive evidence in the public domain of high-level pressure upon the intelligence services to provide the 'right' analysis of Iraq's weapons of mass destruction programmes, the Silberman-Robb Commission insisted, 'The Commission has found no evidence of "politicization"of the Intelligence Community's assessments concerning Iraq's reported WMD programs. No analytical judgments were changed in response to political pressure to reach a particular conclusion.'[42]

If 'security' was the founding rationale for the representation of intelligence, then the media's consideration of security would extend only as far as to whether the handling or mishandling of information jeopardised that intelligence. The possibility that it is not the day-to-day collection and analysis of information but government policy—based on a misrepresentation of 'intelligence'—that affects and possibly jeopardises security is normally out-of-bounds. And that in turn may mean that the media never establishes a critique of intelligence agencies and executive power. While politicisation of intelligence is far from a new phenomenon, the Bush Administration is distinctive in its open advocacy of the policymaker—rather than intelligence collector or analyst—holding the power of interpretation. As Wolfowitz explained in 1996, 'Analysts must always remember that their job is to inform the policymaker's decision, not to try to supplant it, regardless of how strongly they feel about the issue.'[43] A similar example, albeit on a smaller scale, occurred in the United Kingdom when Downing Street 'spin doctors' played a direct role in the framing of the intelligence in the dossiers that would be presented to the public via the media.[44]

This was only part of the extension of the Executive's scope. Within weeks of the attacks on the World Trade Center and Pentagon, the Bush Administration was trying to seize the authority for unlimited detention of 'enemy combatants', for expanded use of rendition and 'coercive interrogation' of suspects, and for expanded surveillance. Officials carrying out the edicts of the Vice President and the Secretary of Defense, used the rationale of the post-9/11 necessity of 'better intelligence' to establish their authority outside legal frameworks and also outside standard procedures of consultation with the CIA. While the manoeuvring for this authority usually took place behind closed doors, the effort was far from secret. Vice President Cheney said on national television on 16 September 2001, 'We...have to work, though, sort of the dark side, if you will. We've got to spend time in the shadows in the intelligence world.'[45] It was only in 2007 that a journalist would chronicle the systematic effort to expand Executive power.[46] While Barton Gellman and Jo Becker's series was widely praised, it did not lead to a sustained critique of policies and tactics in the prosecution of the War on Terror; as we write this, the arguably illegal practices of the Bush Administration have withstood judicial challenges and, in some cases, have been codified by legislative action.

It would be a mistake to represent the media as 'embedded' in the intelligence services. The model of press and broadcasting representatives being placed within military units cannot be extended to covert agencies. Still, any consideration of media-intelligence interaction should begin with recognition of the informal links that have shaped that relationship. Historically, intelligence agencies have tried to ensure both favourable coverage and the placing of stories in overseas outlets through the retention of journalists on its payroll. After the exposure in 1977 by Carl Bernstein of the CIA's ties to 400 American journalists, co-operation continued through both social networks and the granting of privileged access to reporters and correspondents.[47] Yet any construction of this dynamic as one of media dependency is a misleading simplification. It assumes a unitary Government approach when, in both historical and contemporary contexts, the reality is one of bureaucratic tensions. Indeed, such tensions can produce a situation when the media stands as critic of the Executive not in opposition to but in alliance with officials from intelligence services.

More importantly, 'security' cannot provide a stable foundation for media support of intelligence services. Intrinsically, 'security' is always to be pursued, never achieved, for were it to be attained the rationale for intelligence agencies—or, rather, their budgets—would diminish if not disappear altogether. Thus 'security' works hand-in-hand with a permanent fear of insecurity. Provided that this fear of insecurity does not become immanent in 'real' events at home and abroad, this projection may be sustained through media representations of threat and the necessary protections offered by intelligence services and the executive. However, when instability emerges not as an abstracted Axis of Evil but in the breakdown of order, violence, and insurgency, the media-intelligence relationship will have to be reconfigured. Space opens up for critique and even challenges to the projection of the unitary provision of 'security'. This space is limited if the media's attention remains narrowly focussed on the intelligence services rather than the conjunction of intelligence, analysis, and policymaking. Much as the Bay of Pigs disaster could, in the end, be tied to a deficient CIA rather than decisions of Presidents Eisenhower and Kennedy, much as post-Watergate inquisitions would spill blood at the Agency but permit a resurgent Presidential power—linked to a renewal of covert operations—in the 1980s, so the post-9/11 post-Iraq examination could offer the sacrifice of an 'intelligence' for reform while doing little to engage with the manipulation of that system by the Executive.

President Harry Truman, sixteen years after he presided over the creation of the CIA, famously wrote, 'I have been disturbed by the way CIA has been diverted from its original assignment. It has become an operational and at times a policy-making arm of the Government.'[48] For the media, this criticism—initially offered after the Bay of Pigs debacle and then magnified in the aftermath of Vietnam and Watergate—has been the easy way to 'speak truth to power' regarding the intelligence services. Far more difficult is the task of recognising that those services, in the way that they are deployed, manipulated, and sometimes scapegoated, are only part of a much more difficult issue of the State's intervention in both international and domestic affairs.

7

BRITISH INTELLIGENCE AND THE BRITISH BROADCASTING CORPORATION

A SNAPSHOT OF A HAPPY MARRIAGE

Michael S. Goodman

Editors' Notes: Open source intelligence is an increasingly important element of modern day intelligence. As Michael Goodman notes, the earliest forms of modern intelligence (from the Tudor period) might today be classified as news or indeed as gossip. Important information can be gleaned from such sources to triangulate closed source information, and also to provide early warning signals about secret programmes or regional instability. Using previously unseen archive material Goodman explores the utility of the monitoring service through some of its early cold war history, and its importance to Britain and America's 'special relationship'.

The author of this article is currently engaged as an official historian at the Cabinet Office working on the Official History of the Joint Intelligence Committee. As such he has security clearance for access to official records not yet released to the public. This article however, is drawn only from released official records and published sources and the views expressed are those of the author in his capacity as an academic historian and does not represent the views or carry the endorsement of the Government.

There have been myriad writers who have spent entire careers trying to define what it is we mean by 'intelligence'. It is evident that in the English language the term is both a noun and a verb, that it denotes the product, the machinery, and the process. If we look back to the origins of the word, the first recorded usage comes from the middle of the fifteenth century, when 'intelligence' implied news and information. Many would argue that the modern iteration of 'intelligence' is now more than just information or news-gathering, yet has it lost this root meaning? In the Elizabethan period, when British intelligence acquired its foundation, spymasters did not distinguish between 'news' and 'secret information'. With the contemporary debate about the utility of open source, is it time to redress this question? Indeed, in this context it is worth noting that 'the intelligence systems that developed in the later part of the sixteenth century were mainly news-gathering agencies whose functions included not only the work now attributed to intelligence organisations, but also those that in today's society belong to journalism, newspapers, and news agencies.'[1]

The intelligence services and the media in Britain have had a long and often troubled history, yet there are snapshots available of happier times. World War Two was a watershed for British intelligence; it symbolised the birth, death and adaptation of various organisations, but it also signified how the intelligence services had to move beyond their own boundaries to secure knowledge. A good example of this is the monitoring effort undertaken by the BBC. Created in the darkest depths of the late 1930s, the BBC monitoring service was designed to monitor German broadcasts, translate and then distribute them to a wider audience.[2] Of its first customers, and indeed probably its longest standing, were the intelligence agencies. This effort continued throughout the war, when defensive monitoring of foreign broadcasts took on an offensive, propagandistic role, often being used to great effect in deception operations.

In its original 1939 guise BBC monitoring had two primary functions: 1) to provide news and intelligence; and 2) to study worldwide propaganda efforts.[3] The BBC monitoring effort continued to expand throughout the war, largely to meet the demands of an increasing number of government departments. With the end of conflict in 1945 question marks arose as to the level of effort required for the post-war world. Was BBC monitoring still necessary? If it was necessary, what role should it play? Should its costs be borne by the taxpayer or the government? This chapter will provide answers to these questions and, in doing so, focuses on two examples of post-war collaboration between British intelligence and the BBC. The first case-study is the creation of an intelligence sub-committee on BBC monitoring. This, a defensive effort to monitor Communist-inspired communication, is in stark contrast to the second example, attempts in Germany to use BBC broadcasts as a means to encourage defection. Taken together these examples hint at something of the enduring relationship between the intelligence agencies and the BBC, a relationship which involved not just observing broadcasts but actively using information as a means to garner intelligence.

The sub-committee on BBC monitoring

A year before the end of the Second World War the BBC monitoring service was listening to 1,250,000 words a day, in approximately thirty different languages, of which 300,000 were translated and transcribed on a daily basis into English.[4] In August 1945 the Director of Communications and Broadcasting in the Ministry of Information, the body charged in 1939 with establishing the BBC's monitoring effort, produced a detailed report about the shape and nature of monitoring, emphasising in particular the requirements upon amassing information overseas. The heavy wartime costs, the report emphasised, were not due to the listening effort, but rather the typing, editing and publishing of the monitoring efforts. The proposal for the post-war period was not to reduce the amount of monitoring conducted, but instead to have a more frugal policy as to what was actually translated and published. Although listing a number of 'open' countries, the majority of the report concentrated on 'closed' countries, emphasising that monitoring 'continues to fill to a considerable extent its war time function as one of the principal sources of such [gathering] material.[5] In their own internal assessment, the BBC monitoring service came up with similar conclusions.[6]

The report was initially discussed among the Foreign Office, Political Intelligence Department, Ministry of Information and the BBC itself. It was decided that the report should be sent to the 'user' communities. That same month, August 1945, the report was discussed at the Joint Intelligence Committee and wholeheartedly approved.[7] The Joint Intelligence Committee, or JIC as it is commonly known, was created in 1936. Its original rationale was to act as an interdepartmental military committee, subservient to the Chiefs of Staff, and designed solely to produce intelligence for the purposes of military planning. It adopted a Foreign Office chairman just prior to the outbreak of the Second World War and steadily throughout the conflict, extended and expanded its range of powers. By the end of the war the JIC was *the* central forum for British intelligence: its weekly meetings were attended by the heads of the Services' intelligence directorates, together with those from MI5, SIS and subsequently GCHQ.[8]

That the Joint Intelligence Committee should concern itself with BBC monitoring in 1945 is no great surprise. The Committee had become central to the planning and direction of the British intelligence community. Given the sentiments in the August 1945 report—that monitoring provided an exemplary means of intelligence gathering in closed states—it is entirely natural that the JIC would be interested. After August 1945 the matter was not discussed again by the JIC that year. The topic arose once more in 1946, largely, it would seem, as a reflection of the changing Foreign Office perception of the Soviet Union.[9] In March 1946 the Permanent Under Secretary at the FO, Sir Orme Sargent, suggested that something needed to be done to counter Soviet propaganda efforts. The reply was a paper by the Assistant Under Secretary of State, Christopher Warner, who had special responsibility for the Soviet Union. In it Warner wrote how a 'defensive-offensive' position was needed.[10] Such ideas would initially lead to the creation of the Foreign Office's 'Russia Committee'.[11] The decision was momentous, for as the Foreign Office historians have written, 'with the approval of the Prime Minister, an action programme was prepared involving a long-term propaganda campaign against Communism.' To be effective, such a programme had to include not only government departments, but also the BBC.[12]

The Foreign Office ideas were discussed by the JIC in its meeting on 1 May 1946.[13] The timing was apt, for just a few weeks later Sir Kenneth Strong, the Director General of the Joint Intelligence Bureau (responsible for economic and topographical intelligence) issued a minute on the status of the BBC monitoring effort as it was in mid 1946. Strong reported that there were two main types of material produced by the BBC that were of interest to the intelligence community: political and factual. He emphasised, as had the earlier reports, that much of this effort provided intelligence that was inaccessible any other way. Furthermore, coverage was good, though there were two notable 'blind spots': distant regional stations in Russia and Russian Far East broadcasts. More important, though, were Strong's final recommendations, primarily the suggestion that a committee be created, comprised of the intelligence agencies and the BBC, designed to 'determine...intelligence requirements'.[14] The report was discussed by the JIC a week later and Strong's recommendations were approved.[15] It is not entirely clear from the declassified records what happened as a result. We do know that the subject was again discussed within the JIC almost a year later, following another note by Strong. This time the objective was to discuss Anglo-American monitoring collaboration.[16]

Taking the lead from the British example, in 1941 the US government created the Foreign Broadcasting Monitoring Service. That same year a number of US personnel were seconded from this organisation to the BBC.[17] In 1946 the American broadcasting effort, now known as FBIS or the Foreign Broadcasting Information Service, was moved into the Central Intelligence Group, the forerunner to the CIA.[18] At this point it was decided to split the world between the two nations: the BBC assumed responsibility for monitoring the central Soviet service, Moscow's broadcasts to Europe, Soviet bloc outputs, and a spread of stations throughout western Europe, the Near and Middle East; FBIS, by comparison, took control for everywhere else. Both sides then agreed to supply the other with what they received. One American official commented that 'in the character and scope of its activity and in the closeness of its working relationships, the BBC-FBIS combine affords a possibly unique example of enduring Anglo-American cooperation.'[19] Like much else in the Anglo-American special relationship, there was great concern that Britain be seen to be pulling its weight. In exchange for information collected by the Americans, it was proposed, and subsequently accepted by the JIC, that the British maintain their share of the status quo come what may.[20]

By 1948 we can make several observations about the relationship between the BBC and British intelligence. First, and perhaps most importantly, it was recognised that BBC monitoring provided material on the Soviet bloc that was simply unobtainable through any other means. This then was a tacit acceptance of the value of open source material by the intelligence agencies. Furthermore, the Anglo-American relationship was central to the success of the monitoring effort, having split the globe into two areas of responsibility. How did the BBC feel about having their services used by the intelligence agencies? It is in this context that Lt. General Sir Ian Jacob first becomes prominent. Jacob had been the Military Assistant Secretary to the War Cabinet during World War Two, and having retired from the army in 1946 joined the BBC as its 'Controller of the European Service'.[21]

In 1948, having now become the 'Director of Overseas Services', Jacob was the de facto chief of the BBC's monitoring effort. In February of that year he wrote to the Chairman of the Joint Intelligence Committee about what he saw as a critical problem in the relationship between the BBC and the government. 'I am not altogether happy,' he began, '[that] there does not exist at present any arrangement whereby [the intelligence agencies and the FO] can study together the output of the Monitoring Service and express considered views on its merits.' Jacob's suggestion was that the JIC convene a special group to discuss the monitoring effort, its value and where gaps might exist in coverage.[22] The JIC met to discuss the proposal at the end of February and unanimously agreed to the creation of a 'working party' to assess the situation.[23]

Such ideas were not entirely new. In the immediate post-war period several ad-hoc meetings had been convened, held variously at the Foreign Office and the General Post Office, in which members of the FO, BBC, SIS, Post Office and JIB discussed the future of the monitoring service. At these meetings finances had played a major role, as they would continue to do so for years afterwards. Also discussed was coverage, where BBC monitoring had good exposure and where the gaps existed. What is also clear from the minutes of the meetings is that the intelligence agencies and the Foreign Office thought that the BBC material filled an important intelligence gap.[24]

Despite not being as innovative as its members may have felt, the new JIC 'Sub-Committee on Monitoring Requirements' met for the first time in mid-April 1948. It was chaired by a Foreign Office representative, and included members from the FO, the Services' intelligence departments, the Joint Intelligence Bureau, MI5 and GCHQ.[25] The sub-committee's initial remit was to examine how best to co-ordinate guidance for the monitoring effort in order to focus on targets identified by the intelligence agencies. A related consideration, and in a sense one that superseded solely British intelligence requirements, was to ensure that the BBC fulfilled its half of the American bargain. At its essence was the question of cost. Despite its worth, there were only finite resources available to spend on monitoring, hence assessing priorities depended on three factors: those topics of worth to the BBC itself; those useful to the intelligence agencies; and those that the Americans requested. From the declassified record it is not possible to see what the impact of this was, because the next trace of the Sub-Committee on Monitoring Requirements comes from June 1949. We can, however, infer from this that the three factors were still prevalent throughout discussions.

Once more finances were central to the debate. The Americans had let it be known that unless the British were prepared to grant 'increased facilities' for the transmission of material from the monitoring station in Cyprus then they, in turn, would restrict the amount of information coming from Washington. Despite some discussion, it was eventually agreed that 'we had no alternative but to offer the Americans better facilities'. What of the types of material being provided through BBC monitoring? The Cyprus station was extremely useful for capturing Russian regional broadcasts, while a proposed station in the Himalayas would be able to intercept broadcasts from central Asia, thereby filling 'a dangerous gap in Russian coverage.' In summary it was concluded that 'priority must be given, however, to obtaining 100 per cent coverage of the Russian Far East and Caucasian area.' Through the monitoring efforts it was possible to keep abreast, to an extent, with developments at this time in Albania. Efforts focussed on central and southern America were now considered superfluous to requirements, but before a final decision to abandon these regions could be taken it was felt necessary to consult the Americans. Perhaps the most important information was that captured by the American station in Okinawa. By focussing on the Russian regional stations extremely useful intelligence was gathered on the Soviet war potential.[26]

Throughout their deliberations on the value and utility of monitoring, the spectre of the American attitude kept arising, as did the question of cost. The general feeling was that the Americans, with their greater resources at disposal, spent too much time on unnecessary broadcasts. FBIS translated and transmitted everything received, whereas the perception in Britain, due to fiscal implications as much as to its inherent worth, was that topics should be far more selectively picked. For these reasons it was felt essential to second BBC staff both to Washington and Okinawa. A further question, once more based on cost, was how material should be transmitted from the outposts back to the UK. If material was classified as 'intelligence' data, then it had to be transmitted through secure lines. If, on the other hand, it was not classed as intelligence, then it could be brought back by RAF plane. The complicating factor was the material used not for intelligence purposes but for propaganda, for the Foreign Office's view was that it should not be delayed while being physically transported by plane. The result was to split material into that used for 'intelligence' purposes and that used for 'propaganda' means.[27]

At times, reading through the JIC's deliberations on BBC monitoring, it is slightly unnerving how frequently the question of money comes up, especially when compared to considerations of the worth of the monitored material. Further discussions in August 1949 concerned the amount of 'wordage' being transmitted daily from the Cyprus station to London, and once more any decision to reduce the volume came up against the stumbling block that the Americans wanted as much as possible from there. Despite these concerns, the underlying factor was that the material was of undoubted use. The SIS representative at this particular JIC meeting commented on how 'the material received was required urgently by his Department.'[28]

The JIC were equally concerned with Soviet monitoring efforts taking place in the United Kingdom. It was known that a house in Oakleigh Park,

North London, was used by the Soviet government-controlled TASS agency to monitor broadcasts.[29] The question discussed by the JIC was whether this could be allowed to continue, for not only was it felt that TASS monitored British broadcasts, but also that they might be able to observe radar and plane information. The matter was not just the concern of the JIC though; there was also a Parliamentary Question and it was even discussed by the Cabinet. The JIC decided that the best course was to get MI5 to investigate whether any 'illicit activities' were taking place, because if so, it would provide a pretext to close the site down.[30] Eventually, a year later, the Chiefs of Staff decided that the station should close, and accordingly instructed the Foreign Secretary to inform the Russian Ambassador, which he duly did.[31] Subsequently it was decided that the real reasons for closing the station—stopping Russian monitoring—should be concealed from the public.[32] In the end the lengthy deliberations proved futile because just a few months later it was noted that the Russians had moved the monitoring effort from Oakleigh to their embassy in Kensington, albeit on a smaller scale.[33]

By the early 1950s some quarters were beginning to argue that the BBC monitoring effort was becoming less influential in gauging Soviet intentions and capabilities. Sir Ian Jacob was requested to come to the weekly JIC meeting to outline the current status, which he duly did, though the record of his discussion is still retained.[34] By this time the Treasury—who up to this point had been noticeable by their absence from the JIC discussions, despite the frequent recourse to fiscal matters—decided that a financial reduction was imperative for the BBC's sake.[35] The problem, in a sense, was that from the perspective of the intelligence community, the monitoring effort was continuing to produce results. It was commented at this time that the station in Stockholm was producing excellent results with the result that, for the first time, 'one of the biggest gaps in our coverage' was about to be closed. This 'gap' was the Baltic States. A further issue, albeit one that had been omnipresent throughout, was that if sufficient funds were not invested, then the Americans might have to go it alone, with the effect that they might not share the transmissions with the British. Other plans, to create a new station in the Indian peninsular with the objective of focussing on the central USSR, were also subject to procuring enough funding.[36]

Matters were reaching a head. Present at the meeting of the 'Sub-Committee on Monitoring Requirements' were several representatives from the Treasury. One of these, variously referred to in the minutes as Mrs Johnson and Mrs Johnstone, commented that 'in the past there had been insufficient enquiry into the financial requirements of the Monitoring Service', therefore 'the Treasury wanted to satisfy itself that the present expenditure was, in fact, essential'. The response, recorded as 'unanimous', was that 'no economy could possibly be made' with regard to Russia, Eastern Europe, Germany, Austria and the Far East without 'serious injury to vital intelligence interests'. On the other hand, opinion was divided over the utility of monitoring broadcasts in Western Europe, Scandinavia and the Middle East; whereas everyone agreed that efforts in the Americas could be stopped.[37] The Sub-Committee's deliberations were discussed by the JIC two months later, though the presence of the same Mrs Johnson/Johnstone seems to have stifled proper discussion as the conversation was consistently brought back to the financial aspects of the monitoring service. In fact the JIC, with its greater concentration of senior figures, rejected the Sub-Committee's earlier recommendations, arguing instead that everything should continue in its current guise.[38] As a consequence the Sub-Committee had its terms of reference revised, so that it was now responsible for co-ordinating monitoring requirements, looking after liaison matters with the US, and accountable for referring any financial matters to the JIC for discussion.[39]

Tension between the Treasury and the intelligence community over BBC monitoring continued to grow. The first move was made by the Treasury in early 1953 when they blocked the funding required to establish a further station in Stockholm.[40] Though it is not clear what the initial reaction to this was, by November the Sub-Committee issued a report criticising the Treasury and their method of 'financial control' over the monitoring programme. The indomitable Mrs Johnson/Johnstone reported in response, that 'she had never managed to gain a proper insight into the use to which the products of the Monitoring Service were put by [intelligence] Departments'. Her suggestion was that those still involved—the BBC, Ministry of Defence, Foreign Office, War Office, SIS and Security Service—each contribute £80,000 towards the costs of the monitoring programme. The general reaction was not strict antipathy, but a feeling that the departments would not be able to contribute such an amount. Once more the value of the monitoring product was emphasised, with the MI5 representative commenting that they 'derived certain intelligence...which was irreplaceable from other sources.' With the situation at an impasse the matter was referred back to the Treasury for comment.[41]

Once more it is not clear from the declassified documents what the outcome was. We do know that by March 1954 the JIC Chairman, Sir Patrick Dean, informed the Committee that he had been 'obliged to proceed' with negotiations with the Treasury, and that given the haste required to 'forestall quite unacceptable financial cuts', he had not had the chance to inform the Sub-Committee of developments.[42] By mid-1954 the arguments finally left Treasury and JIC hands, with the establishment of a high-level review, to be conducted by Sir William Scott, a former Permanent Secretary at the Ministry of Finance.[43] Scott completed his work over the summer.[44] His report was described by the JIC Chairman as 'an extremely good one' but which, furthermore, 'had been a very valuable study from the point of view of the intelligence agencies'. The BBC monitoring service was far less happy with the report. In an internal review they consistently insinuated that Scott had not understood the role they played in the Cold War, citing a 'number of errors of fact'.[45] Scott concluded that the monitoring programme should continue approximately as it was, but that in order to save money the Foreign Office should assume 'administrative and financial responsibility', thereby providing 40% of the cost.[46] This, then, was the start of a relationship between the Foreign Office and BBC Monitoring that would last until the twenty-first century.

Recruitment in Berlin

While the JIC's involvement with BBC Monitoring was largely defensive, its efforts in Germany were anything but. The BBC had two different roles with the intelligence agencies: the first, described above, concerned monitoring other country's broadcasts; the second, and far more offensive, involved using broadcasts for intelligence purposes. This policy was used to great effect in Germany, though it was not restricted to Germany alone, with similar efforts undertaken in Hungary and elsewhere.[47] In Germany it is entirely possible that the policy started earlier, but the first documented, substantial efforts to use broadcasting for intelligence purposes occurred in 1951. The stimulus was unequivocal: the supply of defectors into British hands had begun to dry up and something was needed to re-inject some vigour into the process. Discussions about how to achieve this were conducted within the Joint Intelligence Committee (Germany). JIC (Germany), as it was known, had been created in the aftermath of the Second World War, ostensibly as an outpost of the main Joint Intelligence Committee in London. In reality the Committee, which would survive until the end of the Cold War, was a more peripheral body. It was concerned almost entirely with military issues, and was composed largely of military officers, being chaired by a senior two-star military intelligence officer in Germany. In addition, SIS regularly attended meetings, unsurprising given their large station in Germany, as did the Foreign Office.[48]

The policy on the 'encouragement of deserters' stemmed from a paper by the Foreign Office's Information Research Department (IRD). This body had been created in the late 1940s to propagate misinformation, directed primarily at the Soviet Union, and designed to enhance Britain's position.[49] The IRD had a representative in Germany and whose role was crucial to the rest of IRD's work. The basis of IRD's work was information; without it nothing could be planned nor the reaction estimated. Once the Iron Curtain had descended across Europe it became increasingly difficult to obtain reliable information. IRD therefore had to work hand in hand with SIS, with one of the most successful operations being the debriefing of those returning from the east. These people generally fell into two camps: the scores of prisoners of war (PoWs) who had been taken to the Soviet Union at the end of the war; and defectors. By the early 1950s the flow of PoWs had essentially dried up, and with the difficulties in recruiting anyone with sufficient access, the burden fell to defectors to fill the void. In January 1951 the decision was made to allow a small IRD team to operate under the Chief of the Intelligence Division in West Germany; previously only a single member been stationed in Germany.[50] The situation was succinctly summed up by the Deputy Head of IRD: 'the shortage of defectors had resulted in a lack of news on which to base propaganda material.'[51]

The IRD's report on encouraging defection was discussed by JIC (Germany) at their first meeting of 1951. It was suggested that one means of encouraging further defection would be to use the dependants of defectors for 'publicity purposes'. Unsure of how this would be achieved in practice, the IRD were tasked with investigating further.[52] At their next meeting the Deputy Head of IRD, Peter Wilkinson, suggested that using broadcasts for encouraging defection was sensible. Encouragingly, he reported, three recent defectors had stated that they had been 'reached'—in other words encouraged—by listening to foreign broadcasts. Furthermore, Wilkinson reported that there had been 'increased authority for certain covert encouragement activities'. In such ventures it was evident that the BBC's role was crucial; equally clear were the benefits of the increased activity: information from defector debriefing had increased, as had the quality of the material itself.[53] Activity in Germany continued to be of importance to the Information Research Department. In late 1951 the director of IRD, Sir John Peck, travelled to Germany to attend the JIC (Germany) meeting. He congratulated the British intelligence agencies operating in Germany, but emphasised that the number of defectors was still small. To try to improve numbers it was decided to find out how the Americans handled their defectors, and for the SIS representative to find out what the policy was on exchanging information with the French.[54]

A further aspect of the BBC's work in Germany involved not just trying to encourage defection, but also to counteract foreign broadcasts. It was reported in early 1952 that the Russians had set up a new station in Kopenick, Berlin, and the JIC (Germany) decided that the BBC, which 'had plenty of resources in reserve', should do something about the Russian broadcasts. At the same time, the BBC had started a new series of broadcasts directed explicitly towards Soviet troops in Eastern Germany; to supplement these, various leaflet drops had been instigated. Yet despite all efforts the results were not encouraging. Major General Kirkman, the chairman of JIC (Germany), reported that 'the unpalatable fact remained that far from increasing, the flow of deserters had become markedly low'. The issue was clear: although it was recognised that Soviet troops were becoming increasingly aware of British broadcasts, there was no information to suggest that this had had an impact on the rationale behind defection. In other words, there was no correlation between the increased effort by the BBC, and the numbers coming across. The problem was equally clear: 'open' propaganda could persuade those who might be thinking about defection to cross over, but it would have little or no effect on everyone else. What was needed was a more ambitious 'secret' approach. At the same meeting, the SIS representative confirmed that discussion with the French should be broached, and that his office would conduct enquiries.[55]

At their next discussion of the problem, it was reported by Peck, the IRD director, that evidence suggested that defectors had 'seemed to have heard or seen our propaganda', but that the 'final motive for defection might be something else'. This was something of a change from the previous discussion, when it had been assumed that British broadcasts might clinch the decision to defect; the implications of this never seem to have been followed up. It was also reported that BBC efforts to encourage defection among Soviet troops in East Germany had stalled because effort had been re-directed towards countering Soviet jamming efforts. BBC broadcasts were still considered as crucial though. It was discussed whether the current series of BBC broadcasts in which defectors spoke about their experiences should be expanded in order to 'appeal to the more intelligent Russians'. At this juncture David Evans, the head of the 'Scientific and Technical Intelligence Branch (STIB)', Germany, suggested that this was sensible given the large number of technicians and scientists in East Germany. STIB was concerned with scientific intelligence in Germany, and would prove to be very useful, especially in the rocketry field.[56]

Evan's suggestion was a sensible one, based on practical experience of the value of Soviet technical defectors. A good example of the types of information provided by defectors occurred in May 1950 with the defection of 'Icarus'. Since the end of the Second World War intelligence on the Soviet atomic weapons programme had been accorded the highest priority, yet much like other targets, obtaining reliable information was extremely difficult. One of the most useful targets in this context was the Soviet mining of uranium in East Germany, for this provided some indication of how much nuclear material the Russians had at their disposal. The defector, codename 'Icarus', was in fact an MVD officer who had originally been located in the Moscow base of the First Chief Directorate, but who had become the Deputy-Director of AG Wismut, the organisation responsible for Soviet mining in Germany.[57]

There are many reasons why someone defects to the opposing intelligence services. Icarus first offered his services because he had been sacked and ordered back to the Soviet Union.[58] Icarus was a joint venture, and while under interrogation by British and American intelligence officers (and incidentally serving them his home-made beef stroganoff) Icarus had heard kids celebrating Independence Day and letting off fireworks, and this convinced him 'he would like to become an American citizen.' The next day however he had completely changed his mind, and soon afterward 'defected' back to the USSR.[59] Thus for three short months—May to July 1950—Icarus was the West's most successful coup against Soviet intelligence.

The reasons for Icarus' disappearance were not immediately clear to British intelligence. We now know that Icarus had returned simply because he was missing his German mistress. Although this seems a simplistic, even silly, reason for re-defection, Western expertise in handling and 'settling' defectors was in its infancy and the process of adjusting defectors to life in the West was under-funded.[60] Icarus had returned to the Soviet zone in Germany where he had been arrested. He was subsequently interrogated by the Soviets and confessed fully; he also provided details of the American intelligence interest in Wismut. For some reason the case was deliberately played down in the Soviet Union where Abakumov, the Chief Interrogator, hid the case from the Central Committee.[61] It is claimed that Icarus was then summarily executed, and the mistress he had returned to was sent to the gulag.[62]

Dr Arnold Kramish interrogated Icarus on behalf of the AEC and labelled him as a 'very distasteful character'. Similarly, he was never fully trusted by Kramish's British counterpart Eric Welsh, who accordingly regarded him as 'very dangerous'.[63] Despite these caveats, Icarus provided some of the most useful current information ever received on the Soviet atomic programme. He provided details of the senior individuals involved in the Soviet programme. A component of this was information on the 'atomic office' located in Berlin, and which enabled British and American intelligence to identify amounts of fine wire mesh transported to the Soviet Union, used for the fabrication of uranium metal.[64]

Despite the fact that the majority of his information was non-technical, Icarus confirmed British and American beliefs that Elektrostahl, a plant just outside Moscow, was involved in uranium processing for production in an atomic bomb.[65] He also provided numerous details on uranium shipping procedures and frequencies. Thus, through his interrogation the processing plant at Krasnoyarsk was identified, as was the plant at Novosibirsk.[66] According to his CIA handler, Harry Rositzke, Icarus provided a 'rare combination of positive and counterespionage information.' From his previous employment in the First Chief Directorate Icarus also revealed information on MVD atomic operations, though these could not have been very specific. In conclusion Icarus provided intelligence that forced a 'sharp upward revision of US estimates of the Soviet atomic energy program.'[67]

This brief example reveals something of the type of information provided by defectors, but also the problems and pitfalls involved in the intelligence agencies' involvement with them. Icarus was not a typical defector; certainly the information he provided was more important that most defector's knowledge. Yet problems at the general level remained. At a subsequent meeting David Evans extended his thoughts, commenting that German scientists who had crossed back over from the East had mentioned the value of BBC Russian broadcasts; JIC (Germany) was, however, reluctant to increase the number of broadcasts aimed at a specifically technical audience.[68] Instead the policy was to appeal to as wide an audience as possible. In September 1952 the BBC launched a new service, broadcast on seven different frequencies, and aimed squarely at the Russian-speaking contingent in Germany. The volume of 'covert propaganda' also increased, though there is nothing in the records to suggest precisely what is meant by this. And, for the first time, leaflets were dropped which specifically incited defection, 'provided that it could be in no way attributable to Her Majesty's Government'.[69]

At the same time, it appears that British intelligence in Germany was going through a crisis of conscience in terms of how to recruit defectors. It was reported by the SIS representative that the Americans had changed their approach in trying to recruit defectors. Instead of appealing to potential defectors by emphasising the material gains of crossing over, the US had started to concentrate on the 'ideological aspects'. Furthermore, the SIS representative stated that 'an examination of defector cases had revealed that the majority had defected because they were in some form of trouble and that there was no evidence to show that our propaganda had any direct influence in making them defect'. The implications were clear, as the representative continued: 'our propaganda was aimed at too wide a target and that the ideological approach should be stepped up and aimed at mental cells of resistance. In other words, to concentrate on the minority who were keen enough to make efforts to listen to BBC broadcasts and not to make a general appeal to all and sundry.' This suggestion, though quite revolutionary given what had gone on before, was greeted with approval, with the Committee deciding to 're-examine our whole propaganda campaign'.[70]

The propaganda campaign in East Germany continued, though it is unclear whether the results ever really matched expectations. The majority of the success stories came in the first five years following the end of the Second World War. Those who crossed sides after this date did so for a variety of reasons. Generally speaking the information they provided was of only limited use. The Soviet system of government, with its emphasis on security and compartmentalisation, ensured that no-one ever knew the whole picture. What was of most use, perhaps, was information gleamed on the Soviet military, and in particular details on the Soviet Order of Battle, yet this information was not restricted to defectors, with huge amounts being provided by other operations.[71] The JIC would continue to be interested in defectors, with a special sub-committee concentrating on the subject from 1950–1990. Furthermore, the BBC would continue its involvement with BBC monitoring, and broadcasting propaganda, more generally, would continue to be used to great effect through various initiatives such as Radio Liberty and Radio Free Europe.

The BBC's involvement with the intelligence agencies in the first decade of the Cold War proceeded along two principal lines, both defensive and offensive. The BBC monitoring organisation at Caversham was used to great effect by the government. Working hand in glove with the government in general, and the intelligence agencies in particular, the BBC was told where to focus its attention. The monitoring service was used to listen to, transcribe and

translate foreign broadcasts, but also to counter the jamming of British transmissions, especially by the Russians. The Soviet Union was the principal target
throughout this period and, working closely with the American FBIS, the
BBC were able to carve the globe into two spheres of influence, thereby ensuring that no serious broadcasts went unheard. Concurrently they also employed
an offensive programme, again at the behest of British intelligence, to appeal
to potential defectors and to encourage them to desert East Germany in
favour of the West. These brief illustrations show that the intelligence agencies, in the middle of the twentieth century, were quick to seize the opportunities presented to them by the media. Furthermore, they show conclusively that
if information lies at the heart of intelligence work, and that if information
and thus knowledge equate to power, then the strength of words is the strong-
est variable of them all.

8

BALANCING NATIONAL SECURITY AND THE MEDIA

THE D-NOTICE COMMITTEE

Nicholas Wilkinson

Editors' Notes: The D-Notice Committee is a typically British invention—it carries no legal or constitutional weight, but its advice is treated by those who receive it as if it did have the full force of the law. As the Secretary to the D-Notice Committee between 1999 and 2004, Rear Admiral Nicholas Wilkinson sat at the apex between the needs of the media and the necessity of government secrecy. Through the two contemporary case-studies of the wars in Afghanistan and Iraq, this chapter demonstrates the careful balancing act that is performed between public disclosure and government secrecy that applies across all western democracies.

Security also lies in the value of our free institutions. A cantankerous Press, an obstinate Press, a ubiquitous Press must be suffered by those in authority in order to preserve the even greater values of freedom of expression and the right of the People to know.[1]

The D-Notice System exists for one purpose only: to provide advice to the media and to officials in the United Kingdom about the publication of national security matters.

Approaching its centenary, it is unique to Britain (although Australia and New Zealand once tried something similar); it has no statutory basis; its use is voluntary for both officials and media, and its advice may be disregarded by them; it is independent in that it answers to no government department or media board, and the five senior officials on it are more than balanced by the thirteen senior press and broadcasting representatives; and it is not perfect either in protecting secrets or in protecting those who follow its advice. Yet it normally works, and it is a preferred interface of the British government and media, for both of whom the unattractively unpredictable and expensive alternative is litigation. A potential addition to such routine use of litigation would be direct or indirect intimidation of the media by the political apparatus, as routinely practised in many other countries, including, alas, some democracies. In Britain, the Official Secrets and other inhibitory Acts are indeed always there, but they have no direct connection with the D-Notice System, and comparatively speaking are rarely used against editors or publishers.

The D-Notice Committee straddles two mutually exclusive aspects of the public interest: the right and duty of the media to publish information about what is being done by government in the name of the public, versus the right and duty of the government to conceal *pro tem* certain sensitive information for the protection of the public. Another inherent dichotomy is that, while national security is a highly political subject, the acceptability of the D-Notice System to the media and the public depends on it being *seen* to be independent of government. Indeed, whenever Prime Ministers have taken too close an interest in its workings, its existence has been seriously threatened.

The system operates too in a somewhat grey area. National Security is a term often used, as an exception or as a justification, including in Acts of Parliament such as those dealing with Official Secrets, Terrorism, Regulation of Investigatory Powers, Freedom of Information and Data Protection. It is however nowhere defined, being what governmental lawyers call 'an ambulatory concept'. This delightful phrase smacks of Humpty Dumpty's 'It means just what I choose it to mean'; but in practice it reflects the difficulty which both media and officials have always rediscovered when trying to encapsulate, in a few lines, a set of criteria which are not either unacceptably broad and all-embracing, or meaninglessly vague and unhelpful.

Both sides of the D-Notice Committee therefore accept that the concept of national security has to be tested and discussed in the light of the particular and often unforeseeable circumstances of each case. Considerations which then come into play include what damage has been or would be done to life or current operations, what impact disclosure would have on future operations, or on the lives of the public and of those working undercover, and how widely known something is already in the public domain. The latter criterion has from the outset been an especially touchy area for the media; as globalisation and developments in electronic technology have gathered even greater pace in recent years, this has directly affected the judgements which the D-Notice Committee has to make. Both sides also accept that the coverage of the system is confined to what is in the Notices and their introduction; it does not apply, for example, to the sort and scale of violence perpetrated by groups like the Animal Liberation Front, nor directly to other parts of the fabric of wider national security such as the economy or (normally) policing activities either.

The History of the Committee

As with so many British institutions, the D-Notice System did not spring suddenly from any one idea, event or group. It started to emerge amorphously, in late Victorian times, from a confluence of trends in world politics, commerce, and the technologies of communications and the military. A much more vigorous press had evolved, partly as a result of rapid improvements in printing processes, and in the railways and linked telegraph system, partly as result of the opportunities this provided to Victorian entrepreneurs with political interests, and partly as a result of Parliamentary action. This included abolition of the tax on paper, educational reform leading to increased literacy and lower middle class prosperity, and nationalisation and cheapening of the telegraph system. The military, too, from the Crimean War onwards, benefited from the telegraph system spreading throughout Europe, and later from underwater cable connections; and the Royal Navy, as the steel frame of the Empire and protector of its trade, moved sedately from the era of sail, wood and broadsides to that of steam, armour, and gun turrets. Encouraged by these developments, the public's interest burgeoned in what today we call national security.

Nevertheless, this progress also brought more sharply into focus the conflict between the two aspects of public interest referred to above. These had been present much earlier, albeit in less stark form. Reporting on military shortcomings in the Crimea was followed by similar openness about other campaigns, in Egypt and the Sudan, and later in the Second Boer War. The disclosure of operational plans and force deployments became a major concern of generals, concerned about the operational implication of such leaks.

Furthermore, in South Africa in particular, restrictions imposed on war correspondents by the Army added to a worsening relationship. Once that war was over, the government and the press made several desultory attempts to find a mutually acceptable system of resolving a situation seen by both sides as unsatisfactory. Each time the Committee of Imperial Defence drafted a Bill to enable some degree of censorship to be introduced in time of tension and war, the hostility of the press and in those days of Parliament to any such infringement of British liberty caused Ministers to postpone further work until a more propitious moment arrived.

When Germany replaced France as the publicly perceived major external threat to Britain and its Empire, the political opportunity to introduce legislation duly arose. The Agadir Crisis of 1911, although directly involving Germany and France rather than Britain, was nevertheless seen by Government, press and public as the brink of war. A new Official Secrets Act was rushed through Parliament with minimal discussion, and the draft Bill to control the press was dusted off. Even at that point, however, Ministers such as Asquith, Churchill and Lloyd George wished to avoid confrontation with an influential press, and the future Permanent Secretary of the War Office, Reginald Brade, was sent quietly to talk to editors and proprietors. From these discussions emerged agreement to set up an informal committee of officials and of press representatives to provide a forum through which informed self-censorship might take place. It met for the first time in August 1912, chaired by the Admiralty's Permanent Secretary, Sir Graham Greene (uncle of the future novelist), with the dominant press members for many years being the owner of the *News of the World*, Lord Riddell, and the Manager of the Press Association, Sir Edmund Robbins.

By the time the First World War began, the Admiralty, War Office, and Press Committee, as it was called initially, had worked out a rudimentary modus operandi and established a greater degree of trust between the official and press sides. Between 1914 and 1918, it operated in tandem with a censorious Press Bureau; the Committee was not entirely liked by the latter, but it spoke effectively on behalf of the press as the Bureau slowly settled down, and resolved many press problems with the Asquith and Lloyd George Governments. It was during this time that the term D-Notice was by chance introduced (the Government was also issuing administrative Notices to the public in other lettered series). The Committee despatched over 700 D-Notices on behalf of the Bureau during the War, dealing not only with military and intelligence matters, but also with diplomatic, industrial, economic and domestic subjects, which comprised a far wider and looser kind of national security concern than has ever since been accepted.

Between the World Wars, this still unpublicised Committee (now joined by the new Air Ministry) remained unknown to the public, to most politicians and officials, and even to most in the press (now joined by broadcasters). For some years it had a low level of activity, concentrating mostly on protecting new technical information of the three ministries attached to the armed forces. In the late thirties, as realisation dawned that another war was indeed possible, the government made half-hearted plans for a wartime Press and Censorship Bureau; the D-Notice Committee was consulted about some aspects, but when War came again was itself placed in suspended animation. Between 1939 and 1945, D-Notices continued to be issued, and several of those involved in the Committee before and after the War were involved in the wartime replacement organisations, and, when the Committee was re-established after VJ Day, some of the wartime aspects (for example giving advice to book publishers) transferred seamlessly into a peacetime mode.

It was the wartime Chief Press Censor, Rear Admiral George Thomson, who was one of the voices suggesting in autumn 1945 that the D-Notice Committee should be reactivated, and when it was he became its part-time secretary. The Security Service (which in such matters also then represented the Secret Intelligence Service and Government Communications Headquarters; all three having been on the periphery of the pre-war D-Notice system) was one of the other early supporters. Its legal adviser, Bernard Hill, and Admiral Thomson worked closely together, but not always in agreement, as the Cold War Notices were developed. The Admiral was held in high esteem by the media, because of his independence of mind and knowledge of their positions, demonstrated from 1940 to his eventual retirement in 1963.

Thus the D-Notice system evolved and operated through all the major turning points and hot and cold conflicts during the post-Second World War period up to the present. The levels of intelligence, security and military activity have been consistently high throughout this period, including those of covert Special Forces, more recently against terrorists. The degree of media interest has usually also therefore been intense, because these activities make good copy, and thus the concomitant D-Notice Committee involvement has been busier than at any period since the First World War. By the mid-1960s, the existence of the Committee was common knowledge, but because its workings and even the Notices were still classified, it acquired a mythological and entirely inaccurate status (much beloved of journalists and television producers) as a shadowy organisation that 'slapped a D-Notice' on anything the government wanted to conceal from the public.

Occasionally the continuation of the D-Notice Committee had been called into question, notably when Harold Wilson became overly involved in the Cable-Vetting Affair in 1967, and when, over the Zircon satellite and similar disclosures in the mid-1980s, Mrs Thatcher demanded more of the system than was consistent with its independence. There have been several politically-commissioned external reviews, including two by the judge Lord Radcliffe (who had overseen censorship in the Second World War), and many internal reviews of individual Notices or of the whole system. There have been several changes of name prior to its current Defence, Press and Broadcasting Advisory Committee (but almost everyone still refers to it as the D-Notice Committee). An internal review held in 1993 led to the previously long-postponed decision to publish the then six Standing Notices, in a further attempt to demystify the system. Since 2000, even greater openness has been the norm; for example a record of the discussion at each of the D-Notice Committee's bi-annual meetings is placed on its institutional website, with much other information about the system.[2]

The Committee's Current Modus Operandi

The only full-time member of the D-Notice System is the Committee's Secretary. He—and they have all been men so far—is usually a retired senior officer from the Armed Services, with the appropriate experience, political clout and security clearances to assess and advise what should not be disclosed, but also when necessary to investigate something officials are telling him, before making any such recommendations. Although he has been accommodated in, and paid for by, the Ministry of Defence for many years now, the Secretary takes every opportunity to stress his and the D-Notice Committee's independence from the Ministry and from all Ministers; his responsibility is equally to the two sides of the Committee, whose individual official and media members are in turn responsible to their parent organisations.[3] The Committee's only collective responsibility is, therefore, to the British public.

The Secretary's week-in week-out advice to media and officials is based on the guidance contained in the now five Standing Notices and their introductory paragraphs (Military Plans and Operations, Equipment (including nuclear weapons), Cryptology, Sensitive Sites, and the Secret Agencies and Special Forces.[4] Every six months he accounts to the full D-Notice Committee for what he has done, very occasionally consulting them in between if confronted with something especially novel or contentious. His normal involvement arises either from a request for advice from a journalist or publisher who wishes to disclose some matter possibly covered by the Notices; or from an official concerned that some endangering information is about to be published; or when the Secretary himself foresees possible damaging disclosure and issues pro-active advice. Only very rarely is a complete story involved, usually just some operational, technical or personal detail which will endanger a life or an operation; never something just embarrassing to the governmental machine. It is equally common for the Secretary to advise an official that there is no reason *not* to publish something, as it is for him to advise a journalist against disclosure. The Secretary also keeps regularly in touch with those in Government Departments who have direct contact with the media over national security (in the case of the secret services, unattributably), to ensure that he is both informed and (if he agrees with what he hears) consistent. It is important to note that a distance is imposed between information the Secretary receives respectively from officials and the media.

In the fast-moving world of international communication, the Secretary lives by his wits and by his contacts. The interest of his job is not just professional, with potentially lethal outcomes, but also anthropological, as he shuttles about in the no-man's land between the skirmishing tribes of officialdom and the media. These differ greatly in role, motivation and priorities, and their sub-tribes also differ as much from each other—MI5 from MI6, *Guardian* from *Times*, Ministry of Defence from Cabinet Office, Sky from BBC—as Glasgow Academy from Eton. Yet all of them also share many characteristics: highly intelligent and articulate, energetic, competitive, dedicated, witty (if rather serious about themselves), ruthless, obsessive about protecting their sources, fierce with those of their own who let the side down, and convinced that to dissemble and to propagandise are necessary weapons in their armoury. They also share an informal view of a third tribe, the politicians, as being lesser, but symbolically necessary and often to be heeded—rather as ancient Egypt's priestly caste must have considered the Pharaonic dynasties.

These semi-frivolous observations are the context necessary to understanding a very serious business: maintaining the right balance between secrecy and the public interest. In the era of ruthless international terrorism this is simultaneously both a clearer and a murkier balance. The observations have a bearing too on how disputes between officials and media arise, on why angry officials occasionally reach too quickly for a court injunction, and why irritated editors occasionally deliberately publish a story without first checking whether it contains details genuinely damaging to national security. The intelligentsia is just as prone to surges of mental testosterone as hooligans are to surges of the physical kind. During the 2003 Hutton Inquiry, a (female) BBC executive excused her delay in responding to a query from me as being because all the top people there and in Whitehall were 'rushing around, beating their chests and grunting loudly at each other'.

Tensions Around Secrecy

In the same way that the security situation in 1911 was such that the British government felt able to introduce measures which would have been unacceptable previously, so since 9/11 governments have taken additional powers they claim to be necessary to combat international terrorism. The media side of the *D-Notice Committee* has reflected the uneasiness about this trend felt more widely by their colleagues. This has been on top of longer-running debates within the Committee, for example over the degree to which information about Special Forces can be protected in an international environment, when the equivalent forces of other countries and their media have different 'rules'. Debate similarly occurs over the grey area between criminal activity (a police responsibility not covered by the D-Notices) and police and secret agencies co-operation on security and intelligence matters, and over whether matters already published in the overseas media may ipso facto therefore be repeated by their British counterparts, and what the public domain means as a concept in our globalised, hi-tech world.

How much secrecy is necessary in a modern state, possessed of shrewd and comparatively well-informed citizens? What is the irreducible core of official secrets necessary to protect national security? Is there sufficient independent judgement of where politicians and officials, grappling obsessively for example with terrorism, choose to draw the line? Where is the dividing line between justifiable whistle-blowing by insiders and disclosures which damage the institutions and operations which are combating threats to security? In the heat of international conflict, is embarrassing ever the same as damaging? Do any tales of past secret activities belong, as part of their personal life story, to those who executed them, or entirely to Crown copyright, or partly to the wider public in whose name they were carried out? Are Crown interest, government interest and the public interest ever the same thing?

These and many others are not just philosophical questions, but regular practical considerations for those in officialdom and the media who deal with national security matters, and therefore also for the D-Notice Secretary and Committee. Events too tend to have a hastening effect on policy, and similarly on new legislation. The nature of any legislation depends, not just on how it is written by governments and their lawyers, but also on how subsequently it is used or abused. Successive Official Secrets Acts have not always been invoked wisely, but, considering the quantity of national security activity since 1911, their use in litigation has not so far been continuously oppressive. Their more insidious effect has been on the minds of many in public service, encouraging them to believe that the authorities require almost all their work, however mundane and undamaging, to be kept from public scrutiny. In the media perception, this has contributed to the *omerta* school of public information policy, habitual to many government departments.

This, and the more recent confusion of factual governmental information (formerly the province of civil service information officers) and interpretive government information (formerly the province more clearly of Ministers, and now called 'spin'), have contributed to a poor relationship between the media and the governmental machine. There are media reasons, too, including the primacy of television (albeit recently weakened by other electronic audio-visual media), with its inherently somewhat superficial, presentational and confrontational handling of political news. Governmental attitudes to the secrecy/openness balance have certainly been coloured by sometimes justified perceptions of poor media practice. All this has been the background to the official/media interaction with which the D-Notice System has in recent years operated.

The Situation Before '9/11'

Operations in Former Yugoslavia and East Timor apart, in the years immediately preceding '9/11', the scope of *D-Notice Committee* activity had been predominantly domestic: leaks allegedly emanating from two former intelligence officers, David Shayler (MI5) and Richard Tomlinson (MI6); the final gasps of Northern Ireland-related terrorism, with skeletons tumbling from the cupboards of the security authorities and terrorists of both stripes; a torrent of books by ex-SAS authors, and Ministry of Defence attempts to enforce a preventive contract; the ex-Director General of the Security Service, Stella Rimington, wrangling with the governmental machine about publishing her memoirs; the Court of Appeal upholding the right of journalists not to hand over source documents to the police; the long tussle over the Freedom of

Information Act (2000), and the Parliamentary Ombudsman criticising government departments for being over-secretive; all these, and even the military intervention in Sierra Leone and the dramatic rescue of hostages there, had a largely *British* tone.

Nevertheless, as direct foreign threats to British national security apparently receded, elsewhere Islamist extremists had been targeting Western interests and influence for some years. The higher visibility incidents included bombing the World Trade Center in 1993, attacks on US Marines in Somalia the same year, bombing the US Embassies in Nairobi and Dar-es-Salaam in 1998 (leading to American missile attacks on targets in Afghanistan and Sudan), and the attacks on *USS Cole* in Aden in 2000 and the American Cultural Center in Calcutta in January 2001. While all this was reported in the UK media, there was little political direction to the UK security authorities to refocus on these areas; while co-operation in monitoring this threat with their American colleagues was continued by the British intelligence agencies, they meanwhile suffered their share of the post-Cold War illusory 'peace dividend'. The direct threat to British security did not re-emerge publicly to centre stage until after the government committed the UK to react to the attacks on the American homeland in 2001. The D-Notice Committee's advisory role was rapidly drawn into this 'new' security situation.

Post-'9/11'

The interaction between officials, media and the D-Notice System went through predictable stages. In the immediate aftermath of '9/11', there was entirely proper media reporting not just of that horrific event, but also of the steps being taken to investigate the background to it and of the nature of the Al Qaeda network and threat. As it became clear that this was centred on Afghanistan, and that military action would be taken there by a coalition including Britain, a less acceptable degree of informed speculation about undercover operations and military preparations began to feature in the British Press. It soon became necessary to advise editors that this could endanger lives and imminent operations, and such speculation then stopped almost entirely, albeit briefly.

After the air strikes against perceived Taliban/Al Qaeda positions in early October, there was renewed speculation about Special Forces (SF) operations, which although mostly inaccurate was nevertheless sometimes prescient, and usually based on insider sources. These practices continued throughout the first phase of the Afghanistan campaign and into the second Iraq war, as did briefing against any senior person (e.g. the British Chief of Defence Staff, Admiral Boyce) who warned of a long haul. At times, the MoD became highly concerned about speculation on SF activity, but in reality much of what was in the newspapers was background SF information already widely in the public domain, and generally the British media avoided publishing endangering specifics on which they had received D-Notice advice.

The next stage was when there was a UK ground force deployment. Initially there was a mixture amongst them of overt SF, which caused some confusion in the media as to what could be reported. After discussion, the agreed DPBAC line was that, if SF had to deploy overtly, they should take precautions not to be recognisable as such to the media. Also in November 2001, there was a successful SF attack on a cave complex elsewhere in the country, in much greater force than their normal preferred small covert groups. There were four SAS casualties, who were immediately evacuated back to the military wing of a National Health Service hospital in UK. Unfortunately the lack of forewarning, and therefore of advice to the media, led to a leak from within the hospital to a local stringer, which was immediately picked up by the local TV station, and thence widely by the national media. By then, it was not possible to do more than D-Notice damage limitation on the detail both of the operation and of the casualties; the publicity caused grief to them and to their families, as well as increasing the possibility of retaliatory attacks by Al Qaeda sympathisers. At one stage, MoD sought a legal injunction against a newspaper, and although this was dropped a few days later, the litigation greatly irritated the wider media, and the number of SF articles and broadcasts increased, albeit almost entirely of material already widely in the public domain.

The same month, the D-Notice Committee discussed SF identification in the context of SBS marines aiding prevention of a mass breakout of Taliban/Al Qaeda prisoners from the Mazar-i-Sharif fort. Advice to the media that publication of close-ups should preferably be avoided, so that at least in the UK the chances of their being recognised were reduced, was generally accepted, but the media side of the Committee did point out that the footage taken by a local cameraman had been syndicated to over 350 outlets around the world. In such irreconcilable situations, intelligent debate at least keeps security considerations in the minds of programme makers for the future.

In due course, ground operations in Afghanistan were joined by greater conventional forces, visible to all. Their visual aspects and activities were in little need of much D-Notice protection from disclosure, other than of certain plans and equipment; indeed both the American and the British authorities welcomed the publicity with which editors were only too happy to fill their hungry columns and air time. The most unwelcome situation, to all concerned, as shown in every campaign from the Boer War to the Falklands conflict to modern Iraq, is one in which there are too many correspondents in theatre with too little to write about, and with editors at home demanding a constant high quantity of reportage.

Iraq 2

Because the sensitive aspects of the run-up to the second Iraq war were largely Political, and the DPBAC is necessarily as far as possible apolitical, its role was initially on the sidelines. About eight months before significant British forces began to deploy to the Gulf in January 2003, it was apparent that war was a high probability, especially to those few journalists specialising in defence and security matters. One role of the D-Notice Secretary was to assist in briefing those other journalists selected by their organisation to stand by for deployment as war correspondents, well before they departed. Most were not experienced in defence or security, and very few themselves had any military experience, even as Reservists. Briefings were provided either individually or en bloc at bigger institutions such as the BBC. The advice concentrated on the unfamiliar areas of potential sensitivity likely to be encountered both before and during the high intensity phase. It was clear that most of the correspondents would be embedded in units of the three Armed Forces, and would therefore have a close personal interest in not disclosing endangering information, as well as being liable to de facto local control of what they saw and reported. It was also clear that those who were not embedded would face problems of access and movement, on a fast-moving battlefield with a dense concentration of high-lethality modern weaponry.

In addition, as the start of the invasion approached, the frequency of media requests for advice and of official requests for assistance increased. There was also once again a spate of mostly spurious SF stories. There were other discussions with journalists about articles on new weapon system capabilities, and about speculation on likely axes of advance and on amphibious landings. D-Notice advice was invariably accepted, and although speculation did not completely stop, it was of a very general nature.

Once the invasion started, its rapidity and success (and the embedding) ensured fewer further security queries. Where there was friction, it was between the international media and the Coalition briefers over access and information. Afterwards the lessons learned were discussed by the D-Notice Committee, prompting comments that included that the following: had the fighting lasted longer, there might have been dissatisfaction with the constraints of embedding; while it had provided plenty of dramatic footage and column inches, journalists had not seen enough of the impact on ordinary Iraqis, even in their vicinity. The initial lack of a strategic overview had been largely corrected at briefing centres in theatre, London and Washington, but the DPBAC Media side felt these centres had still been well behind what was being seen televisually live from the Front in real time. They were also concerned at the Coalition treatment of journalists and camera crews who had not been embedded, in particular those who had attempted to report from inside Iraq. One aspect over which there had been few disclosure problems latterly was UKSF; they had operated covertly and in small teams. Overall, the D-Notice System had played its agreed part throughout, and there had been no serious breaches of operational security by the British media.

And Now?

Judgements about how much secrecy and regulation are required and are tolerable in a mature democracy, in what specific areas they should be focussed, and for how long they should be maintained, have to be looked at in the wider context of constitutional checks and balances. If Parliament is relatively supine in the face of the Executive, the Public looks more to the Judiciary and to the Media for the intuitively desired checks on Power. If all are relatively submissive to the Executive, it is Events which in the end bring retribution.

What has happened since 2001 contains many more 'known knowns' than any other variation in the Rumsfeld lexicon. This is not just hindsight; in strategic terms, as many sources are now revealing, everything which has happened and is happening in the Middle East and in Afghanistan/Pakistan was predicted by those experienced in the regions affected and in nation-building, but was largely 'disbelieved' for reasons of short-term political expediency. The disregarded wise existed in government departments on both sides of the Atlantic and in the regions concerned, in NGOs, and amongst the UK and international media and military. The swamp in which international terrorists and unstable and threatening political leaderships thrive will take many years even partially to drain. Does the D-Notice System have a useful role to play in this ongoing situation?

The few examples above of D-Notice advice provided to the media during the immediate post-9/11 years are the modern part of a continuum since 1912. Many of the fundamentals remain of the conflict between the freedom of the media to report (and comment) to the public, and the responsibility of the Government to keep certain matters secret pro tem in order to protect the public. There are, however, many practical differences from those early days, and to the more recent decades of the Cold War. As always, changes have been driven by technology, both in that available to the governmental machine, even more so to that now possessed by the media, and even more differently in that owned by the public, which gives UK citizens direct access to enormous amounts of international information without reliance on either government or traditional media. It also enables them to 'report' events directly to many others. Even where this is no more accurate and unbiased than news being reported by the traditional media and governments, it is largely beyond the control of either.

And yet in some ways, all this is just a speeded-up extension of what has happened at least since the mid-nineteenth century, when the railways, telegraph, undersea cables, cameras, and wider education started to globalise communication, and to enable individuals to exchange information in and from many parts of the world almost simultaneously. Although battlefields and terrorist activity can now be reported in real time, as can disclosure of sensitive matters revealed in one country in order to discomfit another, the D-Notice System has adapted from the Pre-WWI speeds and methodologies, through the Cold War to the current global security situation. It has moved from quasi-censorship and self-secrecy, to being purely advisory and as open as an organisation dealing with secrets can be.

The D-Notice Secretary now has comparatively even less scope to intervene pre-emptively in particular cases. There is however still a need to limit the damage which certain disclosures, in the traditional and the new media, could do for example to measures being taken to protect the public against international terrorism. What happens in the United Kingdom is just one part of an international campaign (not 'war'), but Britain must play its part, in its own way. As it is impossible to pre-empt every disclosure, the D-Notice Secretary now has more to do in both damage limitation and in spreading awareness among the media of what is likely to be harmful, so that, with or without his specific advice on a particular story, an adequate degree of intelligent self-censorship takes place. The D-Notice Committee also continues to provide the only regular interface where senior officials and senior media representatives regularly meet each other in person, and discuss the difficult practical issues which the current national and international security circumstances throw up.

The governmental side also needs to review its present traditional practices. Greater openness about what is not secret would encourage greater secrecy about what cannot yet be open. The best security, as with that at Bletchley Park and its outstations during and after the Second World War, and later over the Chevaline nuclear missile enhancements, is for no insider to talk about something outside his/her own security circle. This entails both convincing those concerned of the need for the secrecy, and also limiting the secrecy to very specific matters. The frequent official attitude that almost everything about some organisation is secret, no matter how mundane, is seen by those who directly or indirectly work for the Government as untrue, unrealistic and unnecessary. Contempt for blanket non-disclosure then leads to misjudgements and leaks about those aspects which really should be kept secret. Some leaks are inadvertent, but most of sensitive information come either from those at the top for 'political' reasons, or from those lower down for principled, pecuniary or personal reasons; what they have in common is that they come from insiders.

And, of course, once there is one leak, the media will use everything in their armoury to find/encourage others—unless they too can be convinced at editorial level that something really merits non-disclosure. Which is where the D-Notice System will continue to function.

9

REFLECTIONS ON A LIFETIME OF REPORTING ON INTELLIGENCE AFFAIRS

Chapman Pincher

Editors' Notes: As the pioneer of investigative journalism in the defence and security realms, Chapman Pincher is well qualified to write about the relationship between the media and the intelligence agencies. Drawing on a career spanning more than six decades, his chapter provides stories and reminiscences about how this relationship worked in practice. It is quite revealing to see the importance of lunching and shooting with the right people. The story is a two-sided one, for on the one hand Pincher helped the government of the day by preserving national security through a series of articles; yet he remained a thorn in the side of successive governments, revealing information which was meant to remain secret. Throughout what emerges is a fascinating depiction of the role of the journalist as spy, and one cannot help but ponder how different the disciplines really are.

It is satisfying, at the age of 94, to look back on a career in investigative reporting spanning more than sixty years—in various media—and to know that I would choose to repeat it in preference to any other profession. I apologize if my CV sounds immodest but this is how it truly was, as evidenced by many official documents and the thirty-eight large volumes containing all my newspaper and magazine cuttings, which I have willed to my old college—King's College London, where I have been a Life Fellow for many years.

I began my professional life as a biologist, teaching at the Liverpool Institute, pending a return to King's to research genetics. To enhance the salary (then £5 per week) I began freelance writing for agricultural and scientific magazines, learning much about the art of succinct journalism. The outbreak of war ended my academic dream when, in 1940, I joined the Royal Armoured Corps for training as a tank gunner, became a gunnery instructor and, on being commissioned, served a year of regimental duty. As the Army needed some scientifically qualified officers to liaise with the scientists developing new weapons, I was posted to the Military College of Science, where I completed the advanced class in Ammunition and Explosives. Until 1946, I was then involved in the development and field-testing of rocket weapons and other devices, which not only familiarized me with all three Forces but introduced me to the intelligence world. In the process of serving on secret committees I became friendly with several officers and civil servants who would, later, become very senior in the defence establishment, such as Solly Zuckerman (later Lord) and William Cook (later Sir).

While stationed in London, at the Arsenal, I met the editor of the *Daily Express*, and when the German Flying Bombs and V2 rockets began to strike I helped his mass-circulation newspaper to print accurate diagrams of their structure as I had seen the mock-ups made from recovered parts at the Farnborough Aeronautical Establishment. The newspapers had been told, officially, that they could speculate so there were no Official Secrets repercussions.

With remarkable luck, I was posted to a military office in the Mansion House, not far from Fleet Street, to await my release to civilian life and, so, happened to be close at hand when news of the destruction of Hiroshima by an atomic bomb astonished the world. I telephoned Marcus Oliphant (later Sir), who had been involved in atomic bomb research, and he told me that the US government had released a thick report about the whole Manhattan Project—later known as the Smyth Report. He said that the Tube Alloys HQ in London had an advance copy.[1] With the agreement of my Colonel, who was fascinated to know what was in it, I went there and was allowed to see the report and make notes. The result was succession of 'scoops' because there had been a hold up in publishing the report in the US.

For these atomic contributions, which were followed by insider information about the V2, I was offered the post of Defence and Scientific Reporter, which meant that I would be entering national journalism in a specialist role. This was an unusual way of entering Fleet Street, the Mecca to which most journalists could aspire only after service on local newspapers.

Shortly after accepting the post, I was summoned to Woolwich Arsenal by my Brigadier, with whom I had become socially friendly, to be given the shock news that I was to be posted abroad. Though the Americans had seized all the captured V2 rockets and shipped them to the US—along with the chief German rocket scientists—the British had collected enough spare parts to build three, which were to be test fired into the sea at Cuxhaven. The three Services would each have an officer in the team and I was to be the Army's—with the rank of Lieutenant Colonel.

While affecting to be thrilled and grateful, I realized that the project would take so long that I would lose touch with the *Express* so I decided to reject the post if I could, tempting though the promotion was. I wrote to the Brigadier pointing out that the Cuxhaven experience should belong to a soldier who would be staying in the Army, which I was determined to leave. He agreed! A few weeks later I was demobilized and at my desk in Fleet Street the following day.[2]

Through leisurely lunches at a restaurant in Jermyn Street (chosen because it was equidistant between Fleet Street and the Whitehall-Westminster complex) I began by consulting wartime friends who had remained in secret employment. They quickly appreciated that anyone with such access to mass-circulation publicity could be helpful in the defence revolution occasioned by the arrival the atomic bomb and the ballistic missile. The Chiefs of Staff knew that, with Britain financially exhausted by the war, they would have to compete for the money and facilities to construct atomic weapons and new bombers and missiles to carry them.[3] Obviously, a trusted, former insider, keen to support them and their projects, could be helpful in the coming political struggles.

Soon after my appointment, another fluke circumstance provided me with a regular source of exceptional eminence and influence. Before the war I had written and illustrated a simple guide to genetics for farmers called *The Breeding of Farm Animals*, which was published in 1946 as a Penguin Handbook. At the end of a Press facility visit to Farnborough I boarded a bus to take me to the main gate and sat opposite a small man in black, pin-stripe suit and bowler hat. He introduced himself as Fred Brundrett, saying that his hobby was farming and that he had enjoyed my book. He invited me to see his herd of Redpoll cattle on his farm near Emsworth where I found that, during the week, he was Deputy to the Chief Defence Scientist, Sir Henry Tizard, whom he succeeded. Fred and I became firm friends, meeting regularly for long lunches in Jermyn Street, even after his retirement.[4]

The general Whitehall view was that any official information was an official secret covered by the Official Secrets Acts until it was officially released. Fred believed that the taxpayers who would be funding the unusually heavy peacetime defence costs occasioned by the atomic and missile age, were entitled to be kept informed about their investments and the reasons for them. He also suspected that reliance on the nuclear deterrent, which he foresaw, would be difficult for many people to accept without repeated explanation and assurance. He chose me as his medium for imparting that information.

Our relationship was much resented in the higher Whitehall echelons and in the Security Service, MI5, but Fred was his own man and had the backing of Ministers, such as Duncan Sandys. (That would not stop traditional Whitehall mandarins from taking their revenge by denying Brundrett the customary GBE on his retirement.) Fred also introduced me to his chief assistants, who were specialists on various aspects of defence, including atomic weapons, and assured them that I could be trusted.

Over the years, I received—and usually published—such a steady stream of classified information that it precipitated my most cherished professional compliment, made in Parliament—that I was 'a public urinal where Ministers and officials queued up to leak'! Some journalistic critics claimed that I was allowing myself to be 'used' but if the information was true and especially if it was exclusive, I was open for 'use' at any time.[5]

Though not consciously aware of it, I was pioneering a new system of reporting because, previously, Fleet Street had generally regarded most senior civil servants, Forces chiefs and Ministers as leak-proof. A recent flush of released Cabinet, Defence and Prime Ministerial documents has revealed the extraordinary lengths to which officials went, through the so-called 'leak procedures', to discover my sources and, hopefully, deter them and silence me. The amount of time wasted interrogating senior officials and Forces personnel about my reports was so intrusive that, on 27 November 1958, Sir Richard Powell, the Defence Ministry's Permanent Secretary, advised his Minister 'I believe that we must learn to live with the man and make the best of it'. However, that did not deter the Prime Minister, Harold Macmillan, from asking the Defence Ministry, on 4 May 1959, 'Can nothing be done to suppress or even get rid of Mr Chapman Pincher?' The Defence Ministry appeared to answer the question when accredited defence reporters were issued with passes for entry into its buildings. Mine, which I still treasure, was numbered 007.[6]

The danger of being prosecuted for breaching the Official Secrets Acts posed a recurring problem, especially as the Fleet Street lawyers and most editors were seriously scared of them. Fortunately, I found a solution in the shape of Rear Admiral George Thomson, the war-time Censor who had been appointed to operate the peace-time D-Notice system.[7] This involved the issue of advisory notices to editors about areas of defence and intelligence which it would be not only patriotic but wise to avoid. I cultivated the delightful admiral, through regular lunches, and we quickly devised a *modus vivendi*. In those days the D-Notice Secretary was truly independent, with an office outside Whitehall, and Thomson believed it his duty to secure publication if possible without real damage to the national interest. In return, editors trusted him to be telling the truth when he assured them or their reporters that publication would damage security.

So, whatever I was writing about defence or intelligence, I read it over to him by telephone. Sometimes he needed to take Whitehall advice before responding, but, almost invariably, we were able to devise a form of words which permitted publication and allowed me to assure the editor that the copy had been 'passed by Admiral Thomson'. The advantage to the Admiral was substantial because as soon as copies of the first edition of the *Daily Express* reached the offices of rival newspapers—around 10.30 pm—their reporters would telephone him at home to ask if it was safe for them to copy the story. He was able to answer without disturbing Whitehall officials at ungodly hours.

In 1946, while in a London club, I encountered a *Daily Express* foreign correspondent who had been on the island of Tinian, from which the American bomber had taken off to destroy Hiroshima. He and others had been shown the uranium bomb, 'Little Boy', before it was loaded and been told its all-up weight—four tons. That was a major secret which I was keen to divulge because I had figured out, from the Smyth Report, that the Hiroshima bomb had been essentially a gun in which a bullet of uranium 235 had been fired through a hollow cylinder of U 235 to form a critical mass, and wanted to publish a cut-away picture of it. I felt sure that Thomson would veto the weight but he assured me that, since it was an American weapon, I could publish what I liked. Recently, while a guest at the Atomic Weapons Research Establishment at Aldermaston, Berks, I was gratified to see that the official sketch showing the gun-bomb principle was almost identical with mine which had graced the front page half a century earlier.[8] There followed occasions on which, after consulting Whitehall mandarins, the Admiral informed me that if I attributed a leak to an unnamed American source all would be well. It was regarded as even more satisfactory if I could delay an embarrassing revelation until one of my regular visits to the US, when I could give it a Washington date-line. Another source-protecting ploy was to make use of the many international conferences which I attended, those on astronautics, for example, being ideal for releasing secret information about new rocket weapons which I had surreptitiously acquired. One instance was my revelation that, pending the time when the US had developed nuclear missiles with inter-continental range, American forces were to deploy intermediate range Thor missiles at Feltwell, in Norfolk. The fact was sensitive because there was widespread political resentment against such a move as it could increase the risk of a pre-emptive Soviet strike on Britain. Few in Whitehall were fooled by my Amsterdam date-line, giving the impression that I had acquired the intelligence from some scientist at the conference there, but all were relieved that there would be no Parliamentary claims that some Minister had leaked it to me.

When I entered Fleet Street spies were classed as criminals and dealt with by the Crime Reporters. In 1950, however, when Klaus Fuchs was exposed, the *Daily Express* crime reporter asked me to cover the Old Bailey trial because he thought it beyond his expertise. Using information supplied by friends in the Harwell atomic research station, I produced a front-page account headlined 'Fuchs Gave Bomb to Russia'.[9] As the paper's 'spy man' from then on I eventually became the only journalist to cover all the Cold War spy cases from Fuchs, Maclean, Burgess, Philby, Cairncross, Blunt, Houghton, Lonsdale, Vassall and Blake, to the GCHQ traitor, Geoffrey Prime and others. There were also espionage aspects to the Profumo Affair and the Hollis Affair, about which I had inside knowledge from prime sources, including retired officers from MI5, such as Peter 'Spycatcher' Wright.

I remained an investigative reporter throughout my journalistic career because I resisted all efforts to promote me to executive status, even by my proprietor Lord Beaverbrook, with whom I was on friendly terms, spending much time with him in his later years. 'Putting the paper to bed' was night work and held no interest for me. As a life-long countryman I had long been addicted to the chase, having spent most of my leisure time shooting and fishing, sports which, quite unexpectedly, were to be of enormous advantage in my acquisition of prime sources. In the first shooting syndicate which I joined one of the members was an admiral—Sir Hugh 'Rufus' Mackenzie, who was put in charge of the Navy's Polaris submarine project! On joining the Marks and Spencer shooting syndicate in Berkshire I met Lord Forte, who invited me to his shoots, where I met ambassadors and politicians, the Attorney General, Sir Michael Havers, being particularly informative over many years.

Through shooting and salmon fishing with Sir Thomas Sopwith, the air-craft pioneer, I became on terms of regular friendship with Lord Dilhorne, the Lord Chancellor, whose daughter, Eliza Manningham-Buller, (now Baroness) would head MI5. I even encountered my old foe, Harold Macmillan, in the shooting line there and we became friends.

I had met Lord 'Dickie' Mountbatten when he was both First Sea Lord and Chief of the Defence Staff, at formal conferences and interviews but he had always been aloof and conscious of his near-royal status. Then, at a shoot lunch, our hostess, Lady Sopwith, said 'Dickie, sit next to Harry and don't mumble'. From then on he was just another human being. He invited me to shoot on his Broadlands estate and was keen to tell me his own views about defence so that they would colour my reporting. He wanted to know what might be going on in Whitehall behind his back and I was always happy to repay his confidences, as I had been with Fred Brundrett concerning Britain's first H-bomb test in 1957 (in all walks of life 'pay-day' eventually arrives).[10]

I was particularly in debt to Fred for a scoop that the test was to be carried out off Christmas Island in the Pacific, with details of the operation, which was code-named Grapple. So I complied when he summoned me to his country house on a matter of great urgency. There he told me that the Japanese, who were agitated by the dangers of radioactive fall-out, were planning to make the tests impossible by sailing a thousand small ships into the area. If they forced the tests to be abandoned, Britain's entire defence policy would be ruined. Fred explained that the Government had decided to fool the Japanese with a deception operation and needed my help. The object was to convince them, by planted false intelligence, that the tests, which were scheduled for May, had been postponed for several weeks. The effort would be enhanced if I could induce my Editor to print a front-page article by me implying that there had been a delay due to technical problems with the bomb. Various senior atomic scientists had gone through the motions of cancelling their bookings to reach Christmas Island and had rebooked for June, as I 'discov-ered' on telephoning the airline. A front page disclosure ensued and the tests went ahead in May. When I attended the second blast I received some special facilities from the chief scientist there—my old friend, Sir William Cook—for my assistance, which was also acknowledged by the task force commander Air Vice Marshal Wilfrid Oulton, who became another lunch companion.

Shooting also strengthened my friendship with the Air Minister, Julian Amery, and once, when seeking a way of publicising the atomic capability of the RAF, I suggested that a photograph of me leaning against an H-bomb, which no outsider had ever seen, would be helpful. A few days later he asked me to visit an airfield where an official photographer was waiting. We were taken to a hanger from which was wheeled a trolley bearing the RAF's biggest megaton bomb, and the photograph duly appeared, exclusively, in the *Daily Express*.

My long experience has enabled me to understand some of the reasons why distinguished men risked damaging their careers by leaking information to journalists like me. Sometimes, it was to inflict professional damage on an opponent in a competing political party or government department. Frequently it was to take the sting out of something unpleasant which was due to be announced in Parliament, a few days later. Occasionally, it was to publicise something to the leaker's advantage which he had been forbidden to announce for some diplomatic reason. Often sheer vanity was the cause—the vain delight of being in the know and making someone else aware of it. Rarely, it was simply mischievous, as happened in 1953, when Sir Archibald Rowlands, the highly respected Permanent Secretary of the Supply Ministry, retired and, at the invitation of Lord Beaverbrook, joined the *Express Newspapers* Board.

Lunching with him at his favourite Soho restaurant, I asked if he could remember any area where I might profitably dig to which he replied, 'Ask the Ministry of Supply about "Nomination"'. I questioned the Supply Ministry's public relations chief, a friend who, after much delay, assured me that the name was unknown. Other evasive responses convinced me that there was a cover-up but all I could produce in print were a few paragraphs which I quickly forgot. In fact, my inquiry had caused such a rumpus that Rowlands' successor, Sir James Helmore, called me in to say 'Whoever gave you that information is a traitor and it is your duty to give us his name'. Declining to oblige, I assured him that the source could not possibly be a traitor and left.

Years later, when I was lecturing to the War Course at Greenwich, I found myself seated, at lunch, next to Professor R.V. Jones, whose wartime intelligence achievements have been recorded in his classic book, *Most Secret War*. 'However did you find out about Nomination?' he asked. 'It was more secret than the bomb itself.' He then explained that it had been an MI6–CIA group set up to exchange intelligence about Russia's atomic bomb activities and, on the day after my brief report had appeared, was about to hold its first meeting in Washington with Sir William Penney and Sir John Cockcroft in attendance.[11] As Rowlands had died, I enlightened Jones, who then became a friend and my salmon fishing guest in Scotland, where he lived. What had Rowlands' motive been? All that we could suggest was he wanted to cause grief to his successor with, perhaps, a dash of vanity thrown in.

Though Admiral Thomson served me as a tenuous connection with MI5 I had no direct contact until the first public emergence in Moscow of the defector-spies, Maclean and Burgess in February 1956, when he informed me that the Security Service urgently needed my help. I attended his office where I met the head of MI5's legal department, who said that intelligence analysis had convinced MI5 that the two renegades had been produced so that they could be used to make further damaging allegations about the Foreign Office and MI5 itself whenever it suited the Kremlin to sow distrust between the US and Britain. He wanted me to publish a prominent article warning the public that whatever the defectors might say in future would be KGB lies. He admitted that MI5 had acquired evidence of Maclean's treachery over many years and claimed that, though there was nothing legal to prevent the return of Burgess to Britain, he knew that 'he was a bloody spy'. I detected almost a sense of panic in the urgency with which Hill required the publicity—without, of course, any mention of MI5. When he had left, Thomson told me that he and the MI5 man were acting on the instructions of Roger Hollis, then MI5's deputy director general. The *Daily Express* obliged with a front-page news-story, headlined 'Beware the Diplomats!' and the Admiral telephoned me to say that MI5 was delighted.[12] In the result, the defectors were never used to make derogatory statements of any kind.

My regular leaks did not go unnoticed by the Soviet Embassy and I was eventually targeted by a senior KGB officer, called Anatoli Strelnikov, who was posing as a Press officer. Being under pressure from Beaverbrook to secure a visit to a Soviet space research station, I encouraged him but first asked Admiral Thomson to check MI5's views. He discovered that MI5 was very interested and assigned a senior officer, named Michael McCaul, to be my contact. Each time I encountered the Russian I reported the details to my new friend. In the spring of 1961, McCaul suggested a large newspaper feature which could be 'very helpful'. A major exhibition was to be staged in Moscow by leading British electronic companies and there were deep security concerns that the KGB would try to suborn some of the scientists who were, or might later be, involved in defence projects. So, I was provided with a series of case-records, allegedly from MI5's files, showing how, previously, young Britons had been induced into blackmailable situations, mainly sexual, which had been surreptitiously photographed.

It happened to be published, as a large feature, shortly before Strelnikov was due to give me lunch, where he remarked, rather menacingly 'That article you wrote was terrible for peace. What made you write it?' I explained that collecting such information was what I was paid to do whereupon he said 'We will pay you more to write for us—work for us.' I did not respond but when he came to pay the bill he took a bundle of banknotes out of his wallet, flicked them and said 'Don't forget! Work for us.' When I told McCaul he was jubilant, hoping that it might be possible to have the Russian expelled. Sadly, the effort failed.

In April 1962, MI5 received information from a KGB defector to the CIA, Anatoli Golitsin, of the existence of a Soviet spy in the Admiralty. It led to the arrest of John Vassall, a clerk in the Admiralty who had been recruited to the KGB through homosexual blackmail while working in the Moscow Embassy in 1954. When Vassall came out of prison I met him twice for long interviews over lunch and he was such an obvious passive homosexual that he should never have been sent to Moscow, aged thirty, and left alone there, as he was. He was quickly spotted by the KGB and set up at a drunken, homosexual party, where photographs were taken and shown to him later. Threatened with exposure and offered money, he agreed to spy, passing over secret documents, continuing the service when transferred to the Naval Intelligence Division in London in 1957. Vassall dealt with the in-trays and out-trays of naval officers and civilians of the highest ranks and abstracted documents, which, with his previous training as a photographer in the RAF, he copied at his flat in Dolphin Square during lunchtime.[13]

Vassall was arrested on 12 September 1962 and his confession has recently been released into the National Archives.[14] When sentenced to eighteen years imprisonment, it was obvious that he had inflicted great damage over a long period. So, to clear the names of Ministers who had been accused of negligence by some newspapers, the Government set up a Tribunal under Lord Radcliffe, to investigate the case in public. I had previously disclosed that Vassall had been betrayed by a Soviet defector and I was, therefore, required to give evidence. By previous agreement, I was enabled to identify the source of my information about the defector—Lt Col L.G. (Sammy) Lohan of the Defence Ministry. Two other journalists who declined to name the sources for their inaccurate press reports were sent to prison for contempt of court. Later, I was told that Hollis and Radcliffe had ensured that I would not be pressed, when in the witness stand, into revealing any more details about the defector, Golitsin, who was then secretly in London.

One major scoop which I treasure concerned the exchange, in 1964, of Kolon Molody, the KGB officer operating under the name Gordon Lonsdale, for the British MI6 agent, Greville Wynne, who had been held captive in Russia under harsh conditions.[15] The Russians released photographs of Wynne, showing him so emaciated that the British authorities felt forced to offer the much more significant Lonsdale in exchange. The Foreign Office decided to leak the dramatic event in such a way that it would become public shortly after the two spies had each reached Berlin when, it was believed, the Russians would be unable to retract. In choosing me as the medium the Foreign Office reckoned that, as I had a reputation for accurate leaks, the other media would follow up the story—as they did.

While my political sources almost all belonged to the Conservative Party, which my newspaper supported, I managed to cultivate a few Labour Party MPs, against the day when they might be in office. They were most unlikely sources of secret intelligence because they were not normally briefed while in opposition. The maverick George Brown, however, proved to be an extraordinary exception. When George Blake, the KGB spy inside MI6, was sentenced to 42 years imprisonment in 1961, the Tory Government withheld all details of his crimes. Sensing a scandal, the Labour leaders demanded the facts so persistently that the Prime Minister, Macmillan, offered to reveal them to three Labour Privy Councillors on the understanding that while being able to assure their colleagues that silence was being imposed only for genuine security reasons, they would maintain absolute secrecy, as required by their Privy Councillors' oath.

Brown, who was one of the three, lunched with me a few days later, and, gleefully told me the whole story: how Blake had betrayed at least forty agents working for MI6 abroad and, while based in West Berlin, had given the KGB copies of every secret document passing through his office. Brown also revealed that Blake had disclosed details of a tunnel which the Americans had dug under the Russian sector of Berlin to monitor Soviet telephone cables. He wanted me to publish everything, without reference to himself, and it all appeared on the *Daily Express* front page.

Later, Brown told me that he had no regrets about his behaviour, as was also the case concerning his betrayal of my chief contact, Sir Frederick Brundrett. After a series of allegations by Brown, in public and in Parliament, that Britain's independent nuclear deterrent was so insignificant that it was a waste of money, Brundrett asked me to tell him that he was prepared to give him the 'true facts of atomic life'. Brown agreed and I brought them together over lunch where he learned the impressive size and power of the stockpile. However, the gratitude which he then expressed did not stop him from making political capital in Parliament when he asked Macmillan if he was aware that a senior Whitehall figure was leaking the nation's most vital atomic secrets! Fortunately, the wily Fred had cleared his action with Macmillan, who had agreed to it in the hope of silencing Brown and his senior colleagues.

While newspaper readers claiming to have secret information were, usually, time-wasters, one of them, in 1967, was to spark the most bitter and politically charged intelligence incident of my career—the so-called 'D-Notice Affair'. My informant, who drifted into the office off the street, said that he had worked for a cable company and that, every day, all telegrams sent from the Post Office along with private cables, were being made available for scrutiny by the security authorities. The Defence Ministry denied the allegation to me but a fishing companion, who headed the Post Office press department, confirmed it and I deduced that the authority concerned was GCHQ, looking for coded messages to and from foreign intelligence agents.

My front-page disclosure and follow-up stories caused a tumultuous collision between the Prime Minister, Harold Wilson and the entire media lasting six months. Wilson's behaviour, which he would later describe as his 'worst self-inflicted wound', led to a Tribunal intended to discredit me and Colonel Lohan, who had succeeded Thomson as D-Notice Secretary and stood accused of failing to veto the story, true though it was. I and my paper were vindicated by the Tribunal whereupon Wilson, spurred on by the Foreign Office, issued a White Paper repudiating the Tribunal's findings.[16] The intensity of the official response undoubtedly involved an American aspect. Certain cables were being supplied to the US National Security Agency in contravention of the American constitution and the US President was aware of it.

In the late 1970s, when it seemed that Margaret Thatcher might become the first woman Prime Minister, Maurice Oldfield (later Sir), who had become the Chief ('C') of MI6, asked me to arrange a meeting with her.[17] I told her that, should she wish, 'C' would keep her briefed on intelligence matters so that she would be well informed on assuming office. She agreed, provided that the then Prime Minister, James Callaghan would permit it. He did so and the two then met regularly. (Intelligence matters being rarely what they seem, I soon discovered what Oldfield's prime motive had been. He had learned that Mrs Thatcher was already being secretly briefed by a group of his retired colleagues and did not like being usurped.)

After Sir Maurice's death in 1981, I learned that he had repeatedly faked his positive vetting by denying that he was a practising homosexual, which would then have barred him from service in MI6.[18] How this occurred is illuminating about the many ways in which secret information becomes public knowledge.

A year after Oldfield had retired as 'C', in 1978, he had, at Mrs Thatcher's request, courageously, become Co-ordinator of Intelligence in Northern Ireland. This made him a prime target for the IRA, which had previously attempted to assassinate him in 1975 with a bomb in a hold-all slung on railings below his bachelor flat in Westminster. As he was regularly in London and had retained the flat, he required protection there and the Protection Officers supplied by Scotland Yard became suspicious of men who visited the flat, some of whom proved to be homosexuals of the kind known as 'rough trade'. Eventually, the Metropolitan Police Commissioner, Sir David McNee, felt it his duty to warn the Home Secretary that Oldfield might be a security risk and confronted by the evidence, Oldfield confessed. After inquiries produced no evidence that he had been compromised, and as he had only three months to serve in Northern Ireland, he was confronted by the Attorney General, Sir Michael Havers, and gave an undertaking not to misbehave while still in government employment. He was then allowed to finish his tour of duty there and to retire honourably, with his behaviour remaining secret.

In 1984, while researching a book about the motivations for treachery—later published as *Traitors*—I heard of moves to expose the Oldfield case from a reliable source who wished it exposed. I raised the matter in Havers' hearing at a pheasant shoot and he confirmed it, in front of others. After much thought, I decided that it would be professionally dishonest to suppress the case in *Traitors*, where consideration of the role of homosexuality in treachery was essential, just because Oldfield had been a friend.

My statements were widely disbelieved, especially by his former colleagues but Mrs Thatcher confirmed, in Parliament, that in March 1980, Oldfield had admitted that, from time to time, he had engaged in homosexual activities and that his positive vetting had been withdrawn because his behaviour had made him a security risk.

Through my friendship with the second Lord Sieff (Marcus) I met Lord (Victor) Rothschild, formerly of MI5, who, among other facilities, secured me an 'audience' with the Shah of Iran, which proved to be of intense intelligence interest to the Foreign Office. In September 1980, I answered an unexpected telephone call from Rothschild at my village home in Berkshire, to which I had retired for the shooting and fishing. He told me that an overseas acquaintance, who was visiting him at his home in Cambridge, wanted to meet me. The consequences were to engage the attention of the media for years and lead to major changes in regulations governing official secrets.

Rothschild explained that the visitor was a retired member of MI5 domiciled in Australia. He showed me a slip of paper bearing the names of many spies and asked me if I would be interested in talking to his friend about them. The visitor, Peter Wright, whom I had never met before, then explained that he had become so concerned about the Soviet penetration of MI5 that he had begun a book about it but, after completing only ten short chapters could not proceed with it, through illness. He also stressed that he urgently needed £5000 to prevent the bankruptcy of a small stud farm he had started in his retirement in Tasmania. He therefore suggested that I should write the book on some profit-sharing basis.

As nobody from MI5 had ever told its secrets before—except to the Russians—I provisionally agreed but only on condition that I would not be responsible for paying any money to him. He would have to be paid directly by the publisher. To my astonishment, Rothschild undertook to set up a banking arrangement so that Wright's identity could be kept secret from the publisher and from everyone else.

I visited Wright's home in Tasmania, where he and his wife had moved to be near their married daughter, staying there for nine days, becoming the first journalist to be taken into the confidence of an MI5 officer prepared to tell everything he knew. The result was *Their Trade Is Treachery*, published in 1981, which caused a furore. It exposed the fact that the former Chief of MI5, Sir Roger Hollis, had been seriously suspected by some of his own officers of being a GRU agent throughout his 27 years of service and had been recalled from retirement to be interrogated.[19]

The Cabinet Secretary, Sir Robert Armstrong (now Lord), described the book as 'a bombshell' and, to counter it, the Prime Minister, Mrs Thatcher, assured Parliament that the book was speculation and insinuations when, in fact, an inquiry had been set up to discover my MI5 sources, which had quickly identified Wright. She then announced the first independent inquiry for twenty years into the efficiency of the safeguards against further penetration of the secret services by foreign powers. Carried out by the standing Security Commission, the inquiry did not produce its thick report until May 1982 when the Prime Minister reneged on her promise to publish it. Instead, a statement listed a large number of improvements while indicating that there were others so secret that they could not be revealed to Parliament or anywhere else. I—and many others—thought it crazy that major changes affecting MI5, MI6 and GCHQ should have had to await the publication of a book by a freelance investigative writer.

I responded in, 1984, with a much more detailed book called *Too Secret Too Long*. Two years later, Wright, who had cut contact with me, decided to reissue his disclosures under his own name in a book called *Spycatcher*, which induced the Government to stage an expensive court case in Australia, which it lost, with the publicity making the book a certain best-seller.[20] The three books eventually led to a new Official Secrets Act, and many other procedural changes concerning security and classified intelligence with some degree of Parliamentary oversight.

With the release of so many classified documents in the UK, US and Russia (where I was recently elected to the Moscow Academy for Defence, Security and Law and Order) I am able to continue my research in intelligence affairs.[21] One result has been the final exposure of the former Labour Minister, John Stonehouse, as a Soviet agent who spied for money. Stonehouse was exposed by Czech defectors in 1968 but his Prime Minister, Harold Wilson, managed to suppress any effective investigation by MI5, even when the traitor had been jailed for fraud. In a newspaper article which I wrote in 2006 I stated that the proof lay in the Czech Intelligence records in Prague, whereupon the *Mail on Sunday* investigated there and discovered a copy of Stonehouse's 1,000 page record.[22] Known by the code-name Twister, he had been recruited soon after becoming an MP and was taken over by the KGB after being appointed Aviation Minister.

My whole experience of the intelligence world over so many years has been like constructing a giant jigsaw puzzle, with so many of the missing pieces hidden behind near-impenetrable barriers or even deliberately destroyed. It continues to entrance me.

10

BEDMATES OR SPARRING PARTNERS?

CANADIAN PERSPECTIVES ON THE MEDIA-INTELLIGENCE RELATIONSHIP IN 'THE NEW PROPAGANDA AGE'

Tony Campbell

Editors' Notes: In this article Tony Campbell, the former head of intelligence analysis in Canada's Privy Council, outlines the perils facing governments in the twenty-first century, the 'information age', now that intelligence is not the sole guarantor of information sovereignty. Campbell charts the evolution of the media-intelligence relationship in Canada and how it has changed before and after 9/11. The chapter argues that despite efforts to move the two sides closer together, we should be wary about letting them get too close, lest we forget what each is designed to do. Furthermore, Campbell outlines the development of the Canadian government's attempts to use propaganda, and notes how such moves, though slow, are beginning to catch up with other western countries.

'Democracy, for all its faults, is incapable of the Big Lie which is the hallmark of totalitarianism.'[1]

We have been living through a global convulsion of seismic proportions appropriately known as the Information Revolution. It has catalysed a change in the place of information in the calculus of power and statecraft. 'Soft

power', 'public diplomacy', 'information warfare', 'total information dominance', and 'spin', among other terms, have become defining concepts of our
age. As an extension of these ideas, whatever polite term might be preferred,
propaganda has moved from the periphery to centre stage as a tool of, as well
as a threat to, national governments. This development has inevitable consequences for the media and for state intelligence services and for the relationship between them. This chapter will explore these issues in a Canadian
context.

In earlier reflections about the impact of the Information Revolution, I
suggested that there is a new dimension to the concept of state sovereignty
described as 'information sovereignty'.[2] I defined that term as the condition of
a 'country's governors, legislators, and people having the autonomous capacity
to have access to the information and expert knowledge needed to make
sound and independent decisions in all areas of their interests'. From that
perspective, I proposed that 'made in Canada' information for decision-making and judgement, the quintessence of the traditional intelligence function,
was now more necessary for Canada than ever before. But in democratic
countries, intelligence is not the sole guarantor of information sovereignty.
Several national institutions are needed. Of these, none is more important
than the mass media because of their public information and education functions and their capacity to shape public opinion that drives political, economic and social consensus.

It follows that achieving an appropriate relationship between those two
vital national institutions is a matter of public policy importance. This chapter
will explore the nature of their relationship in the Canadian context, drawing
lessons of possible relevance to other countries. It will do so from the perspectives of a former career public servant and 'practitioner' of intelligence and,
more recently, as a teacher of strategic information and communication in the
field of human security and peacebuilding.

The relationship between the media and intelligence services is by no means
an issue of novel significance in the twenty-first century. Sir Francis Walsingham, Queen Elizabeth I's Principal Secretary, is said to have 'invented the art
and science of modern espionage' including by means of establishing a web of
information providers who were 'no 'secret service' (but) men of affairs and
men of the world (who) were less spies than reporters'.[3]

Broadly speaking, both intelligence and the media are in the same business.
They collect, analyze and disseminate information and knowledge. Therefore,
some degree of relationship between these institutions has long been logical

and sometimes necessary for national security purposes. But despite these areas of compatibility, there are crucial differences between the institutions, notably their distinct 'ownership' (public versus private), customer focus (government decision-makers versus the public) and modus operandi (closed versus open). These differences quite naturally establish a tension between them, one that is usually healthy and to be desired in a democratic state. This is because of the role the media play, or ought to play, in helping to expose government power to public accountability, and equally because of the role intelligence can play inside government of countering distortions caused by the commercial pressures on the media to please corporate owners, bow to powerful advertising or investment interests, and cater to public enthusiasms and the popular thirst for uncomplicated information and amusement.[4]

While in varying degrees over the years there has been this partial compatibility of interests balanced by a healthy tension and scepticism in the relationship between intelligence and the media in all democratic countries, I argue in this chapter on the basis of recent experience in Canada that this relationship has taken on vastly greater importance and sensitivity in recent years. A new and less accommodating balance may need to be struck in future because of the emergence of four forces of change. The first factor is the global information and knowledge technology revolution. Secondly, there has been the emergence of a closely associated 'new propaganda reality' in which governments and media are not only targets of propaganda from each other, but are routinely under pressure to aim propaganda in the 'black' sense of the word against their own publics. Third, as evidenced in recent years in Britain and the US, there is increased temptation in democratic governments to politicise intelligence in support of favourable public opinion goals. Finally, there is increasing concentration of (often ideologically driven) media ownership at both the domestic and global levels.

Underpinning this argument lies an important 'paradigm-shifting' idea that goes to the heart of the question of contemporary intelligence–media relationships.[5] Prior to 9/11 the paradigm in that relationship, reflecting attitudes coming out of the Cold War and the Vietnam War, could be described as the 'oversight paradigm'. The media saw intelligence as state power whose potential abuse needed to be guarded against in the public interest. The immediate post-9/11 paradigm shifted to what might be described as the 'cautious collaboration paradigm' because of the recognition of partial compatibility of information interests between the media and intelligence services especially at a time of a national security threat

In Canada, this post-9/11 paradigm of defensive but cautious collaboration gave way to a much more closed and adversarial relationship after the occupation of Iraq and the revelations of the Maher Arar public inquiry. It will be suggested that this 'arm's length paradigm' will continue to apply indefinitely in today's world. Spurred by a propaganda- and entertainment-oriented media in an era of 'infotainment', the role of intelligence in government needs to be adapted to include a specific function of guarding governments and through them public knowledge and opinion against 'wrong information' generated by national and international media. Such wrong information results from unintentional misinformation and intentional disinformation in the propaganda senses of the words, as well as from commercially distorted information and propaganda coming from their own media.

On the other side of the ledger, the risk of politicisation or propagandising of intelligence by government requires that the remaining serious professional media must develop and maintain a more robust capacity for independent information-gathering and analysis. They must also have strong expertise capable of scrutinising government intelligence services–capable of 'asking the right questions'–to protect the public against temptations in government to use intelligence to manipulate public opinion.

Despite important and even desirable complementarities between them, the need for a firm arms-length relationship between the media and intelligence seems to be the more compelling public interest. I will suggest that these forces are not temporary and call for much greater media investment in reporting capacity and expertise in areas relevant to intelligence, much greater attention by intelligence services to domestic information sources and flows, and much greater internal independence of intelligence services within government to ensure objectivity and avoid '1984' outcomes which are an ever-present danger.[6] They call also for a greatly improved awareness on the part of the public of its vulnerability to the manipulation and deception of contemporary propaganda practices by both government and the media. More than ever in this Information Age, an informed citizenry is the only reliable bulwark of democracy.[7]

These themes will be picked up again in more detail later in this chapter, which is divided into four main sections:

1. Background on the Canadian and UK/US intelligence and propaganda relationships
2. Broad impressions of the evolution of intelligence-media relationships in Canada prior to 9/11

3. Impressions of media–intelligence relationship post-9/11
4. Implications of 'the new propaganda reality' for personal and
   national 'information sovereignty' in Canada

1. UK and US intelligence and Propaganda Activities: The Canadian Connection

There are strong historical and strategic reasons why Canadian intelligence experience remains relevant to the UK and the US and may well offer helpful comparative insights in a volume of this sort. First, although Canada was established in 1867, the mother country retained the formal constitutional powers for foreign affairs and defence until as late as 1931.[8] This meant that Canada's early experience with intelligence was firmly within a British military context and tradition. The relationship between intelligence and the media in the First World War not only had Canadian participation, but was literally *shaped* by Canadians. This was because Lord Beaverbrook, the 'British' multimillionaire and press baron, came from New Brunswick, Canada and served in the Wartime Cabinet of David Lloyd George as the first ever Minister of Information. As such, he played a key role in the development of new propaganda techniques linking media and intelligence functions.[9] Revelations about these techniques were published after the war by Sir Campbell Stuart, a Canadian military officer (i.e. in the British Army during the war) who Beaverbrook befriended crossing the Atlantic by steamer and in 1917 arranged to locate in the hush-hush world of nascent British propaganda operations.[10] The result was that the development of intelligence in Canada remained highly influenced and, in some respects, controlled by Britain for the first fifty years of Canada's existence.

Seen from a strategic angle, Canadian familiarity and sympathy with British institutions and ways clearly had important advantages. Canada for most of its history quite consciously worked to reinforce strong links with the UK as a general foreign policy objective because of its interest in building and reinforcing a Trans-Atlantic community. This compelling logic applied and still applies to Canada's intelligence relationship with the UK. It goes hand in hand with Canada's familiarity and sympathy with American institutions and ways that flowered through the twentieth century and that naturally prevail with regard to shared continental interests and perspectives. Together, these twin qualities gave rise to a type of intermediary or 'bridging role' in which Canada has occasionally acted as an 'honest broker' between the two sometimes divergent UK-US intelligence perspectives.[11]

This intelligence bridging role had its genesis at the outset of the Second World War when a Canadian businessman from Winnipeg, Sir William Stephenson (the self-styled 'Man called Intrepid'[12]) was entrusted by Sir Winston Churchill to play a crucial role on behalf of Britain in cementing the UK-US intelligence relationship throughout the War. He was selected to represent MI6 (SIS) in New York, beginning in June, 1940. (This was not unprecedented: another Canadian, Sir William Wiseman, had similarly taken up the SIS liaison position in the United States in1915.) 'From here Stephenson directed SIS's liaison with the Americans, an undertaking that was to develop into an umbrella organization entitled British Security Coordination....'[13] This in turn developed into a very important relationship between the 'Commonwealth' and US intelligence services known sometimes as the AUSCANUKUS or 'four eyes' intelligence relationship.[14] It has played an important role in intelligence cooperation throughout the Cold War and continues to this day. Moreover, the post-9/11 'Global War on Terrorism' has in many respects intensified the value of this intelligence relationship which combines the cooperative advantages of services using a common language and having a strong degree of shared cultural affinity with the advantage of dispersed geographic perspectives. The historical and cultural affinity that paved the way to cooperation among these intelligence services has influenced how they approach the organization and practice of intelligence, including how they respectively relate to important national institutions like the media.

2. The Intelligence-Media relationship in Canada pre-9/11

At a conference organized in 2000 by the Canadian Association for Security and Intelligence Studies (CASIS),[15] a panel of well-known Canadian journalists discussed media-intelligence relationships in Canada. Each of the three speakers adopted a distinctly different strategy in their working relationships with intelligence services which can usefully serve as a model of possible approaches to intelligence-media relationships in Canada from the media perspective. At one end, there was what we might call Position 'X' or the 'embedded model'. It involves a journalist or broadcaster working more or less intimately with the intelligence services, and vice versa. In effect, the reporter trades a more sympathetic touch in covering intelligence services and issues in return for more trusted and privileged access to information from intelligence sources. At the opposite end of the spectrum is Position Z, or the 'adversarial model'. Here the reporter views the intelligence services as a threat to individual rights, noxious and even dangerous institutions hiding behind a wall of secrecy that are naturally prone to working against the public interest unless thwarted by vigilant media. The reporter anticipates and accepts distrust and resistance from the services and uses every possible tool to expose them to public scrutiny. The middle or Y position in this spectrum could be called the 'sceptical model'. This journalist or broadcaster covers intelligence issues in just the same way as s/he covers any other public interest issue or institution: that is, by applying sceptical but balanced and objective analysis to accessible information.

It is an important point that all three positions on the scale do not differ on the fundamental journalistic mission of seeking and revealing 'truth' in the public interest. But they differ on how they can best accomplish that mission in dealing with intelligence services. Similarly, none of these positions will differ in terms of respecting the inescapable imperative of media owners being profitable by attracting readers, viewers and/or listeners. The other common interest to be recognized in each case is the need reporters may feel to reflect the values and opinions of editors, and, when apparent, of corporate ownership.

Model Depicting Media Options for Covering Intelligence Services and Activities:

X (embedded)   Y (sceptical but balanced)   Z (adversarial)

The other dimension in seeking an analytical model of intelligence-media relationships is the position of the intelligence services themselves. Here again we can describe a three position spectrum. 'Position A' is the 'open model' where the services seek actively within the bounds of appropriate security constraints to be as open and transparent as possible with the media. This will include identifying and facilitating access to sensitive information by trustworthy and knowledgeable reporters. It will be characterized by proactive as well as responsive transparency. 'Position C' is the opposite, and can simply be called the 'closed model'. Here, relationships with media are evasive, non-cooperative, adversarial, and at a very long arms length: a relationship of no relationship. 'Position B' in the spectrum is the 'cautious model' in which intelligence services treat media relationships contingently and tactically, more or less on a case by case basis according to the benefit a relationship might bring the service, trusting some reporters or news organizations more and others less, according to their demonstrated track record, but in all cases erring on the side of less cooperation and openness, not more.

As in the case of the media, intelligence services can be taken to share certain common underlying interests no matter which of these three positions they choose. First, and foremost, intelligence services need to protect their 'sources and methods'. If these are publicized, lives and national interests can be endangered and valuable sources of information lost. Second, intelligence services in democracies know that they serve political masters and are not the final deciders on the appropriate strategy for relating to media. Third, in law-based societies, intelligence services know that they must abide by the prevailing laws regardless of policy or strategic interests.

Model of Intelligence Service Options for Dealing with Media:

A (open)   B (cautious)   C (closed)

Applying these relationship models to five distinct phases of Canadian history between 1939 and 2001 provides a snapshot of the nature of the intelligence-media relationship in Canada over that time period:

1. Second World War (1939–45)—the relationship was 'CX'—closed and embedded
2. The Gouzenko Affair (1947–1948)[16]—the relationship was 'CY'—closed and sceptical
3. The Cold War–pre-Vietnam (1948–1967)—the relationship was CX—closed and embedded
4. The Cold War–post-Vietnam, post FLQ 'dirty tricks' Crisis(1968–1989)—the relationship was CZ—closed and adversarial
5. The post-Cold War (December 1989–September 11, 2001)—the relationship was BY—cautiously open and sceptical

A few conclusions can perhaps be drawn from this snapshot. First, there would appear to be a greater degree to which Canadian media accept the embedding model in a situation of national military conflict, and a corresponding tendency to adopt the scepticism model in periods of perceived relative peace. Second, media-intelligence relationships in Canada have been highly influenced by the political moods and cultural attitudes to intelligence services prevailing at any given time in key allied countries like the US and the UK. Third, intelligence-media relationships have deteriorated markedly when there have been significant intelligence failures or scandals. Fourth, public and corresponding media attitudes to intelligence services seem to have deteriorated during periods in which the services have opted for the closed or 'C model'.

3. The Canadian intelligence-media relationship post-9/11

3.1 Phase 1: From 9/11 to the Iraq Invasion

In order to analyze the post-9/11 intelligence-media relationship in Canada, as in other countries, one has to distinguish between (at least) two distinct phases. The first was the immediate aftermath of the 9/11 attacks (September 2001 to March 2003) and the second was the post-Iraq invasion period (April 2003 to 2008). Applying our relationship models to these two phases, I would describe the first phase as being characterized by a BX–cautiously open and embedded—relationship. The second phase can be characterized as 'CZ'–a return to closed intelligence faced by adversarial media, similar to the latter Cold War period.

In Canada, as in the UK and the US, there was a marked rallying of supportive media interest in security matters and therefore intelligence issues after the shock of 9/11. Perceiving a state of emergency, the media were eager to play a helpful public information role and respond to the high level of public nervousness and demand for security related information. The Canadian intelligence services responded to this unprecedented level of public and media interest by taking a much more open approach to the intelligence-media relationship than ever before.

A private interview with a close professional observer of intelligence-media relations during this period indicated agreement that the traditional Canadian media 'default position' of 'comforting the afflicted and afflicting the comfortable', especially from a human rights point of view, had given away at least temporarily after 9/11 to a much broader view of Canada's security interests, including the social ramifications of national security. There was more interest in the actual security function and the pool of media people with some insight into security issues expanded even though almost all of the newly assigned reporters were 'not full time' on the beat. Nonetheless, many saw that the issues were more complex and 'some even recognized that they should be as sceptical about non-government organizations, lawyers and lobbies as they traditionally were about security and intelligence services'.

3.1.1 The Budget Factor

There were several additional factors that worked to open the intelligence-media relationship in this period. The first was a matter of budgets. Security related budgets, including those of intelligence organizations, were significantly expanded by the Canadian government immediately following 9/11.

These new resources allowed for more proactive public communication activities.

The post-9/11 budget increases reversed a decade of severe post-Cold War cuts to Canadian intelligence capacity. Those cuts deserve to be seen as among the most misguided policy responses of that period in all countries, including Canada. The logic of the so-called 'peace dividend' was widely accepted following the disappearance of the Soviet Union and the emergence of a 'new world order'.[17] All this was summed up by the optimism reflected in a well known article by Francis Fukuyama titled 'The End of History'.[18] These policy perceptions were misguided because of the blindness they reflected about the likely emergence of a variety of security threats, especially of a nationalistic nature, previously suppressed by bi-polar ideological conflict. These were clearly anticipated around the world because of the notoriety of an article (later a book) by Samuel Huntington who questioned whether or not the world faced a 'clash of civilizations'. However his arguments were discounted in Canada because of their pessimistic view of cultural conflict.[19] This policy blindness and misjudgement in the Canadian government in the 1990s was of course exacerbated by the reduction in intelligence capacity that took place in that period.

In Canada the severity of the cutting of intelligence capacity went well beyond other countries because the chopping started from a much lower base to begin with. It reflected the Chretien government's undisguised anti-military/security tendencies which meant that intelligence received virtually no policy attention whatsoever at the top.[20] This was all the more extraordinary and deserves to be considered a major failure of the Chretien era when one considers that twice within a twenty-year period Canada had experienced major terrorist attacks, first with the abduction of a British diplomat and murder of a Quebec government minister in 1970 by Quebec separatists, and then with the bombing of an Air India flight flying from Canada to the UK in 1986 by Sikh terrorists with the loss of 329 lives including 160 Canadians.[21] It is against this background that one can see the significance of the Chretien government's decision to increase its security and intelligence expenditures after 9/11. However, funding by itself could not produce overnight changes and there was a lengthy period of 'catch-up' required to turn around years of neglect, including in the area of intelligence-media relations.

3.1.2 The Era of Asymmetric Security Threats

Another important factor accelerating changed approaches in intelligence-media relationships was the changing threat environment. Although Western intelligence services were already well aware of it, the chief message of 9/11 was that the new millennium would see a security environment characterized by asymmetric threats (whether security, criminal or natural). The implications of this evolution were enormous for intelligence services accustomed to the bipolar ideological conflict of the Cold War. For one thing, they would need to know more and more or at least have ready access to insight about relatively 'granular' issues ranging, for example, from AIDs in Botswana and South Africa, to migration in the Philippines, to organised crime in Nigeria, to animal rights extremism in Italy—and the possible links among all these topics. Faced with this multifaceted threat environment, the intelligence services in Canada and elsewhere needed urgently to expand their networks for understanding real time issues. The same imperative faced the media, which were frequently faced with digging up information on a wide variety of issues for impatient editors and readers. Inevitably, this created a dynamic interest on the part of both intelligence and media in Canada to look to each other more positively for assistance than ever before.

3.1.3 Open Source Information and Communication Technologies

A third contributing factor to a greater degree of openness and reduced adversarial conflict between intelligence and media in Canada immediately following 9/11 was the emerging realisation that the 'information and communication technology revolution' (ICT) was imposing needed change in the traditionally inward and secretive work style of intelligence services. In Canada our experience by the late 1990s was that at least 90% of 'raw' information input to intelligence analysis was from open, not secret, sources. The use by analysts of unclassified, freely available information from the internet or other open sources was not just desirable but essential to understanding developments or threats in a globalized world. However, getting access to open sources from within 'secret organisations' required a range of changes in longstanding methods, attitudes, rules, structures and processes and these took time.

3.1.4 The Connecting the Dots Imperative

Another driving force of change in the relationship between intelligence and media in this period was recognition by one inquiry after another in the United States that 9/11 had been possible because of the failure of intelligence services 'to connect the dots'. 'Stove-piping' or 'silos' and the typical inward focuses within intelligence services, and their lack of connection with outside actors, were seen as key factors in the intelligence failures of 9/11. These messages from the US were recognised as applying to other countries, like Canada, and they were reinforced subsequently in the subsequent Hutton and Butler inquiries in the UK. This common diagnosis resulted in heavy pressure on the services in Canada and elsewhere to 'open up' to each other and to the outside world. Just as there was a need for intelligence to connect more with the media, so was there a corresponding need, for the same reasons, for the media to have greater connection with intelligence. There was a perception of a new degree of compatibility if not interdependence of interests between the two professions and this reinforced a partial opening up in both directions.

3.1.5 The Academy

For the same reasons, it might be noted, there was also post-9/11 a significant opening up in the intelligence-academic relationship in Canada, with much less 'knee-jerk' suspicion in both directions than had been the case since the McDonald Inquiry in the early 1980s. This was important because academic 'security experts' (as they are called by the media) played a disproportionally important role in Canada in post-9/11 media communication with the public compared to other Western countries. Academics provided expertise to the Canadian media that they had neglected to develop over the years but they needed access to intelligence-based information to be able to offer this service. So, academics became for public education purposes an extension of the media during this period.

In short, in the new global, financial, security, technology and political realities post-9/11, intelligence services found they had much greater need for media access, academic expertise, open source information and access to global knowledge networks than ever before. Similar forces were at work in the media and this encouraged intelligence services and media to look for ways to work together more constructively than in the past. While these powerful forces justified an improved relationship and significantly greater openness and trust between media and intelligence in Canada, it could be said that the balance in that relationship swung too far immediately after 9/11. As is well documented, the US media responded to 9/11 with a patriotic rallying to the flag[22] (with some honourable exceptions, notably the Knight Ridder news organization[23]) that clearly departed from normal exacting standards of professional news and opinion coverage. The self-censorship and vulnerability to manipulation reflected in the case of Judith Miller of the *New York Times* was only the most egregious of many examples of this phenomenon.[24] Post-9/11 experience in Canada's media closely paralleled the embedded and uncritical mindset of most of the US media. While an improved degree of media-intelligence cooperation was to be welcomed in this period, an embedded or 'bedmate' relationship proved manifestly contrary to both the media and public interests in Canada.[25]

3.2 *Phase 2 in the Post 9/11 Period: Iraq Occupation to the Present*

The Canadian Prime Minister of the day, Jean Chretien, made his career's single most popular decision when he decided that Canada would eschew participation in the American occupation of Iraq in the absence of a UN mandate. Although not clear at the time, this decision was partly based on some Canadian intelligence analysis that found no evidence of weapons of mass destruction in Iraq.[26] However, two main factors brought about a distinct cooling in the media–intelligence relationship in Canada in the period after the invasion of Iraq. First, the revelations that suggested that the staffs of both President Bush and Prime Minister Blair had 'sexed up' intelligence to justify public support for the attack on Iraq appalled Canadians. Politicisation and skewing of intelligence in this context was a black eye to the image of intelligence as a truth telling institution in these other countries and Canadian media had no reason to believe that Canadian intelligence services would be any different, notwithstanding Canada's non-participation in the Iraq occupation.

The second factor was the gradual public unfolding of the case of a Canadian citizen, Maher Arar, who suffered 'extraordinary rendition' to Syria by American agencies partly as a result of 'raw' intelligence supplied inappropriately (as it was later found in a public inquiry[27]) by the Royal Canadian Mounted Police. Revelations about this case placed in further question the public and media view of the objectivity of Canada's intelligence services.

On the other side of the equation, the Canadian government also went through a major shifting of attitude around public information policy, severely affecting the current media-intelligence relationship. At all times, the general disposition of a government to openness and transparency naturally has a key impact on the readiness of intelligence services to cooperate with the media. Canada has had an Access to Information Program (ATIP) on the books since the 1970s that is costly for government and frustrating for citizen users but at least it establishes the principle of the desirability of public openness in the Canadian government. The law forces intelligence services to disclose information that cannot be withheld under several ample exemption clauses.

However, the Stephen Harper government took a quite extreme position against public openness and access to information, and this severely chilled the intelligence community's earlier efforts to be more transparent. Some intelligence community insiders see this chilling effect as tantamount to 'unilateral disarmament' because it limits public communication opportunities for pre-empting or responding to attacks on intelligence services coming from 'single issue advocates' or lawyers trying to position their clients' cases in the public mind through the media. According to a person interviewed for this study, 'this means that we allow opponents to frame the argument'.

An additional important factor affecting the degree of media-intelligence transparency post-Iraq/Arar is the increasing legalisation/litigation of Canadian government policies because of the operation and interpretation of Canada's Charter of Rights and Freedoms. This is not only a matter of the role played by the courts but also by intelligence oversight machinery, and a seemingly Charter-obsessed legal community inside and outside government. An atmosphere of unremitting legal challenges forces intelligence services to be more cautious and closed than they might otherwise prefer.

These various factors would appear to have had a significant cooling effect on the relationship between Canadian media and the intelligence services since the Iraq occupation. It prevails as of the time of writing. In terms of the relationship model outlined above, the situation in Canada has come around full-circle, reverting to 'CZ'–closed and adversarial.

4. The media-intelligence relationship in Canada faced by the 'New Propaganda Reality'

Prospects for a shift back to a less adversarial and closed relationship in the near future seem remote. At a seminar in Ottawa sponsored by the Canadian Journalism Foundation and the Canadian Association for Security and Intelligence Studies on April 1, 2008, Ward Elcock, the former head of the Canadian Security Intelligence Service (CSIS) and one of Canada's most experienced intelligence officials, expressed the personal view that there can never be anything better than a wary, arm's length relationship between intelligence and the media. This is because of the 'inherent' conflicts of interest between the two functions, one oriented to the open and public, and the other oriented to the needs of government and secrets. He likened his sometimes negative past experience with media to feeding alligators–'sometimes they can't tell the difference between the food and your arm'.

Jeff Sallot, an Adjunct Professor in the Carleton University School of Journalism and distinguished journalist covering security and intelligence issues, was the media representative on the same panel. He made it clear that while journalists need and want access to intelligence and security information, they need a vastly improved 'Access to Information Program' to achieve it, as well as continuing private personal contacts to the degree possible with intelligence sources. However, he drew a deep line between that kind of one-way cooperation and anything tending towards two-way cooperation between media and intelligence. In other words, intelligence services should be as transparent as possible to media but not vice-versa.

Is the distancing and estrangement that these views suggest 'a bad thing'? Is greater cooperation between media and intelligence 'a good thing', something public policy should encourage in spite of the inherent differences of perspective? Is there a higher public purpose to be served by greater cooperation between these two major 'truth telling' institutions? These questions bring us back to two issues raised at the beginning of this chapter: the public policy imperative of 'information sovereignty' amidst 'the new propaganda reality'.

In his fine book Michael Herman outlines the historical evolution of 'intelligence as news'.[28] He points out that 'the diplomatic system which became institutionalized in Europe in the sixteenth and seventeenth centuries was largely a response to nation states' need for information'. By the eighteenth century, 'secret intelligence was never clearly separated from other kinds of government information. Before the emergence of private newspapers and press freedom, governments tended to see all information as their property, secret to some extent; the distinction between information 'in the public domain' and 'classified' official information is a modern one'.[29] This suggests that the concept I am proposing of information as a necessary pre-condition for national sovereignty is not new, and neither is the idea of the desirability of mixing sensitive state information with news from all sources. Under ideal circumstances, a high level of cooperation between effective intelligence services and well-informed media would contribute to Canada's information sovereignty.

However strong the case for close cooperation in today's information-centric world, I believe that there is an even stronger case for media and intelligence to be carefully insulated and distanced from each other. The emergence of a world in which there is an unprecedented level of 'white' and 'black' propaganda practised by all institutions, government and private sector alike, makes it important to encourage distrust and competition, the absolute minimum of collaboration, between the media and state intelligence services. This is a regrettable but necessary response to the risk of information distortion and manipulation coming at the citizen from governments or, equally, coming at governments and the public from the media.

Propaganda is defined here as 'the deliberate, systematic attempt to shape perceptions, manipulate cognitions, and direct behaviour to achieve a response that furthers the desired intent of the propagandist'.[30] 'White propaganda' comes from a source that is identified correctly and the information provided tends to be accurate. However, it is skewed to present the sender in a favourable light or to build up a positive image or credibility with the audience that can be manipulated at a later point. 'Black propaganda is credited to a false source and spreads lies, fabrications and deceptions. Black propaganda is the 'big lie', including all types of creative deceit.'[31] 'Grey propaganda is somewhere between white and black propaganda. The source may or may not be correctly identified, and the accuracy of the information is uncertain...it is not limited to governments...'[32] Disinformation is associated with propaganda, usually of the black variety, and means 'false, incomplete, or misleading information that is passed, fed, or confirmed to a targeted individual, group or country.'[33] Spin has become a common term in relation to the manipulation of political information with propagandistic implications. Spin refers to '...a coordinated strategy to minimize negative information and present in a favourable light a story that could be damaging'.[34]

Propaganda is by no means a new phenomenon. As noted earlier, it came to the modern forefront in the First World War but had its origins in the classical liberal art of rhetoric.[35] What is significant about modern propaganda is, first, its adoption of the insights of psychology (e.g. Edward Bernays, the self-described 'father of public relations' and who was the nephew of Sigmund Freud) and, second, the augmentation of its potential as an instrument of power ('soft power') because of the globalisation of electronic information systems.[36]

Information as power has taken on new importance in contemporary international and domestic affairs. It led in the 1990s to adoption and development in the United States and elsewhere of the military concept of information operations (IO)'. IO is based on the idea that 'the global information environment has become a battle space in which the technology of the information age...is used to deliver critical and influential content in order to shape perceptions, influence opinions, and control behaviour'.[37]

None of this is unfamiliar to observers of world affairs in the opening years of the 21st-century. The 9/11 terrorist attacks were themselves primarily intended to have a propaganda effect and much of the subsequent response by political leaders such as President Bush and Prime Minister Tony Blair can now clearly be seen as rooted in propaganda. However, what needs to be underlined in this evolution is what I am suggesting is a 'new propaganda reality' in which democratically elected politicians primarily target their own publics even more than their countries' external adversaries, and this may include using intelligence to give extra credibility to their propaganda or spin.[38] As noted above in the example of Lord Beaverbrook, Britain's first Minister of Information, propagandising a country's own citizenry was far from unprecedented in authoritarian states or during wartime.[39] But doing so in a democracy without a war underway and using intelligence to do it, as in the recent American and British cases prior to the attack on Iraq in 2003, would seem to be an important departure.

While the American military seized on the issue of information warfare (or information operations as it later came to be known) in the 1980s, the British military appear to have followed their example after observing American psychological operations in the first Gulf War. The Canadian military were much slower to follow these examples in any significant way until relatively recently. Similarly, at the civilian political level, spin efforts during nearly ten years of the Chretien government were relatively old fashioned and traditional–a speech here, a press release there, plus advertising together with regular public opinion polling—but little that could be regarded as sophisticated propaganda. Even during the Quebec Referendum on separation, a direct threat to national unity, the Chretien government appeared surprisingly oblivious to advanced communications methods as practised in the United States, the UK, Israel and elsewhere. Consequently, it caught many Canadians by surprise to observe the 'spin master' examples of the Bush and Blair governments and to see information operations being practised in military settings overseas following 9/11. The Martin government that succeeded Prime Minister Chretien showed signs of imitating some of these practices, but the real 'propaganda moment' for Canada has really come about with the advent to power of the Conservative government of Stephen Harper in 2006 and the appointment of General Rick Hillier as the Chief of the Defence Staff.

At the political level, PM Harper's government has routinely adopted advanced American public relations, political marketing, and propaganda influences. It appears to have imported its strategies and techniques from American conservative counterparts, including a strategy of tightly controlling all messages from government to the public, keeping ministers and backbenchers on very tight communications leashes, and selectively briefing favoured media. At the military level, Canadians were entirely unprepared for the new, sophisticated and aggressive approach to marketing itself and its policy interests that has emerged out of the Department of National Defence over the last two years. Concretely, the armed forces adopted a programme called 'Operation Connection' which has been described as 'part of one of the greatest military promotion efforts in Canadian history'. Its goals are ostensibly to shore up recruitment and public support for Canada's dangerous Afghanistan role, but 'Operation Connection is also trying to reshape the very way Canadians see their military'.[40] This is a decidedly political agenda and voices have unsurprisingly been raised within Canada about the appropriateness of General Hillier's unabashed propaganda offensive.

Interestingly, General Hillier is a charismatic army leader who wanted to find a way to move Canada's neglected military closer to its American and British counterparts. He served on exchange with the American CENTCOM in Miami where it seems likely that he was influenced by US military 'hearts and minds' thinking and information operations concepts. He brought these ideas home to his new position and, no doubt with good intentions, has launched his communications blitz on an unsuspecting Canadian public. He believes that insurgency warfare needs to ensure that the home front is supportive and optimistic about outcomes even if this is not immediately justified by the realities on the ground. The best way to achieve this support and optimism is to manufacture and control the messages received by the public using every marketing and propaganda technique in the book including the embedding of journalists in the field.

The scale of the Operation Connection programme directed at Canadian public opinion is unprecedented. It has a budget of $23 million (CDN) per year and according to the CBC, it employs 500 uniformed and civilian public affairs officers. In short, the programme has all the trappings of full scale propaganda, white, grey and black. Its roots are in the domestic propaganda work of the Creel Commission and of Lord Beaverbrook ninety years ago. Canadians still hardly know what has hit them. The point is that Canada, with no real tradition or sympathy for propaganda, least of all from government sources, has quietly moved into the propaganda reality which has gripped many countries in recent years.

It is not just government propaganda, however, that is of concern. Private sector marketing verging on propaganda has long been commonplace and citizens are more or less equipped to deal with it, including by ignoring it.

However, efforts to persuade the public have become more subtle and less overt than mere marketing. This is particularly noticeable in the news and opinion mass media where in recent years in Canada there has been increasing concentration of ownership accompanied by overtly political corporate strategies.[41] This press concentration reduces opportunities for journalists and makes it easy for them to be intimidated because of their quite limited work alternatives. This in turn makes them more susceptible to propaganda barrages congenial to their employers' political leanings.

In Canadian television and radio, the public information situation has been degraded by the movement coming out of the US to 'dumb down' or politicize broadcasts into highly ideological, simplified scripts. Many Canadians get their information from American television where programmes on the Fox Channel and equivalents seem more interested in one-sided news coverage, and outright propaganda dressed up as entertainment. Canadian television and radio inevitably compete with similar audience-building strategies.

Within such a bleak information and communications environment in which government has taken to propandising its own public, how is the Canadian citizen to be adequately informed? And, with media lending themselves to propaganda interests from corporate and other special interest groups, domestic and foreign, how are government and the public it serves to be adequately and accurately informed? And where does media and intelligence cooperation come into this picture? Do any of these institutions actually have anything approximating 'information sovereignty'?

The answer to these questions, which I draw from the contemporary propaganda reality in Canada and internationally and which, I do not think, will be temporary, Canada has no choice but to intentionally sustain and reinforce all the key information institutions in our society. They must be empowered to work independently within their respective spheres, and to be as little dependent as possible on each other. The personal sovereignty of the individual and the collective sovereignty of the state depend on both having access to competitive sources of information and a better understanding of information distortion at the personal and institutional levels. As common law courts and universities have long ago discovered, adversarial debate and peer review are the surest way to get to the truth. In summary, competing information sources, not collaborating organisations, seem the best prescription for maintaining a realistic appreciation of contemporary realities among Canadians and their government. If this is true, it means that the relationship between the media and intelligence in Canada and elsewhere for the foreseeable future should remain 'CZ'–closed and adversarial–sparring partners in the public interest.

11

THE CLANDESTINE CLAPPERBOARD
ALFRED HITCHCOCK'S TALES OF THE COLD WAR

Pierre Lethier

Editors' Notes: In the first of two chapters concerning the portrayal of intelligence on the big and small screens Pierre Lethier explores Alfred Hitchcock's spy thrillers in the context of Cold War history. He highlights the importance of Hitchcock in establishing the spy-thriller genre, and also in blending the operational and diplomatic realities of the 1960s into mass consumption entertainment. Lethier also alludes to the extent to which the CIA, FBI and former British intelligence insiders assisted in the development of characters and storylines—raising question marks over the social utility of this form of entertainment, which are further examined in the next chapter.

Alfred Hitchcock's considerable frame, simultaneously reassuringly rounded and startlingly misshapen, clearly had the capacity to contain several personalities, and all of them as fascinating—some would also say complex—as one another. Hitchcock has always been a remarkable entertainer who operated both within and without the mainstream classical tradition, but was also recognised as an *auteur* unanimously acclaimed as much for his precocious creation of cinematic forms as for his intellectual explorations of the burgeoning medium. Armed with the wealth of knowledge he had acquired from working alongside older colleagues in German expressionist cinema or had picked up from the Russian pioneers of *montage*, Hitchcock soon mastered the most complicated elements of camerawork and the finer techniques of the cutting room, and adapted immediately to the needs and formulae of American studios. With this threefold technical experience he was to be as successful in Islington as he was in Hollywood. Starting out as an illustrator and screenwriter, then a Jack-of-all-trades of the film industry, and then, at the age of twenty-six, a film director, Hitchcock always had a tremendous gift for storytelling.

He never tired of reiterating that he had initially drawn inspiration from Edgar Allan Poe, one of the many (and certainly one of the most widely acknowledged) founding fathers of the conjoined literary genres of detective and spy story. He soon became an accomplished adaptor of the vast riches of middlebrow literature, reinventing and elevating texts and plots to entertain or terrify audiences who had quickly become entranced by his works of suspense, mystery, tension, betrayal, crime and romance. What Hitchcock probably succeeded at more than most of his contemporaries was to enable spy literature to accommodate simultaneously both the somewhat conservative demands of classical cinema—notably the romance and the formation of the heterosexual couple—as well as a more socially liberal viewpoint which occasionally swelled into anger against abusive state institutions. Indeed, the cinema-going public embraced his rebellious humanism, which often derided the authorities or the powerful as well as the police, and he rightly became celebrated as the defender of the wrongfully accused. Hitchcock offered his fugitive heroes ample compensation for their pains and anxieties, usually in the form of willing and desirable women, all of them nevertheless connected with espionage or crime in some way or other.

Ultimately Hitchcock—the son of a wealthy East End grocer—was a smart and shrewd businessman who exploited American television to make his fortune,[1] and, for all the extraordinary cinematic inventions he devised and the terrible risks he took—far more than I could possibly enumerate here—he never lost or wasted his personal fortune in the course of his long career in film. Hitchcock's continual drive to innovate is attested to in the ever-growing number of works written on him, ever since Andrew Sarris, Robin Wood, Eric Rohmer and François Truffaut turned their attention to him in the 1960s. Unsurprisingly, Hitchcock still remains the most widely studied of all filmmakers. Some critics, such as Jonathan Freedman and Richard Millington, go as far as to see in him a latter-day Alexis de Tocqueville, an acerbic commentator on 'imperial America'.[2] The aim of this chapter, which will place Hitchcock's last spy films in their wider context, is to highlight one of his many innovations, one that has been largely overlooked until now, but is no less important for that—his creation of the CIA film, a subgenre of the spy film which was to become utterly dominant from the mid-1960s onwards.

Nearly a third of Hitchcock's output took secret intelligence as its subject—53 feature films of which no fewer than 14 were espionage or counterespionage tales. The first five spy melodramas he directed for Gaumont British from 1934 to 1938 made his reputation, paving the way for a glittering career in Hollywood from 1939 onwards.[3] Towards the end of the Second World War, he made a brief return to Britain in order to direct two anti-Nazi and pro-Free French spy and resistance allegories.[4] After this he went to Hollywood to direct seven espionage and counterespionage thrillers and humorous melodramas.[5] At the very beginning of his journey in espionage, the driving force behind Hitchcock was a group of pioneer screenwriters, veterans of the British Military Intelligence Service—Charles Bennett and Angus MacPhail, for example—who under the aegis of global-market-oriented producers, successfully created humorous, elegant heroes, often both rugged individualists and agents of the civilisation that continuously resists their individualism. After recounting the adventures of individuals thrust into counterespionage—of which Richard Hannay, the hero of John Buchan's novels, is the most distinguished example—Hitchcock first brought a professional agent to the screen in *Secret Agent* (1936), a very free adaptation of Somerset Maugham's adventures in Switzerland as an agent of the War Office Intelligence Service.

In 1946, after deep and detailed negotiations with FBI mogul Edgar Hoover himself, Hitchcock was to cast a second organisation man in *Notorious*—the counterespionage agent Devlin, whose mission consists of infiltrating and then exposing a network of Nazis in Rio de Janeiro who are secretly building a nuclear bomb. Then, in 1956, Hitchcock returned once again to his old mould of hero—the naive but resilient amateur, the innocent victim of the shadowy manipulations of the special services—in the remake of his first spy thriller, *The Man Who Knew Too Much*. A new backdrop conveys overtones of Hungarian premier Imre Nagy's assassination by Soviet secret agents that year. However, the film appears to challenge the American version of the first phase of the Cold War rather than champion it. While in retrospect the political context of the film might seem to be the Hungarian crisis, chronologically and visually the film is at least as suggestive, if not more so, of the unusual and brief Anglo-French alliance which in those days led, for example, to the bold and foolhardy Suez expedition, or of the unprecedented proposition of the political amalgamation of Britain and France under the governments of Guy Mollet and Anthony Eden. Then came an ambitious American remake of *The 39 Steps*—*North by Northwest*, in 1959—one of Hitchcock's biggest successes, a film whose tone and register belong as much to the American tradition of marriage and remarriage comedies as they do to the spy genre. Both *The Man Who Knew Too Much* and *North by Northwest* provide a useful indication of the evolution and fragmentation of the genre at the point when the Film Noir cycle was drawing to a close, but before spy mania—with its often burlesque or parodic tones, ploughing the furrow of the James Bond series—had started to inundate cinema screens in the early sixties. The specific context invoked in *North by Northwest* is very clearly post-McCarthy America, a nation gradually emerging from the debilitating trauma of the witch-hunt age. While *The Man Who Knew Too Much* dramatises a close collaboration between Special Branch (overt mention of MI5 in films was censored in 1956) and the SDECE (Service de Documentation Extérieure et de Contre-Espionnage—which Hitchcock was still careful to refer to by the old moniker of the Deuxième Bureau), *North by Northwest* was, by contrast, the very first film to suggest the CIA's covert activities on American soil.[6] Hitchcock's compatriots Ian Fleming and Eric Ambler were so fascinated by the film that they attempted to talk Hitchcock into directing the film originally intended as the first James Bond adventure, *Thunderball*, in that same year of 1959. However, Hitchcock had just become a naturalised American, and had other plans—henceforth the spies who interested him were from Langley, Virginia, rather than Broadway, London.

At this exact point, not only the Cold War but also its representation in the espionage film genre were becoming more complex than had previously been the case. A number of different narrative strains were developing which, in the case of the spy film, gave a peculiar sense of each of the Western powers pursuing its own version of the Cold War. In this peculiar context of disharmony, Alfred Hitchcock embarked on a transatlantic espionage trilogy with *Torn Curtain* (1966) *Topaz* (1969) and *The Short Night*, which unfortunately he was unable to complete.[7] *Torn Curtain* and *Topaz* are not considered to be Hitchcock's best work, far from it in fact. Although their perceived lack of artistic merits has been quite harshly criticised, these films nonetheless represent particularly interesting documents for the significant contribution they make to an understanding of the ideology and metamorphosis of the spy genre. In these films Hitchcock recaptured two critical developments in the long-drawn-out crisis of the East-West confrontation, and showed himself to be an enlightened commentator on the geopolitics of nuclear power, the dangers of undermining nuclear equilibrium and, as a result, the fundamental fragility of the notion of peaceful coexistence. Hitchcock's commentary begins by tackling the crucial question of anti-missile defences in *Torn Curtain*, then proceeds to depict the threat to an already shaky nuclear parity with the Cuban Missile Crisis in *Topaz*.

Torn Curtain is a work of pure fiction, almost entirely invented by Hitchcock and written under his watchful eye—one could almost say on his dictation—by Brian Moore; unlike all of Hitchcock's other spy films, it is not based on a pre-existing literary or journalistic text. Like many other screenwriters who worked with Hitchcock, Brian Moore had worked in British military intelligence. Without a shadow of doubt, given the thematic kinship and the structural similarities of the two narratives, *Torn Curtain* invites immediate comparison with *Cloak and Dagger*, a film Fritz Lang made in a one-off collaboration with the now-defunct American Office of Strategic Services (OSS). One notable feature of *Cloak and Dagger* reproduced in *Torn Curtain* is the boffin committing an act of violence. The man of science, Michael Armstrong (played by Paul Newman), must assume the mantle of a spy for the task in hand and commit a murder in order to have any hope of completing his sacred mission. Hitchcock lingers over the act of murder, at once wishing to show the immense physical and moral difficulty involved in the act of killing, and to offer the audience, who are cast in the role of the voyeur, the immense guilty pleasure of witnessing the slaughter of the beast—the Communist cop—by a couple—the Western spy and the anti-Soviet resister—thrown together by circumstance. Here Hitchcock takes the Shakespearean situation of a male protagonist driven to murder an older man by the essentially suicidal impulse of a woman, but pushes it to a level of spectacle far beyond, say, that of his contemporary and rival Anthony Asquith in *Orders to Kill* (1958).[8]

Hitchcock's film recounts the stealing of secret research into anti-ballistic missiles from a group of East German atomic scientists, all of whom are willing instruments of Soviet intelligence, in the mould of the real-life characters Manfred Von Ardenne and Gustav Hertz.[9] As a matter of fact, in the 1960s Moscow was already beginning to claim that it had devised a technological innovation akin to the anti-missile shield America developed at the turn of the millennium—instead the Kremlin overstated its claims to such an extent that its ill-advised and deceptive propaganda ended up compromising its own interests. Indeed, Moscow had developed and refined its anti-aircraft missiles to such a degree of effectiveness that its preposterous claim of possessing an anti-ballistic arsenal might have seemed credible, for a time at least, to its Communist partners.[10] When *Torn Curtain* went on international release, the monthly journal *Red Guard*, supported by the secret services in Beijing, published a carefully argued indictment of the alleged Kremlin's anti-Chinese policies.[11] *Red Guard* took violent exception to the fact that the Kremlin had failed to install anti-aircraft or anti-ballistic defences in Vietnam, and, citing Russian military hierarchs, the revolutionary Maoist paper insisted that its Communist 'brothers' in Moscow had anti-ballistic missiles in plentiful supply, which if they had been deployed would have driven the American military back or out of Asia altogether. *Red Guard* claimed that the United States had not yet managed to develop an equivalent arms system or perfect anti-ballistic missile technology, and insisted that an anti-ballistic system was so expensive that the United States government had recoiled at the spending involved.

Ironically, Hitchcock's plot uses the dialectic proposed by Communist ideologues only to destroy it more effectively. In *Torn Curtain*, the pretext given for the false defection of Michael Armstrong/Paul Newman to East Germany is America's abandonment of its anti-ballistic missile research programme, although this is obviously not explained in terms of the budget cuts alleged in *Red Guard*. When he arrives in East Berlin, Armstrong announces at a press conference that he intends to offer his considerable learning to the Leipzig University Professor Gustav Lindt—played by Ludwig Donath—a leading authority in his field. Armstrong proposes that they work on producing a defensive weapon that will make all offensive nuclear weapons obsolete and thereby abolish the terror of nuclear warfare. In order to win the trust of the East German authorities, Armstrong launches a scathing attack, stating unambiguously that Washington has no wish to abandon the nuclear arms race, and that this is the sole reason the American government dropped the project he had devoted so much of his energy to. However, Armstrong confesses later to the head of the pro-Western resistance espionage network *Pi*, which is supporting him, that his research into anti-ballistic missiles has failed to produce any results, while he is convinced that Lindt's work has been successful. Yevgeny Velikov, one of the Soviet Union's most eminent scientists, was to declare twenty years later, on 3 March 1986, to the XXVIIIth Congress of the CPSU, that the USSR had possessed a sufficiently capable scientific base to develop adequate countermeasures to the American Strategic Defense Initiative, the so-called Star Wars program. And now, forty years after *Torn Curtain*, the highly polemical and relatively complex subject Hitchcock chose to tackle seems to have retained much of its relevance, especially now as Russia is once again bludgeoning the world with its bellicose rhetoric, an outrageous reminder of the Cold War.

Torn Curtain also provides a rare and informative illustration of some of the peculiarities of its age. The year in which the film was made, 1966, was one of particular significance where the question of East Germany was concerned. Walter Ulbricht, First Secretary of the East German Communist Party (SED), made the first of several formal requests for the GDR to join the United Nations. His successor eventually obtained recognition in 1973. However, Hitchcock's purpose was to portray the true and despicable nature of the East German regime. The NVA pump round after round of automatic fire into the crowd of civilians into which Armstrong and his fiancée have slipped, helped across the border by the non-violent resistance network *Pi*. At the University of Leipzig atomic research centre, scientists who would normally reign supreme in their institution are in fact reduced to the status of mere lackeys of the Stasi. The contrast between the orderly omnipotence of the secret service and the feebleness of the scientists frames the development of the plot. *Torn Curtain* is indeed a manifesto against the police state. There are very few contemporary accounts from when the film was made, and in this regard *Torn Curtain* is an original and unusual work. After the popular uprising which was crushed on 17 June 1953, the repression which was then brought to bear on all resistance movements gave the West reason to believe that police order had prevailed.[12] For example, in his work of 1968, the historian Ralf Dahrendorf claims that by the end of the 1960s 'the East German regime appeared to be quite legitimate in terms of the assent, or at least the absence of active dissent, on the part of the citizens'.[13] This was not Hitchcock's opinion. Nor, indeed, is it that of Christopher Andrew and Vasili Mitrokhin who in their study paint an entirely different picture, recalling that in the mid-1970s the Stasi still believed that 500,000 GDR citizens remained hostile to the political system.

In *Topaz* as in *Torn Curtain*, Hitchcock constantly plays with the historical elements of his film, employing tricks of plot structure; in this film, too, it emerges very clearly that his purpose was to support the idea that obtaining information would allow a peaceful resolution to a crisis. The more you knew, the better chance you had of averting war. This paradigm of intelligence may seem obvious today, but the same could not really be said of the 1960s. The problem always lay in establishing the facts, and this is what really interested Hitchcock, inspiring him to make a film essentially about a major crisis of intelligence, coupled with a crisis of confidence. The first distinctive quality of the film is its choice of subject matter: the Cuban Missile Crisis, which had been ignored by film studios up to this point; and the second is its rejection of the illusory sense of relief which followed the resolution of the affair. Unlike many other espionage and counterespionage films which portray this period, *Topaz* is not remotely a film of détente. Furthermore, it unquestionably offers both a representation of America's soft power and a vision of America triumphant, portraying it as a powerful and attractive model.[14] The historian Ernest May once declared that 'the United States considers itself the greatest power in Europe'.[15] A generation or so separates May, whose work on *The Kennedy Tapes* inspired Roger Donaldson's film *Thirteen Days* (2000), and Alfred Hitchcock, but they bear comparison as observers of the delights of American superiority and hegemony, in Europe especially. In Hitchcock's version of the events of October 1962, the famous 'thirteen days' are gently stretched out, giving him space to depict human intelligence at work—Hitchcock, unlike May, gives these activities a central role. While May is almost exclusively interested in intelligence acquired by the CIA's U2 spy planes over Cuba from 14 October 1962, Hitchcock's prime concern is to represent human intelligence as a powerful and successful instrument of American hegemony. It is worth remembering that when Hitchcock conceived his Cold War triptych, spy stories were considered among the safest vehicles for presenting America's reassuring power in the best possible light. Furthermore, the Kennedy era that the film truly allegorises was a time for the United States to hold forth on the threats it faced with a dose of humour, even mockery, and certainly with a dash of glamour and fantasy, and even a liberal sprinkling of brutality and light-hearted sadism for good measure. It comes as little surprise that in his reconstruction of the missile affair of October 1962 and the simultaneous revelation of Soviet infiltration of the Western democracies, Alfred Hitchcock chose to present the resolution of these two major crises as in every respect a triumph of American espionage.

The screenplay of *Topaz*, based on a number of realistic geopolitical intrigues, follows an unusual structure, which Hitchcock and Samuel A. Taylor organised into five geographical sequences, in which the Atlantic is crossed in both directions: beginning (as in *Torn Curtain*) in Copenhagen with the defection to the CIA of the Kuzenovs, then in Washington with the clash between counterespionage and diplomacy, in New York with the clandestine obtaining of information from the Cuban delegation to the UN, in Cuba with the dramatic outcome of subcontracted secret operations, and finally in Paris, where the diplomatic and counterespionage intrigues reunite and then resolve. Unusually, these five strands are manipulated not by the lead character, the French diplomat-secret agent, but by the *One Who Knows*—the Russian defector. *Topaz* shows no propensity for spectacular physical action or explosions. Unlike action-adventure spy films of the period, there are no formidable villains—in *Topaz* the antagonists are of debatable skills and intelligence, and lack dignity; they are merely infatuated politicians and pompous activists. One of the film's qualities is to demonstrate how the very peculiar ethics of espionage and diplomacy can come into conflict, but above all how both can invade, confront and transform people. In *Topaz* the characters are at once actors and slaves to the whims and deceptions of politics. Whether their response is one of surrender or acceptance, or, on the other hand, of rejection and defiance, for different reasons almost all of them try to hide behind these moving screens in order to lead private lives fashioned from very similar deceptions.

Topaz is in effect a prototype whose singularity is the accuracy with which it reveals the very nature of the culture of the CIA and its workings, an especially rare feat in cinema at that time. Until 1960–1, the general public had known very little about the CIA since its creation in 1947.[16] Not until the disaster of the Bay of Pigs expedition were the agency's clandestine activities brought to wider attention.[17] The question of human intelligence, like that of Soviet intentions before the revelation of the missile installations on 14 October 1962, has been the subject of many studies and been interpreted in several different ways. Commentators have been unanimous in their condemnation of the work of the National Security Council analysts who, in the famous intelligence estimate of 19 September 1962, placed their faith in the fact that the Soviets had never installed offensive missiles outside their own territory. The National Security Council, ignoring the advice of CIA Director John McCone, estimated that the Soviets would continue to behave in the same fashion. Opinions are more divided, however, on the value of the intelligence provided by agents: the debate among experts has focused essentially on the usefulness of information supplied by the CIA's Russian sources and by French agents, who were known to have a spy network in Cuba at a time when the CIA had only a handful of contacts in Cuban labour unions. American historian Michael Beschloss—basing his arguments essentially on statements made by National Security adviser McGeorge Bundy—contends that GRU officer Oleg Penkovsky, an important source shared by Britain's SIS and the CIA in Moscow, had furnished, well beforehand (in 1961) valuable information

which allowed the interpreters of the U2 photographs to make an exact identification of the MRBM (SS4) installations spotted on the crucial flight of 14
October.[18] Only John McCone, so it seems, had foreseen that Moscow would
be unable to resist the temptation of installing strategic and tactical nuclear
weapons on Cuba.[19] When the presence of conventional Soviet ground-to-air
missiles (SAM2) was detected on Cuba in the summer of 1962, McCone
immediately concluded, going against the prevailing opinion, that the purpose
of these missiles was to protect nuclear missile sites. Believing that the French
had access to a useful network of informers in Havana, McCone took the
initiative, meeting the French ambassador in Washington, Hervé Alphand,
and then seeing the head of the French secret service, General Paul Jacquier,
in Paris. There are several conflicting theories regarding the nature and extent
of France's involvement, which provided Hitchcock with the basis of a significant part of his screenplay. French historian Maurice Vaisse claims that on 10
August 1962 the French ambassador in Havana, Roger du Gardier, reported
to the State Department that Slavic-looking troops, clearly Russians, had
landed in several Cuban ports by night, and that there had also been sightings
of Chinese and Algerians. Most importantly, du Gardier reported the arrival
of missile-launching equipment. In his account of the diplomat's report Vaisse
does not mention which type of missile had been spotted by French observers,
but there can be little doubt that they were ground-to-air SAM2s and most
definitely not nuclear SS4s, since the latter did not arrive on the island any
earlier than 4 October. Drawing on the account by the French military attaché
in Washington, General de Rancourt, who had once served as General de
Gaulle's aide, Vaisse insists that the French military delegation to the United
States, which also claimed to have a number of Cuban informers, passed the
Americans more information on the missiles.[20] What is striking in the testi-
monies gathered by Vaisse is both the vagueness of the nature and the date of
the intelligence which was passed on, and the complete obfuscation of the role
played by the secret services. Hitchcock to an extent corroborates the French
historian's account, but he also goes against it by making the French intelligence agent Philippe Thyraud de Vosjoli (who, under the name André
Devereaux, is the character played by Frederick Stafford in Hitchcock's film)
the genuine source of the intelligence. Similarly, Hitchcock supports certain
elements of the CIA's version of events, but in places he diverges from the
official American account. Thyraud de Vosjoli is in fact never mentioned in
works by historians close to American and French political and administrative
institutions—either in terms of the role he played or as a person—since on

the one hand the French officially consider him a rogue traitor who sold out to the US, and on the other hand the CIA have constantly denied that it had ever recruited the SDECE's representative in Washington (and Cuba), claiming consequently that he could never have played any role which would have been of use to them. For reasons of diplomacy, on both sides of the Atlantic Thyraud de Vosjoli was soon seen as a pariah, somebody whose name should never be spoken.[21] However, the original adventure of the French agent—which Hitchcock reinvents in his film, editing out or mollifying the most controversial elements—was nevertheless to appear in unexpurgated form in three documents which made news headlines between 1967 and 1970—first, in Leon Uris's best-seller *Topaz*,[22] then in the cover story run by *Life* magazine on Philippe Thyraud de Vosjoli,[23] and finally in Vosjoli's own published account, *Lamia*.[24]

Hitchcock faced difficulties of historical re-enactment and characterisation which his screenplay needed to resolve, but there was an even thornier problem—that of representing a further character, one even more controversial than the French agent and the CIA men: the Soviet defector Anatoly Golitsin. The KGB defector adds substance to the plot, bringing to the film a viewpoint which one might reasonably take to reflect the filmmaker's own view. After the discovery of the nuclear sites, and the revelations by Golitsin that some of the highest levels of French power had been penetrated by Soviet espionage, it suddenly became extremely important for the Americans on the one hand to keep secret the findings of the U2 and all the supporting intelligence, and on the other hand, and apparently in complete contradiction, to mobilise their allies Great Britain and France against the challenge which Khrushchev was furtively preparing—one of the delicious ironies which are a hallmark of Hitchcock's treatment of the subject of espionage. Hitchcock and screenwriter Samuel Taylor understood this fundamental contradiction in the workings of intelligence and reproduced it very skilfully in *Topaz*. It is one of the film's undeniable riches.

Hitchcock transformed considerably for his own dramatic ends the story of Golitsin upon whom Kusenov's character in the film is modelled. The Golitsin affair has been interpreted in a variety of different ways—more often than not very negatively, depending on the country and the time—but it cannot be denied that Golitsin's defection to the CIA has had extraordinary repercussions in the recent history of Western counterespionage. Although in 1968/9 Hitchcock was keenly aware of the dramatic potential of the defector's sensational revelations, he might never have imagined the extremes of manipulation went to by the CIA's head of counterespionage, James Angleton, and the Special Investigation Group, based on the clues provided by Golitsin, who clearly had some knowledge of what espionage operations the KGB was targeting, but knew little—next to nothing, even—of the results these operations had yielded. His defection came a year after that of the Polish intelligence officer Michael Goleniewski—a claimant to the imperial throne of Russia—who had enabled British counterespionage to identify the mole at the heart of the SIS, George Blake (who was to provide Hitchcock with a main character in his next screenplay), as well as the Portland spy ring. Following Goleniewski, Golitsin compounded the extraordinary climate of suspicion which had invaded and paralysed every intelligence headquarters in the West, leading to a flood of fresh accusations.[25] He insisted, but without being able to supply a name, that the KGB had a mole high up in the CIA, as well as agents who since the Second World War had infiltrated not only the Anglo-American secret services, but also those of France, Canada and Norway, as well as Western political circles, in NATO in particular.[26] A long and devastating hunt for spies within the CIA was undertaken under DCI Richard Helms, which lasted until 1973. After the arrest of Penkovsky in October 1962 and the defection of Kim Philby to Moscow in January 1963, the terrible trauma turned into an incurable paranoia.[27]

One of the most sensational of Golitsin's revelations was the existence of the spy ring 'Sapphire' (alias Topaz). Golitsin was unable to give the names of the Soviet infiltrators among General de Gaulle's entourage in France, agents who were acting against NATO and American defence interests, yet the clues he provided were sufficient to launch a mole hunt in France like that which was taking place in the United States. All of this was quickly hushed up by the political authorities. Hitchcock kept out of this peculiar French controversy. Apart from his striking depiction of the two most significant traitors, he represents a number of dubious and arrogant French officials, who are subtly anti-American or at least indifferent to America's plight in Cuba. Adopting a strikingly realistic viewpoint in his depiction of these French diplomats, Hitchcock portrays their function as that of creating ever more obstacles for the hero André Devereaux, reinforcing the sense of his isolation. The crisis of confidence represented in the film is such that the hero's greatest fear in France is more of the police than of the diplomats. Indeed, when he first encounters the dead body of one of the traitors—Henri Jarré, played by Philippe Noiret—who has been thrown from a window and landed on a car roof, Devereaux's main preoccupation is to keep the police out of the affair, and indeed to keep himself out of the secret police's way. This entirely factual event is particularly interesting, since here Hitchcock re-enacts an incident that took place in Paris in 1969 rather than 1962. Colonel de La Salle, a hero of the *Normandie Nié-men* squadron and senior staff member of the combined Allied air force until 1965, but, crucially, also a Soviet agent, committed suicide by throwing himself from the window of his Paris home just as the DST (Direction de la Surveillance du Territoire) were arriving to arrest him. His broken body was found on the black roof of the police car. Hitchcock must have seen pictures of this defenestration of the Soviet agent, and reproduced the scene in his film.

The traitor Jarré is inspired more by a prominent French NATO official, Georges Pâques, who was arrested in 1963 and condemned to life imprisonment, although he was soon granted an amnesty by his *normalien* classmate President Georges Pompidou.[28] In his memoirs the former assistant director of the French secret police, the DST, Raymond Nart states that it was indeed Golitsin who provided the necessary leads for him to unmask Pâques,[29] whereas his superior at the time, Marcel Chalet, says that the traitor within NATO denounced by Golitsin was the Canadian professor Hugh George Hambleton.[30] Hitchcock is categorical in his revelation of the identity of the head of the Topaz network—Jacques Granville, played by Michel Piccoli, who is given the codename Colombine in the film, and escapes punishment. There is, of course, no shortage of suspects, and the list of eminent politicians aligned with Moscow has lengthened considerably since Eastern Bloc archives were opened up at the end of the Cold War.

Yet the main element of Uris's novel and Vosjoli's account erased from the screenplay is Golitsin's declaration regarding the KGB's plans to get hold of American nuclear secrets. This statement was made at the same time he revealed the existence of the Topaz network. Vosjoli devoted his energies to uncovering the network until October 1963, when his country ordered him to discontinue all such activity and concentrate solely on spying against United States interests.[31] The scandal derived from the perfect match (according to Vosjoli, Golitsin and Angleton) between French and Russian intentions towards American nuclear capabilities.[32] Vosjoli refused to bend to his new orders, and resigned on 18 October 1963. Unlike Leon Uris, Hitchcock decided not to make use of this last twist to the Vosjoli story—which was in those days scandalous and unverifiable—for the character of André Devereaux.

The screenplay of *The Short Night* was initially written by Ernest Lehmann, who had previously written the script for *North by Northwest*, and then by

David Freeman.[33] It is based on the novel of the same name by Ronald Kirk-bride (1967), and also draws on Sean Burke's account entitled *The Springing of George Blake* (1970). The event Hitchcock intended to recreate took place in October 1966, and sent shockwaves across the world—the spectacular escape of the British SIS officer George Blake, who had been condemned to forty-two years in prison for spying for the Soviet Union.[34] According to Free-man, what this screenplay in fact offers is a set of highly personal ideological and narrative conclusions which Hitchcock had reached. The proposed nar-rative for *The Short Night* was intended to combine the clarity of classic cin-ema and the extreme thrills offered by cinema in the late 1970s: the clarity would be reinforced by the film's linear construction, as it followed the pursuit of Blake across the wide open spaces of Finland, while the thrills were to take the form of a torrid and explicitly portrayed love affair far beyond anything Hitchcock had previously attempted.[35] The structure of the screenplay was to be similarly rigorous and simple. British double agent Gavin Brand, based on the infamous George Blake, escapes from Wormwood Scrubs prison and flees to Finland, where his beautiful wife and children are waiting for him. In New York, Joe Bailey, a sportsman and a playboy 'who can easily get very angry' and whose young brother, a CIA operative, was one of the traitor's many victims,[36] is recruited by the American intelligence executive Zelfand and subcontracted to intercept Brand by finding his family, and to terminate the traitor with extreme prejudice. The first part of the script, whose structure takes the form of a fast-paced, enthralling series of action sequences, investigations and sud-den twists, draws to a close when Bailey finally finds Brand's wife, Carla, in Finland. The encounter with Carla Brand initially creates emotional confu-sion, and quickly evolves into a passionate and compulsive carnal relationship, depicted explicitly. The second part sees the return of Brand to his family, only to come close to killing his wife, and then snatching his boys away. Bailey eventually manages to overcome the obstacles placed in his way by the Finnish police, who are anxious to ensure that the laws and neutrality of their country are respected.

The explicit violence which is to be found throughout the screenplay begins with the first scene, in which an innocent, naive girl, an Irish Communist, is raped and murdered by a sex-starved Blake/Brand, and continues with the attempted murder of Carla Brand by a hitman working for the Russians. The story of the pursuit ends with a breathless chase towards the Russian border in which Bailey leaps onto a train bound for Moscow, where he confronts Brand, who is under the protection of a group of Russian officers. The screenplay's melodramatic climax leaves the reader in little doubt about Hitchcock's vision regarding the fluctuation between violence and knowledge in espionage narratives. What Bailey finally achieves is to trade and save the two children from the contagion of Communism by taking them away from their father, whose life is spared. The red spy, portrayed essentially as a criminal, no longer poses an immediate threat to the security of the United States or Great Britain—after five years behind bars he has become nothing more than a slightly sordid has-been, a psychopath and a burden the Russians can now look after. Hitchcock's Soviet characters' main concern was to avoid a diplomatic incident and so they let the American and the two children go scot-free. In May 1979 the script was ready for filming, but Hitchcock had obviously noticed nothing heralding the abrupt change in the international situation which was to take place, to almost everybody's surprise, that December. Hitchcock therefore painted a more interesting picture, that of the West's traditional system of espionage and counterespionage on its last legs. When his characters Bailey and Carla utter the evocative lines 'Spying and espionage, everybody suffers from it. The gains are vague and abstract and the losses are all personal,' Hitchcock is simply bearing witness to the temporary but nonetheless genuine collapse of conventional American intelligence for a significant part of the 1970s, i.e. from Watergate until the Soviet invasion of Afghanistan, which gradually gave the CIA a much-needed boost.

Another particularly interesting feature of this unfinished trilogy was to have been the shift from the lighter, more carefree atmosphere of the 1960s—the years following the peaceful resolution of the Cuban crisis, a time when an illusion of peace and tranquillity was preserved—to the new anxieties of the Cold War and the conspiracy obsessions of the 1970s. With *Torn Curtain* and *Topaz*, Hitchcock modified and refreshed the genre as a whole, and in so doing created a distinct new genre—the CIA film—a golden goose which laid countless eggs for Hollywood from that moment on. With *The Short Night* Hitchcock would not only have pushed still further the change of atmosphere which was reflected in the trenchant political thrillers of the decade, but also have represented for the first time the profound and trivial contingencies which are the lifeblood of espionage. What Hitchcock did achieve was to cultivate the cinematic ground on which future dramatists and cinematographers ply their trade, blending—as Hitchcock did—the real world with fictional accounts.

12

FROM VAUXHALL CROSS WITH LOVE

INTELLIGENCE IN POPULAR CULTURE

Robert Dover

Editors' Notes: This chapter addresses the nature of the recent televisual interest in spy dramas, focusing, in particular, on the American series *24* and the British series *Spooks*. Both are considered and their inaccuracies evaluated. Dover then moves on to contemplate why it is that the public have a thirst for such programmes, and what benefits they can offer governments on both sides of the Atlantic. Are such programmes, films like James Bond and the myriad computer games where you assume the role of a special forces' soldier, mere escapism, or are there other factors at play?

Intelligence and entertainment is an explosive mix of the secret and the powerful. This is sovereign power executed often with maximum secrecy and sometimes covert military tools. Such combinations are always going to be attractive to those who commission and write television and cinema drama and to governments seeking persuasive propaganda outlets as they tap into popular feelings and insecurities about terrorism and policing, threats to the homeland and the projection of power abroad. The main thrusts of this chapter are two-fold. First, that depictions of intelligence in popular culture provide a fragmentary and distorting view of intelligence activity, which leads the viewing public to think that it understands the agencies and what they do.

And second, that this fragmentary view helps to create new realities within which policy-makers then start to operate.

The depiction of armed force, war and terrorism on television and in the cinema has been the subject of some scholarly work—mostly in the sphere of cultural and media studies[1], but also by some international relations scholars who explore the political messages that lie beneath the cultural representations of war dramas[2] and science fiction[3], or that underpin the speeches or statements of governments and international organisations.[4] What I take from these sophisticated scholarly efforts is that the cultural representations of intelligence that one might observe have several important political and social purposes. The first is to provide an understanding of who threatens us, and why they threaten us. The second is to forge an understanding of a common national bond with common values, and the thirs to assert a means by which that threat can be contained, rolled back and ultimately defeated. More particularly it is to assert a particular set of methods through which the threats can be overturned.

Through the examples of the BBC Drama 'Spooks' (known as MI5 in America), '24' and the James Bond series of films, this chapter examines how intelligence has been represented by mass consumption cultural outlets, and what this tells us about the politics of intelligence and the way the public has been conditioned to understand it. The main point I wish to convey is that the act of policing or disciplining behaviour through the use of secret intelligence services is not a value neutral one. The politics of state intelligence are every bit as political as those of the terrorists or dissidents they seek to contain and defeat. Just because liberal democracy, free trade and free speech are advertised as positive norms, this does not mean they are received as such universally; after all, many millions of Chinese presumably think positively about the Chinese system of government and economics, they cannot all be oppressed into acquiescence. So I'm seeking on the one hand to make a reflexive point that 'our' politics are contested and that we should understand that our adversaries are, in ways we understandably do not like, challenging our politics and our social system. In return *we* challenge their conception of politics when the government and its policing and intelligence agencies place them under surveillance or curtail their ability freely to associate; these are the disciplinary aspects of *our* way of politics.

The second point I advance is that the cultural representations on screen do really matter. They are not just fictitious fluff and nonsense; they have a real world impact in respect of how they help to condition the public to think about intelligence, the use of state sanctioned violence, and counter-terrorism (and influence those who might join the intelligence agencies) and how that in turn conditions media perceptions, and ultimately the perceptions of the political classes and those in the agencies. So, far from being a value neutral portrayal of intelligence, these representations help create the reality they operate in. Exploring the characters, the scenarios and the politics behind these cultural representations gives us insights into what might be called real world politics, and into the conditioning of society into certain political and philosophical positions. For example, one clear set of messages involve a sense of all-encompassing threat, that at any moment in time the United States or United Kingdom could be brought to its knees by terrorist atrocities. Moreover, that these terrorists seek to 'end our way of life' and that we are engaged in a life or death struggle.[5] When polled, the vast majority of western populations believe these things to be true—without the time and space to study evidence in detail the public's perceptions is surely influenced by news and popular media messages?

The American Administration clearly thinks that these popular media outlets are of some use in their war against terrorism. Just as the British and German governments invested time in the Second World War placing political propaganda within popular films, so Hollywood enjoys a close relationship with both the Pentagon and the White House.[6] After 9/11 the White House invested some time in cultivating US movie makers into representing the war on terror 'properly', sharing key ideas and concepts.[7] One might question how successful they have been in achieving this—the majority of the output has indeed portrayed terrorism as a clash of civilisations. The result is a strange mix of a corporate film industry, with a public service broadcasting strand that focuses on terrorism as a new place to play out its vulnerabilities and then create its heroes and the mythology of a fight between good and evil. The role of the government in creating this propaganda is not advertised, which is not to suggest some kind of conspiracy—it is another way of the government discharging its public information function and trying to shape public debates. What is under-explored is exactly what we, the voting and viewing public, is being asked to sign up to by these messages, and this will be examined later.

24, Spooks and James Bond

24 and Spooks have a similar subject matter but different ways of presenting their world views. 24 centres on the activities of an entirely fictional Los Angeles

Counter Terrorism Unit (CTU) and so far has followed them, in real time, over full days (so six series of twenty-four, one hour shows). On each of these fictionalised days Los Angeles and America has faced a catastrophic terrorist event that CTU has had to identify, contain and prevent. All of the terrorist attacks depicted by *24* are unprecedented in their size and scale in the real world. The human resources open to CTU are scarce while the technological resources available to them are vast. Everything is conducted at a breathless pace, and no one seems particularly affected by sleep deprivation, the needs of personal hygiene or the constraints of cell phone battery life. The story lines, which mostly focus around terrorists trying to use nuclear or biological weapons, trying to assassinate the President or Presidential candidate, have some believable elements to them. The drama is high, and as I will discuss later, ticking time-bomb rationality features heavily in the motivations for the actions of the lead character, Jack Bauer, and his team.

The BBC Series '*Spooks*' is set in the British Security Service (MI5), in a fictitious Section D—although the real Section D used to deal with threats from political subversives. Amusingly the building the series shows as the MI5 building is actually the headquarters of the British Masonic movement—the Grand Union Lodge—no doubt fuelling some Internet conspiracy theories about how these two secret organisations interact. *Spooks* is somewhat more grounded than *24*; its threats are smaller scale, consisting of more 'run of the mill' terrorism, although it is quite inventive in places. *Spooks* has also been careful to show some of the interplay between politics and intelligence although Sir David Omand complains about their representation of his old post in this book. Finally, the James Bond series, as everyone surely knows, depicts an MI6 agent deployed in all manner of exotic locations, with a 'licence to kill' on behalf of the British state. There are, of course, many more examples of intelligence programming and films, but these examples allow for a broad brush analysis to be presented.

The time bomb is ticking

The 'ticking time bomb', or the emergency situation is a device used constantly in popular representations of intelligence activity. The idea that a Jack Bauer from '*24*' or Adam Carter from '*Spooks*' would have allowed the 'CREVICE' plotters—bent on blowing up a large British shopping centre and nightclub—to develop their plot and reveal so much of their network would be unthinkable. Jack would have tortured and/or killed them early, resulting in the plot very nearly succeeding, while Adam would use perfect satellite imagery, sigint and surveillance to rein them in at the very last moment, his powers of detention a direct distortion of MI5's need for police help in these circumstances. Of course the CREVICE plot was allegedly somewhat hastily disrupted when the CIA threatened pre-emptively to bring the network down if MI5 did not do so immediately—something surely worthy of being drama-tised.[8] Such interactions have been played out on the small screen in series like the BBC's *The State Within* (2006).

The importance of this 'ticking time-bomb' mentality is the conditioning effect it has on the viewers and the trickle-up effect it then has on policy-makers; what one might call a fog of perception, echoing the fog of war. It helps to condition and to shape what Slavoj Zizek describes as objective vio-lence—that which secures the state and certain modes of trade—while por-traying the violence of adversaries as exceptional and shocking—to use his terminology, 'subjective violence).[9] *24* has attracted opprobrium from liberal quarters for the easy way it slips into torture scenes and the flimsy rationale it has for doing so. There is no place here for Alan Dershowitz's judicially justi-fied torture—these decisions come down to an individual officer making an immediate decision; there is only a hint of accountability in the previews for Series 7.[10] By contrast, in *Spooks* torture is often meted out by the adver-sary—in series 6, and by way of an interesting twist, by American rogue agents, but in earlier series by Syrians and private military company personnel. Tor-ture carried out by British officers is done reluctantly, and is carefully discussed by ad hoc committees of senior intelligence officers. The signals being given out respectively by *24* and *Spooks* are plain to see—everything in *24* is subor-dinate to the national interest, whereas in *Spooks* derogations of human rights are agonised over, and the extraordinary rendition of two British officers at the end of Series 6 is meant to echo loudly and morally the American practice of judicially sanctioned kidnapping, much as the film *Rendition* (2007) has done in cinemas. Furthermore, in the last episode of Series 3 of *Spooks* (2004) the writers clearly show that terrorist activity is the result of the war in Iraq—linking into mainstream British concerns about 'blow-back'. We can see these different messages in the news media too where Britain's role in GWOT is portrayed as restrained and responsible while the American approach is depicted as cavalier and without judicial sanction.

There is a curious difference between the producers of *Spooks* and of the film *Rendition* who clearly wanted to send a political message, questioning government-sanctioned kidnap and torture, to spur a political and moral debate among the viewers, and the producers of *24* who argued that their dramatised and fictional account of torture has no impact on the public, because they can discriminate between reality and drama.[11] This is a puzzling position, mostly because it shows a lack of reflection. We know, as individuals, that we mediate and discriminate between pieces of information on the basis of our experiences, be it through schooling, parental preferences, personal trajectories, newspaper reportage or whatever. Some of these experiences are now delivered through television, cinema, and, for youths, via video games. To create a credible, dramatised, scenario involving terrorists and weapons of mass destruction in the context of speeches by President Bush[12] and then British Prime Minister Blair[13] and assume that the public will not use them to form judgements and opinions on 'real-world' threats is a complete nonsense. The two are necessarily bound together; this is, after all, one of the key attractions of both *Spooks* and *24*—they are near enough to real world scenarios to engage our fears and interest in situations of the here and now.

So where to draw the line? In the second series of *24*, the prevailing scenario involves terrorists threatening to detonate a nuclear bomb in Los Angeles. This ties in closely with the threats described to us by British and American politicians and in effect we are being challenged to consider what measures we would find acceptable in identifying, containing and preventing these threats. It is a classic utilitarian conundrum—the question of how far to derogate the human rights of one or several individuals for the protection of many tens of thousands. When we are asked to consider what we would want the state to do to protect our family and friends, our responses are likely to be at the disproportionate and unrestrained end of the spectrum—entirely naturally, I would suggest. Aside from the functional utility of torture (and there is no evidence that it works), amongst the other false premises drawn in these scenarios are the immediacy of the emergency, the idea that the intelligence agencies would know about the plots in this detail and also the notion that they would know that a particular detainee was connected to a particular plot.[14] A stark binary is drawn therefore between torturing a suspect and potentially foiling the terrorist attack, or allowing it to proceed. If we take this forward, the 'Islamic' threat is presented by western populations as being both immediate and all-encompassing, which deprives the public and indeed policy-makers of the critical space to consider strategy. The public's desire is to see threats ameliorated—so being assured that the current strategy is the best will suffice—while the reinforcing cycle of securitized responses makes it very hard for politicians and civil servants to suggest non-security tactics. A good example of this can be seen in the debate between Michael Rainsborough and David Martin Jones and the critical scholars Tarak Barkawi and Richard Jackson.[15] In this instance, those challenging the prevailing counterterrorism orthodoxy were myopically labelled as unwitting sympathisers with jihadist causes, despite the wealth of evidence to the contrary. Not only does this sort of labelling make no practical sense, it tells us something significant about the disciplinary and conditioning aspects of counter-terrorism—namely the politics of who is to be protected and who is to be regarded as an adversary, and on what grounds these decisions are made.

We might interrogate this conditioning in the following way: who is the 'we' that is to be protected? Are gypsies and anarchists, for example, to be included in the 'we' and if not, why not? Are there core values to which 'we' have to adhere? Who are the 'they'? What conditions need to prevail before 'they' can be categorised as 'us'? What are the limits to the actions the state can take to protect 'us' from 'them'? None of this should indicate that I am opposed to the political system we use in the west—but it is important that we understand that these political positions are ultimately contested, or contestable. The choice to defend them is a political position in its own right, not the stuff of unassailable common sense as it is presented now by our political leaders and our media. For us rigorously to consider the politics we are being asked to defend should be a commonplace of a responsible citizenry.

The fact that democratic neo-liberalism is seen by the vast majority of European and American western populations as common-sense does not remove the contests around these key values. After all, if China and not America was the global hegemon it is likely we would offer critiques of their conceptions of 'democracy' and 'human rights'. It is because Europe and Europe's historic colony, the United States, have dominated the wider world for 500 years that we assume our views and beliefs to be universal. What is more, western societies also believe their essentially liberal beliefs can be occasionally bypassed for their own protection—witness the US Patriot Act (2001) and the British Terrorism Acts (2000 and 2006). No better statement of this pragmatic attitude towards these core values can be found beyond Vice President Cheney's 2001[16] declaration that:

We also have to work sort of the dark side, if you will. ...A lot of what needs to be done here will have to be done quietly, without any discussions, using sources and methods that are available to our intelligence agencies if we're going to be successful. That's the world these folks operate in. And so it's going to be vital for us to use any means at our disposal...It is a mean, nasty, dangerous, dirty business out there, and we have to operate in that arena.[17]

Ticking time-bomb rationality has allowed us to part with our core values in the name of protecting them. In the language of the markets, we have had to issue a correction into the market, in this instance via unpleasant or illegal methods. Do such moments fundamentally undermine the liberalism they seek to protect? Absolutists would suggest they do, moving us closer to the barbarism we seek to oppose. The alternative view is that by accepting casualties and opposing the terrorists within a human rights framework, we maintain the higher moral ground, and ultimately undermine the terrorists' moral and political claims. Serious measures are not something that should necessarily be opposed outright; after all, they provided the core of some successful but controversial strategies in the Second World War. From a cultural perspective, the mainstreaming of certain core messages—of what the state is fighting for, and how we should fight for it (which refers back to Zizek's objective violence), is interesting. The intangible is how these signals filter around the polity, percolating through the public, the political classes, the military, the security sector, and the news media in the 'fog of perception'. The impression often given of intelligence officers and government elites being immune to these kinds of cultural messages falls at the first hint of reflexive thought. Intelligence does not operate in a vacuum and officers are not immune from the created realities of media invention.[18] So, while it is useful for the CIA to meet with and advise the producers of *24* on story lines, eventually the new reality they create—through *24* and other broadcast media—and the public response to it, eventually constrain them into certain ways of working. If torture works on *24*, the argument might go, why is it not being used by counter-terrorism professionals in America? Evidence of this is just emerging from Philippe Sands, who has examined whether the Pentagon took cues from American television drama about the acceptability of torture in Guantanamo Bay.[19]

If we are trying to draw lessons for real-world intelligence then ticking time bomb rationality is not a good starting point. To start with, the routine and the mundane is a far safer intellectual premise; it avoids sensationalising the work and offering false and dangerous binaries. The majority of intelligence work on counter-terrorism is concerned with the less sexy elements of this field and for very good reason. Ironically one film that does show this side of intelligence activity is *The Lives of Others* (2006) the award-winning film about the Stasi, in which the routine collection of intelligence is shown to very good effect. A focus on supply lines, support networks and financing routes (like narcotics and charities) provides a far bigger intelligence target to hit; it also provides a far wider opportunity to wrap up whole networks, rather than just the individual fanatic willing to sacrifice him or herself. So while the real-world picture is focussed on a network-centric view, the focus of popular culture is the individual fanatic, which skews the public perception of what intelligence officers spend their days doing, and how they should do it.

New variant: 'Reds Under the Bed'

Popular cultural representations of intelligence suggest to the viewers who to classify as enemies and what to do about them. An extreme example of this occurs in series 6 of 24 when we are introduced to an Asian family being harassed by 'red-neck' locals. Our sympathies are channelled towards the Asian family, who seem, via their wide-eyed son, Ahmed Amur, to be the innocent victims of bigotry. The white American who steps in is portrayed in a positive light and all our liberal sensibilities are satisfied. But in a curious twist, Ahmed turns out to be aiding terrorists, which signals to us that these new variant 'reds under the bed' can be literally found anywhere; hardly a progressive message and one that validates racial profiling. Spooks is not immune to these tendencies either: in Series 2 it controversially portrayed the radicalisation of young British Muslims in Birmingham[20], which concludes in the young adolescent blowing himself up in a playground, while in Series 3 they depict terrorists from the former Soviet Union acquiring WMD from university researchers. This has real-world resonance due to the security clearance now required by PhD students to work with certain types of materials, although it is interesting that it is former Soviet citizens being portrayed—no one seems willing to portray Russia as the adversary any more, despite the rhetorical war that is raging between Britain and Russia. It is similarly notable that the British government's schizophrenic approach to immigration is brought to the fore by programmes like Spooks, namely the tension between what is seen as on the one hand an open door policy to migrants, and on the other a fear of these migrants becoming terrorist threats. The inconsistency does not need to be explained away—it is just an observable feature of the British political system, much as it is in America and Western Europe.

So, the depiction of counter-terrorism operations, save for Series 6 of Spooks, which focussed on the interaction between intelligence and diplomacy, has enough real-world content to convince the audience of its believability. But as, Sir David Omand has said in this volume, the depiction of his former job bears little relation to the bureaucratic realities of intelligence work in the western hemisphere. Oliver Mace, excellently played by Tim McIn-nerny, is an arch-Machiavellian character full versed in the dark arts, having served in Northern Ireland and is forced to resign when he is caught trying to send seven terror suspects to Egypt, without going through legal due proc-ess—something which is now commonly described as 'rendition' (Series 5, 2005). We can extend this idea of a slither of believability on to the depiction of racial groupings. The threats faced in *Spooks* and *24* are from recognisable 'others': Saudis, Iranians, Lebanese, Syrians, Turks, Algerians, 'generic' Mus-lims, Serbs and post-Soviets provide the mainstay of the threats in these pro-grammes. The outliers in these groups are the Serbs and post-Soviets who fit outside of the now classic Islamic 'other'. Yet they do fit neatly into groups who have been 'othered' by western political and media circles—the Serbs notably in 1999 in the run-up to the Kosovo campaign and in 2008 again over Kosovan independence, while the post-Soviets have been demonised as a hangover from the Cold War and because of the suggestion of endemic organ-ised criminality in the area. All of these adversaries are portrayed as being resourceful, indefatigable and without humanity. In the instances where these particular groupings are not involved, *Spooks* often reverts to an extremist and deranged character type—so Neo-Nazi groups (Series 1), Internet hackers (Series 2), extremist environmental campaigners (Series 5) and non-Muslim religious fundamentalists (also Series 5) become the adversary, still very much the 'other'. The two prevailing messages are that threats to 'our' society ema-nate from the Muslim world (both internally and externally), and from those with strongly-held views, which sit outside of mainstream liberal norms. Were Michel Foucault still alive he would have a field day—these messages clearly resonate with prevailing government ones and so it can be argued that they help to condition public responses to these particular groups, alerting them to the immediacy of the threats and dampening down their willingness to con-test the approaches adopted by the state.[21]

The threats from these adversaries is further exaggerated by the portrayal of the acts they are willing to commit against British and American targets. The easy use of weapons of mass destruction puts them beyond any sympathy the audience might have. In *24* the terrorists have twice been willing to use nuclear weapons against America and twice to use biological and nerve agents. In *Spooks* their adversaries have also tried to use nerve agents, radiological devices and to unleash a flood in London. It would be ridiculous in these circum-stances for the programmes to have engaged in a sustained moralising debate about whether American or British foreign policy may have precipitated these attacks.[22] The extreme actions of these fictional terrorists remove the possibility of debate and thus further cement the 'othering' of these adversaries. This is a shame, not for any hand-wringingly liberal reason, but because one of the key lessons of successful counter-insurgency campaigns is the ability to take the heat out of insurgencies and other politically motivated violence through understanding and countering the political grievances of the enemy and either appeasing enough of the moderates to make the insurgency unviable or to counter the grievances altogether. The messages coming out of these intelligence-focussed entertainment programmes does not allow the public, and by extension the policy sphere, to consider these questions properly.

Re-writing Imperial Grandeur—James Bond

Winston Churchill famously said he wanted to set the continent alight with the Special Operations Executive (SOE), a series of stay-behind armies and force multipliers aimed at providing robust resistance to the occupying Nazi armies of the Second World War. The SOE was given free reign to conduct guerrilla operations, assassinations and to arm and assist resistance movements as they saw fit. It was the perfect breeding ground for a different kind of intelligence-led special forces, one that made the most of the resources available to it, and thought on its feet to create devastating effects.

One such exponent was Patrick Leigh Fermor, scourge of the German Wehrmacht on the island of Crete. Classically educated, polite, and dapper Leigh Fermor could have been the template on which James Bond was modelled. As a fluent Greek speaker, he helped to organise the Cretan resistance in 1943–44, but Fermor was more than just an adept guerrilla fighter and organiser; he was a true gent, and after the war proved himself to be a very able scholar and writer too.[23] The qualities that he and other members of the SOE showed during the Second World War were taken forward in exaggerated form into the Cold War by the cinematic portrayal of Ian Fleming's James Bond, and the characterisations were also a product of the author's experience in naval intelligence, although not completely autobiographical, as contemporary debates have pointed to a number of figures who might have provided inspiration for the James Bond character.

Bond was the ultimate Cold War warrior, the threat from SMERSH—an organisation that recruited from the USSR but was dedicated to trying to engineer war between the west and the Soviet Union—was ubiquitous. This can be construed as a proxy for the fear of the USSR which was all-pervasive in political and media circles. In a similar way to the present day the threat was immediate, and as per the logic of mutually assured destruction, all consuming. The cumulative effect of these factors is a suffocating quality. The Bond films were the perfect relief for this kind of tension. It also repositioned Britain from the post-imperial and bankrupt world power it was after WWII, to a vigorous and centre stage character in the international system. The corollary of Bond would be seen in Michael Caine's portrayal of Harry Palmer, a spy who suspects his own agency of foul play with leading scientists in the *Ipcress File* (1965). Caine becomes the anti-establishment hero to Bond's inherently establishment hero.

One of the social utilities of James Bond was that he provided some welcome relief to the drudgery of post-war Britain, for internal British consumption and also for export around the world. Bond was well dressed, well groomed, smart, witty, resourceful and a hit with the ladies. The sexual politics of James Bond films belong to an era where warrior heroes rescued damsels in distress, and homosexuality was illegal and socially taboo. Honor Blackman's character 'Pussy Galore' was a lesbian who Bond 'converts' to heterosexuality, something that Germaine Greer argues is the ultimate straight male fantasy.[24] Jeremy Black argues that Fleming's ambivalence towards homosexuality comes from two sources. First, that he saw heterosexuality as *normal* and homosexuality as *problematic* and second, that the homosexuality of Guy Burgess (a high profile British intelligence defector) rendered all gay men inherently untrustworthy.[25] Thus Bond is constantly confronted by adversaries who are gay. For example, Blofeld is protected by lesbians in *Diamonds are Forever* (1971), and in *From Russia With Love* (1963), gay intellectuals are highlighted as the enemies of progress. Progressive politics this ain't, but an accurate portrayal of mainstream societal values in the 1960s and 70s it is. Indeed James Bond can even be seen as a violent reaction to the sexual liberation of the 1960s. He presents a particular model of heterosexuality, as the straight male hero figure, who all women want to be seduced by. The Bond films of the modern era, *Die Another Day* (2002) and *Casino Royale* (2006) observe this misogyny with an irreverent air, signalling just enough distance from it to make it acceptable viewing for politically correct twenty-first century audiences.

What any of this tells us about intelligence is open to question. On one level the description of intelligence officers as being Bond-like is fanciful, although we can see these super-hero character traits leak forward into 'Tom Quinn' and 'Adam Carter' in *Spooks*, and to 'Jack Bauer' in *24*. Bond represents a clear example of how some parts of the British security apparatus, military and *Daily Mail* and *Daily Express*-reading Britain sees itself on the international stage, while Bond's sexual politics can still be seen in the so-called 'lad's mags' of *For Him Magazine (FHM)*, *Loaded*, and *Nuts*, among others. So there are clear resonances with other popular cultural reference points, but the operational elements depicted in Bond films lend themselves far more to the experiences of the SOE, than they do to any intelligence reality since. Ironically one has to look to a film about the Stasi for a more accurate view of intelligence methods.

The public relations function of intelligence programming

Suggesting that television dramas serve a public relations function for government and intelligence agencies might sound like the stuff of conspiracy theories. Indeed, one of the more lurid claims made during the 1990s was that the popular SF drama *The X-Files* was softening the public up for revelations that humans had made contact with alien life forms.[26] However, in the case of intelligence dramas there is good evidence for this link. One early example was in the drama *The FBI*, which ran from the mid-1960s to mid-1970s, which was endorsed and advised by J. Edgar Hoover, the head of the FBI until his death in 1972.

Soon after the 9/11 attacks President Bush's political counsellor Karl Rove met with the Motion Picture Association of America and various film producers to ensure that the war on terror was represented in a certain way. Rove was allegedly keen to ensure that the movie houses did not present GWOT as a Samuel Huntingdon-esque 'clash of civilisations'. This clearly has not happened, with the movie houses depicting GWOT exactly in these terms. It has not been unhelpful to the Bush Administration—helping to reduce levels of opposition to counter-terrorism legislation. Similarly there has been some interaction between the Security Service in the UK and the actors and producers of *Spooks*, although, there is no evidence of these government sources suggesting particular story lines. The writers of *Spooks* have been inspired by certain events in the real world, such as the conspiracy theories surrounding the death of Princess Diana, the July 7, 2005 London bombings and the current diplomatic impasse with Iran. They have moved from being dramatists to docu-dramatists, engaging with half understandings of news stories and privileging the role of intelligence agencies in dealing with such threats. They offer snap-shots or faux glimpses into the secret world of intelligence that serve to exaggerate some of the threats and reassure us, the viewing public, of the bravery and competence of intelligence officers, their agents, and their political handlers, which are all useful messages for the vigilant state to have circulating.

Worryingly, though, the production teams believe themselves to be accurate portrayers of intelligence and counter terrorism activity. The *24* team is said to compose of writers who have done 'heavy research' in counter-terrorism, while *Spooks* script-writers play down their links to the intelligence agencies and play up their skill as informed writers of pacey drama related to news stories of the day.[27] Such over-confidence feeds into the assuredness of the drama, and through to the viewers so that both the public and some expert audiences believe that this is how counter-terrorism is done in the real world—a reality that is created through the absence of better information.

One aspect of intelligence work that is overlooked by popular programmes is the role of private intelligence in society. The growing number of private intelligence companies and their publicly revealed activities against, for example, the McLibel protesters, the Campaign Against the Arms Trade, and more recently against the environmentalists 'Plane Stupid' all point to a significant level of activity that is now part of the total intelligence picture.[28] Some of the things private intelligence officers have been accused of doing might make for reasonable television; the 'Romeo agents' used in the McLibel investigation would be just the sort of thing for late evening television drama.[29] But this now important area of intelligence activity only appears in the public's consciousness when a perfect storm of private intelligence officer error—which is common across all the examples above—is coupled with entrepreneurial activists and a receptive media. These activities, as the proliferation of business intelligence companies and articles attest, are now mainstream. The fragmentary view of intelligence presented by the media would lead you not to think so, focussing as it does, on government intelligence.

The representation of intelligence in popular culture has proved to be useful for government and the agencies alike, as it shows them in a good and often heroic light. The public relations work of explaining threats and profiling adversaries, coupled with positive depictions of intelligence work, has gone a long way to make the official case for the war against terror. These efforts should be seen as being highly political: they use outlandish examples and offer little reasonable space for the viewer to consider alternative approaches, something that should be of concern to all those who do not wish uncritically to support all government activity. Furthermore, these representations show only one type of intelligence activity—covert state activity leading to an intervention. They do not show routine state intelligence, nor do they show the work of private intelligence firms. This myopia skews public perception of intelligence work, revealing a mere fragment of what goes on, leading to a general false consciousness about government security and intelligence. In other words it is a diversion from reality masquerading as an interpretation of reality.

Being Bond—the rise and rise of video games

The personal computer and the games console have come a long way in the last twenty-five years. The realism of their graphical depictions of scenarios, enemies and towns means that games-players, including this author, can be temporarily transported into imaginary worlds to confront all sorts of digital enemies, albeit with a very 'real world' feel to them. There are not many intelligence titles. There are *24* and *James Bond* concessions, and there are also *Tom Clancy* covert-ops games and those that utilise the art of the special forces on intelligence-led missions. At the other end of the spectrum there are strategy games, involving some kind of basic intelligence information and judgements to be made by the player—these include the highly successful *Medieval Total War* (2007) game on personal computers. The majority of titles to be discussed in this short section come from the military genres and, appear on personal computer and Sony Playstation consoles, solely because they are the ones I have experience of.

The importance of these games are the opportunity they present for players to practise at real-world scenarios, without the obvious penalties of the real world, such as injury, death or judicial process. They allow the player to mull over appropriate tactics and ethical concerns in a world devoid of human contact or social mediation. What struck me about these virtual realities was that the concern for the safety of innocents all but vanished in an instant playing games such as *Men of Valor* (2004) and proportionately as a principle of war disappeared remarkably quickly when playing *Call of Duty 4: Modern Warfare* (2007). Being a virtual gunner in the AC-130 ground-support aircraft, with thermal imaging, and a graphic representation that looked eerily like that one might see on the television news, brought to mind that these games might indeed be training the next generation of games-playing adolescents to be effective unmanned aerial vehicle operators. It is surely no coincidence that the Predator's controls are very similar to those of a Playstation games console; a readymade supply of UAV operatives is growing up among us, just as the casual violence of games like *Grand Theft Auto* has been linked to incidences of violence among teenagers. The kill-chain on one of these games is, for obvious entertainment reasons, very short. Nick Broomfield's film *The Battle for Haditha* (2007) showed a similar picture of UAV operators engaged in the Haditha theatre—the line between the virtual and real worlds in this regard is alarmingly slim and our response to these activities, if they were happening in London or New York, would be loud and sustained. The relative value of life is an issue that has been brought up by human rights activists but is one that remains underexplored by society and unacknowledged by the political classes. The potential for retributive responses from Muslim communities who see their human rights as worth less than those of secular or Christian citizens is profound—and yet both the media and political signals we receive suggest that this disparity really exists.

The realism of cities, as in *The Getaway* (2002), a game about organised crime in London, allows one to become even more involved in the action and the story line, while the *Grand Theft Auto* series has similarly been remarked upon for its reality—certainly in terms of the way the gamer can interact with virtual characters and cities. The *Call of Duty* games advertise themselves as having been developed with the US Army as training tools, much as *Close Combat* (2002) and *Armor Battle* had been in 1983, allowing tank commanders to move around a virtual battlefield. The links between military utility and video games seem legion and presumably the nearer we get to a robot infantryman, rather than just UAVs, the nearer we will come to utilising the legions of gameplayers honed on moving around cities and making kill judgements on what they see on screen.[30] The messages we receive about people and governments from the developing world and people of different faiths become particularly important in operational scenarios, and indeed in activities that play out policing and counter-terrorism, for example.

So, what does the player gain from these games, and what are their limitations? The games force the player down a series of proscribed choices. For example, titles covering insurgencies in the Middle East do not offer the player an opportunity to try to create some kind of localised political solution, or to remove local support from the insurgents. The choices are somewhat more limited—whether to engage with the enemy or go round him. The go-round option, both in conventional military and policing terms, usually means delaying the aggressive contact until a later time. The game play is also linear—moving from one scenario to another, hence measuring success is established from the outset. Now, a game in which one can negotiate with an enemy, engage in patient diplomacy and conceive an elegant solution is not going to be *that* entertaining. Indeed, aside from the *Total War* strategy games it might be more interesting to watch paint dry. Given that these games are played obsessively by teenagers, and academics in their early 30s, I think it is important to question the political messages that are propagated by them and in particular, how these entertainment formats contribute to the mix of educational messages about security and military power, and indeed about how one treats 'others'?

Watching *The Battle for Haditha*, any of the main television news channels and then playing *Call of Duty 4*—it is astonishing how close they are in their visual representations of insurgents and battlefields. We will only know the effects of the repetitive and dehumanising aspects of these video games in ten to fifteen years time, when the youths who have played them become functioning adults in society and members of the security and military apparatus. As societies we have not equipped them to challenge and question militarised responses to counter-terrorism problems; all of their cultural cues suggest the answer involves overwhelming force.

Popular culture and intelligence—where's the beef?

Watching programmes and films about the panoply of intelligence activities is an enjoyable diversion from reality, which is why so many are made, and why they are so widely watched. The more serious point about this genre is that it does have a real world effect on those watching it. Films and television programmes provide sometimes the only information the viewer has about the intelligence services and counter-terrorism policy. So the way that intelligence, intelligence officers, agents, politicians, terrorists and adversaries are portrayed can be viewed as a version of the truth, a form of docu-drama. This does not happen in a vacuum: the 'education' of the masses about intelligence is informed not only by popular culture, but by the media (of all hues), literature, prejudice and even on occasion by humble academics. More important perhaps is that these dramatised accounts create new realities in which policymakers and intelligence officers work. Phillipe Sands' book on torture, *Torture Team: Uncovering War Crimes in the Land of the Free (2008)*, shows an alarming account of how far the imagined reality can influence the real world.

So, popular culture is but one of many ways into the subject, but it forms the most persuasive, and the most immediate. For a programme like *24*, which is filmed in real time, the suspense and the rapidity of the plot twists and the

217

seriousness of the stories force the viewers to make emotional rather than rational decisions about the events. Torture becomes a rational mode of intelligence collection when mapped out against the ticking time-bomb we can see on the other half of the screen. But we know, from the Second World War experiences of Latchmere House in London and subsequent psychological studies, that torture is a hopelessly unreliable means of intelligence collection. This delusion of counterterrorism is unhelpful to our understanding of intelligence practice today and feeds notions that the viewing public is being conditioned to accept certain unpalatable practices. Of course, viewed in a wider context, this moment in history is one of the few times when torture has been viewed as being unacceptable. Stepping back to the time of Sir Francis Walsingham—the father of modern intelligence—and suggesting that torture was taboo would have been deemed to be some kind of heresy. Indeed, right up to the Second World War there was seen to be a utility in the practice. The modern prohibition on torture is almost an historical anomaly—hence it would be curious if the entertainment industry eschewed something so visually striking, emotionally resonant and historically engrained as this. There is however an interesting disjuncture between the human rights agendas espoused by all western governments, their easy recourse to torture and extra-legal measures in these 'extraordinary times' and their depiction in counter-terrorism dramas. It seems likely in this instance that the public is more reticent about these tactics than the government, which is often not the case.

So, we should cast a critical eye over an industry that establishes and repeats ad nauseum such cliches. Intelligence officers that always show perfect judgement, senior officers who are always politically involved, but who tend to ignore their flawed political masters, are not an accurate or positive set of signals about the nature of government intelligence. Furthermore, agents are to generally be mistrusted, and moles and double-agents invariably end up dead. Politicians are driven exclusively by electoral advantage and ill-thought schemes (*Spooks* and *24* bring this out nicely), while the enemy is invariably without scruple, pursuing a political agenda one would be hard-pressed to find in any sanatorium. The technologies involved in state espionage are always flawless—satellites are always positioned in the right place, at the right time. Imagery and signals intelligence is always in perfect view, giving clear sight to the analysts, who are able to bring incredibly disparate pieces of information together at lightning speed into cogent and actionable intelligence. The only time the British Joint Intelligence Committee is mentioned is when it suddenly acquires rogue tendencies (*Spooks*) and no intelligence agent has yet to undergo a Scott (1996), a Hutton (2003) or Butler (2004) inquiry (save for one court case in *Spooks*) and officers can be killed off with only the minimum of fuss and accountability. All are a vast distance away from the realities of modern western intelligence.

Ultimately what purpose does this entertainment serve? Is it purposely designed to reinforce a certain view of the world, or does it just do that incidentally? It would be an extreme leap of faith to suggest that the entertainments industry was rigged by governments to shape our view of the international system, although we can look to *24* to see what happens when former intelligence officers are brought in to help with the scripts and the influence this has on the policy arena. No, these programmes are part of a 'fog of perception' that reinforces a securitized way of thinking about the world and about issues of terrorism and by extension migration. As this fog gets thicker our politicians and security professionals have far less scope to de-securitize their responses. All the cultural indicators validate the status quo and the public also believes that these tactics work. But these docu-dramas are merely diversions from reality, showing fragments of intelligence activity—as a result we should enjoy them, but guard against their seductive but counterproductive charms.

AFTERWORD

Are the professions of spy and journalist really that different? Both strive to seek knowledge, to increase understanding, and to better inform their consumers. Both professions have a range of contacts through which they garner knowledge. Information is central to both and has to be subjected to the same sorts of questions, commonly known as the Ws: What is the information? Where was it gathered? Why has it been volunteered? When was it obtained? How was it acquired? Who was involved? Such basic questions are not restricted to these disciplines alone, yet they are central to assessments of source material. Historically there have been obvious differences in the ways and means by which information is obtained, but in an increasingly fast-paced world, the gulf is not as large as it once was. Sources are cultivated in both worlds, as is the need to prioritise targets. Both jobs have the verification of sources as a common concern. In both it is crucial to admit what is not known. Similarly issues of timeliness, accuracy and reliability are central tenets. Dissemination is equally as important, in particular knowing who the audience is, gauging at what level a subject should be pitched, and the delivery method itself.

Despite the similarities, there are, however, a series of crucial differences between the professions of spy and journalist. Perhaps the largest difference concerns the implications of getting it wrong—a journalist can offer an apology or issue a revised report; the spy, by contrast, has far greater weight on their shoulders. One need only consider the series of intelligence failures in the early 21st-century to see the implications of a false call. Furthermore there is a subtle difference in the nature of what is reported—is it mere news or rather opinions? In theory the former should be more objective than the latter, but which is more important for the policymaker and the member of public to receive?

AFTERWORD

While there are similarities and differences in the nature of the work, a more important question is to consider how the 24 hour news culture has affected the culture of intelligence. Carmen Medina, an analyst in the CIA, has written about the different circumstances engendered by this process. In the Cold War, she argues, policymakers needed a service to tell them what was happening in the world: this could only be provided with any degree of accuracy by the intelligence agencies; today, the media can fill such a task and probably, in all likelihood, faster. In the Cold War policymakers needed assistance in understanding the nuances of foreign cultures and what events meant; today the plethora of 'experts' in the media fulfil such a role. In the Cold War intelligence agencies had unique information; today journalists can access areas and people that government officials cannot.[1]

Does this mean that the profession of intelligence is doomed and all that is needed is an expansion of the journalist cadre? Obviously not. Intelligence is arguably more important today than it has ever been. The urgent need for information is far greater than it was during the Cold War, with its emphasis on strategic observations of the Soviet Union, due to the broader range of concerns. Does it mean that the two disciplines should move closer together? Perhaps a greater amount of reciprocity would be useful; after all, how can the performance of the intelligence community be judged, and more importantly how can trust be regained and retained, if the public are left ignorant of what is done on their behalf? There are problems of getting too close, as several chapters in this book demonstrate, but with information being the mode of warfare of the twenty-first century, is enough being done to bring the battle to the airwaves? With the pace of the world speeding up after 9/11 we can all only hope that answers will become clearer before it becomes too late.

GLOSSARY

ATIP	Access to Information Program
AUSCANUKUK	Used to describe the relationship between Commonwealth and US intelligence.
BBC	British Broadcasting Corporation
BND	German Federal Intelligence Service
CASIS	Canadian Association for Security and Intelligence Studies
CBC	Canadian Broadcasting Corporation
CENTCOM	United States Central Command
CIA	Central Intelligence Agency (US)
CSIS	Canadian Security Intelligence Service
CTAG	Combined Threat Assessment Group (New Zealand)
CTG	Counter Terrorist Group
CTU	Counterterrorism Unit
DGSE	*Direction Générale de la Sécurité Extérieure*
DNI	Director of National Intelligence (US)
DST	*Direction de la Surveillance du Territoire*
ECHR	European Convention on Human Rights
EU	European Union
EUCOM	European Command (US)
FBI	Federal Bureau of Investigation (US)
FBIS	Foreign Broadcasting Information Service (US)
FCO	Foreign and Commonwealth Office (UK)
GCHQ	Government Communications Headquarters (UK)
GTAZ	German Joint Counterterrorism Center
GWOT	Global War on Terror

HUMINT	Human intelligence
IAEA	International Atomic Energy Agency
ICT	Information and Communication Technology revolution
IRD	Information Research Department (former department of the UK's Foreign and Commonwealth Office)
ITAC	Integrated Threat Assessment Center (Canada)
ITV	Independent Television (UK)
JIC	Joint Intelligence Committee (UK)
JTAC	Joint Terrorism Analysis Centre (UK)
KGB	Committee for State Security (Soviet Intelligence)
MI5	Common denomination for the UK Security Service
MI6	Common denomination for the UK Secret Intelligence Service
MVD	Russian Ministry of Internal Affairs
NATO	North Atlantic Treaty Organisation
NCTC	National Counterterrorism Center
NNWS	Non-nuclear weapon states
NPT	Non-proliferation Treaty
NSA	National Security Agency (US)
NTAC	National Terrorism Analysis Center (Australia)
NYPD	New York Police Department
OSC	Open Source Center (US)
OSINT	Open Source Intelligence
OSS	Office of Strategic Services (US)
OWA	Operative Working Arrangement
PCTEG	Policy Counterterrorism Evaluation Group (US)
RAF	Royal Air Force (UK)
RICU	Research Information Communication Unit
SAS	Special Air Service (UK)
SBS	Special Boat Service (UK)
SDECE	*Service de Documentation Extérieure et de Contre-Espionnage*
SHAPE	Supreme Headquarters Allied Powers Europe (NATO)
SIPRNET	Secret Internet Protocol Router Network (US Department of Defense)
SIS	Secret Intelligence Service (UK)
SOE	Special Operations Executive (UK)

STIB	Scientific and Technical Intelligence Branch (UK, Cold War)
TASS	Telegraph Agency of the Soviet Union (Soviet era newspaper, that is now the official newspaper of Russia)
UAV	Unmanned Aerial Vehicle
WMD	Weapons of Mass Destruction

NOTES

INTRODUCTION

1. Ed Husain, *The Islamist: Why I Joined Radical Islam in Britain, What I Saw Inside and Why I Left*, Penguin: London, 2007; Omar Nasiri, *Inside the Global Jihad: How I Infiltrated Al Qaeda and Was Abandoned by Western Intelligence*, Hurst: London, 2006.
2. William Dinan and David Miller (eds), *Thinker, Faker, Spinner, Spy: Corporate PR and the Assault on Democracy*, Pluto: London, 2007; Nick Davies, *Flat Earth News: An Award-winning Reporter Exposes Falsehood, Distortion and Propaganda in the Global Media*, Chatto & Windus: London, 2008.

1. REGULATION BY REVELATION? INTELLIGENCE, THE MEDIA AND TRANSPARENCY

1. Murrey Marder, 'The Press and the Presidency: Silencing the Watchdog', *Nieman Reports* (The Nieman Foundation for Journalism at Harvard University), Spring 2008. http://www.nieman.harvard.edu/reports/08–1NRspring/index.html accessed 2 April 2008.
2. Those who took an upbeat outlook include Alvin Toffler, *The Third Wave* (New York: Morrow, 1980); Walter Wriston, *The Twilight of Sovereignty: How the Information Revolution is Transforming Our World* (New York: Charles Scribner and Sons, 1992); Nicholas Negroponte, *Being Digital* (New York: Knopf, 1995).
3. Matthew Aid, 'The Time of Troubles: The US National Security Agency in the Twenty-First Century, *Intelligence and National Security*, 15, 1 (Autumn 2000), pp. 1–32.
4. Alastair Roberts, *Blacked Out, Government Secrecy in the Information Age* (Cambridge: Cambridge University Press, 2006).
5. J. Scahill, *Blackwater: The Rise of the World's most Powerful Mercenary Army* (New York: Nation, 2007); R.P. Young, *Licensed to Kill: Hired Guns in the War on Terror* (New York: Crown, 2006); R.I. Rotberg *Battling Terrorism in the Horn of Africa* (Washington: Brookings, 2005).

6. Margaret Keck and Kathryn Sikkink, *Activists Beyond Borders* (Ithaca: Cornell University Press, 1998).

7. Private information.

8. Gordon Stewart, *The Cloak and Dollar War* (London: Lawrence and Wishhart, 1953).

9. Hugh Wilford, *The Mighty Wurlitzer; How the CIA Played America* (Harvard University Press, 2008), pp. 225–48.

10. An example was Claire Sterling's book, *The Terror Network* (1981) which was translated into 22 languages, and argued that Soviet Union was a major source of direction and backing behind terrorist groupings around the world. Some have alleged this made uncritical use of material that had originally been generated as propaganda.

11. Oleg Penkovsky, *The Penkovsky Papers: The Russian Who Spied for the West* (NY: Doubleday, New York, 1966); A. Foote, *Handbook for Spies* (London, Museum Press, 1949). Much of the material on Foote's book is now available at KV2/1616, PRO.

12. Memorandum for the Record by DCI McCone, 'Discussion with the President', 1 September 1964, Doc.49, *FRUS*, 1964–1968, Volume X, National Security Policy, 1964–8 (Washington DC: GPO, 2001).

13. *Final Report of the Select Committee to Study Government Operations With Respect to Intelligence Activities*, (Washington DC: GPO, April 1976) pp. 191–201.

14. Loch K. Johnson, 'The CIA and the Media', *Intelligence and National Security*, 1, 2 (May 1986), pp. 146–7.

15. Johnson, 'The CIA and the Media', pp. 162–3.

16. Roy Varner and Wayne Collier, *A Matter of Risk: The Incredible Inside Story of the CIA's Hughes Glomar Explorer Mission to Raise a Russian Submarine* (NY: Random House, 1978).

17. William Casey, DCI, Presentation of the American Society of Newspaper Editors, 9 April 1986, File 1, Box 27, William Odom papers, Library of Congress.

18. However, these files never materialised, 'C.I.A. Is Slow to Tell Early Cold War Secrets', *The Washington Post*, 8 April 1996. In 1998 George Tenet would announce that this promised declassification had been cancelled, citing among other things, concerns voiced by allied services and different priorities.

19. Christopher M. Jones, 'The CIA Under Clinton: Continuity and Change', *International Journal of Intelligence and Counterintelligence*, 14, 4 (October 2001), pp. 503—528.

20. Joshua Dean, 'Assault on the Mountain', *Government Executive*, 1 July 2000, http://www.govexec.com/features/0700/0700s3.htm accessed 23 April 2008.

21. The most famous example is perhaps John Young's Cryptome at http://cryptome.org/

22. Marcus Franda, *Governing the Internet: The Emergence of an International Regime*, (Boulder, CO: Lynne Rienner. 2001).

23. David Robb, *Operation Hollywood: How the Pentagon Shapes and Censors the Movies* (New York: Prometheus Books, 2004).

24. Kate Houghton, 'Subverting Journalism: Reporters and the CIA', *CPJ Special Report 1996*, http://www.cpj.org/attacks96/sreports/cia.html accessed 28 April 2008.

25. R. Jeffrey Smith and Dafna Linzer, 'Dismissed CIA Officer Denies Leak Role: Official Says Agency Is Not Asserting She Told of Secret Prisons', *The Washington Post*, 25 April 2006.

26. Matthew M. Aid, 'Declassification in Reverse: The US Intelligence Community's Secret Historical Document Reclassification Program', 21 February 2006, National Security Archive http://www.gwu.edu/~nsarchiv/NSAEBB/NSAEBB179/accessed 21 April 2008.

27. Anthea Temple, 'The spy who loved me', *The Guardian*, 2 October 2002.

28. P. McDermott, 'Withold and Control: Information in the Bush Administration', *Kansas Journal of Law and Public Policy*, 12 (2002), pp. 671–4.

29. Matthew M. Aid, 'Declassification in Reverse'.

30. Robert M. Chesney, 'State Secrets and the Limits of National Security Litigation', 75, 5/6 (2007), pp. 1249–1334.

31. Ted Gup, 'Investigative Reporting About Secrecy', *Nieman Reports*, (The Nieman Foundation for Journalism at Harvard University), Spring 2008. http://www.nieman.harvard.edu/reports/08-1NRspring/index.html accessed 2 April 2008.

32. Alastair Roberts, *Blacked Out*, pp. 129–30.

33. Thomas Fenton, *Bad News: The Decline of Reporting, the Business of News, and the Danger to Us All* (NY: HarperCollins, 2005).

34. Walter Pincus, 'Increase in Contracting Intelligence Jobs Raises Concerns', *The Washington Post*, 20 March 2006.

35. Steve Weinberg, 'The Book as an Investigative Vehicle for News', *Nieman Reports*, (The Nieman Foundation for Journalism at Harvard University), Spring 2007. http://www.nieman.harvard.edu/reports/07-1NRspring/index.html accessed 2 April 2008.

36. Seymour Hersh, *Chain of Command: The Road from 9/11 to Abu Ghraib* (London: HarperCollins, 2003); George Packer, *The Assassin's Gate: America in Iraq*, (New York: Farrar, Straus and Giroux, 2005).

37. Valerie Plame Wilson, *Fair Game: My Life as a Spy, My Betrayal by the White House*, (New York: Simon and Schuster, 2007); Joseph C. Wilson, *The Politics of Truth: Inside the Lies that Led to War and Betrayed my Wife's CIA Identity: A Diplomat's Memoir*. (New York: Carroll and Graf, 2004).

38. R. Jeffrey Smith and Dafna Linzer, 'Dismissed CIA Officer Denies Leak Role: Official Says Agency Is Not Asserting She Told of Secret Prisons', *The Washington Post*, 25 April 2006. Interestingly, at the request of the government, *The Washington Post* suppressed the details of the specific countries where the secret prisons were located.

39. Philip Shenon, 'Times Reporter Subpoenaed Over Source for Book', *The New York Times*, 1 February 2008; Philip Shenon, 'Leak Inquiry Said to Focus on Calls With Times', *The New York Times*, 12 April 2008.
40. Bob Drogin, *Curveball: Spies, Lies, and the Con Man Who Caused a War* (New York: Random House, 2007).
41. S. Aftergood, 'Classified Documents: Secrecy vs. Citizenship—In the digital age, there is an appetite for direct access to source documents', *Nieman Reports 2008*, (The Nieman Foundation for Journalism at Harvard University), Spring 2008. http://www.nieman.harvard.edu/reports/08-1NRspring/index.html accessed 2 April 2008.
42. Ibid.
43. The full story is narrated by Cryptome at http://cryptome.org/cia-iran.htm accessed 25 April 2008.
44. White House transcript, 'President Meets with Cabinet, Discusses National and Economic Security, The Cabinet Room', 7 October 2003, 11:42 A.M. EDT, available at http://www.whitehouse.gov/news/releases/2003/10/20031007-2.html accessed 27 April 2008.
45. Robert D. Novak, 'On the Shield Law, Good News and Bad', *The Washington Post*, 17 April 2008.

2. INTELLIGENCE SECRETS AND MEDIA SPOTLIGHTS: BALANCING ILLUMINATION AND DARK CORNERS

1. See Chapman Pincher chapter.
2. Such as the exposure of the role of Commander Buster Crabb in the botched and fatal frogman operation of 19 April 1956 to inspect the hull of the Soviet cruiser *Ordzhonikidze* in Portsmouth harbour that resulted in the resignation of the Chief of SIS.
3. http://www.aarclibrary.org/publib/church/reports/book1/pdf/ChurchB1_10_Domestic.pdf, accessed March 2008. See also the Richardson amendment to the Intelligence Authorization Act for Fiscal Year 1997 (H.R. 3259).
4. Andrew Defty, *Britain, America and Anti-Communist Propaganda 1945–53* (London: Routledge, 2004) and for a more downbeat view Paul Lashmar and James Oliver, *Britain's Secret Propaganda War: Foreign Office and the Cold War 1948–77* (London: Sutton Publishing, 1998).
5. Arjan Dasselar, *The Fifth Estate: on the Journalistic Aspects of the Dutch Blogosphere*, http://www.isopeda.nl/thefifthestate.pdf, accessed March 2008.
6. Marie Gillespie, *Audiences, Publics and Citizenship*, ESRC Research Report, at www.mediatingsecurity.com accessed March 2008.
7. Jeremy Paxman, 'Never mind the scandals: what's it all for?', The James MacTaggart Memorial Lecture, Friday 24 August 2007.
8. The insult from Sir Robin Day that caused Defence Secretary John Nott to storm out of such an interview in 1982.

9. Tony Blair, 'The challenge of the changing nature of communication on politics and the media', Reuter's speech, 12 June 2007, available at <http://news.bbc.co.uk/1/hi/uk_politics/6744581.stm>, accessed March 2008

10. Quoted by the BBC Political Correspondent Andrew Marr in the 2008 Bagehot Lecture, Queen Mary College, London

11. Paxman, op. cit.

12. For example, Henry Porter, 'The UK Government's manipulation of the case for longer periods of pre-charge detention', *The Observer*, 11 Nov 2007

13. Matthew d'Ancona, *Confessions of a hawkish hack: the media and the war on terror*, Philip Geddes Memorial lecture, 27 October 2006

14. A clumsy expression, but it avoids conceding to the extremists their self-appointed status. See Dr Douglas E. Streusand and Lt. Col. Harry D. Tunnell IV, *Choosing Words Carefully: Language to Help Fight Islamic Terrorism*, US National Defense University Center for Strategic Communication 23 May 2006

15. Simon Jenkins, 'These Fear Factory Speeches are Utterly Self-Defeating', *The Guardian* 7 Nov 2007

16. *Countering International Terrorism: The UK Strategy*, (London: HMSO Cm 6888, July 2006) para 5

17. As reported in *The Daily Telegraph* of 12 and 13 February 2003

18. General Sir Rupert Smith, *The Utility of Force*, London: Allen Lane (2005), p. 391

19. (Ayman al-Zawahiri to Abu Musab al-Zarqawi, 9 July 2005)

20. Donald Rumsfeld, citing Ayman Zawahiri, in The US Army Professional Writing Collection, http://www.army.mil/professionalwriting/volumes/volume4/july_2006/7_06_2.html accessed in March 2008

21. Marie Gillespie, *Audiences, Publics and Citizenship*, ESRC Preliminary Findings Report at www.mediatingsecurity.com

22. Jeremy Black, *The Politics of James Bond: From Fleming's Novels to the Big Screen* (Westport, CT Greenwood, 2001). Cited by Professor Peter Hennessy, The Hinsley Memorial lecture 2005, Cambridge St John's College.

23. Hansard, House of Commons 5th series, vol CLXXIV, 15 Dec 1924, col 674.

24. As discussed in Sir David Omand, 'Can we have the pleasure of the grin without seeing the cat? Must the effectiveness of secret agencies inevitably fade on exposure to the light?', *Intelligence and National Security*, Vol. 23, No. 3 (2008).

25. Mike McConnell, 'Overhauling Intelligence', *Foreign Affairs*, July/August 2007

26. For example, in the UK, Peter Oborne, *The Use and Abuse of Terror: The Construction of a False Narrative on the Domestic Terror Trail*, London: Centre for Policy Studies (2006) and for the US, John Mueller, *Overblown: How Politicians and the Terrorism Industry Inflate National Security Threats and Why We Believe Them* (New York, Free Press, 2006).

27. Sir David Omand, *The Dilemmas of Using Secret Intelligence for Public Security*, in Hennessy (ed.) The New Protective State, (London: Continuum, 2007)

28. I first heard this approach outlined by Mike Grannatt, former Head of the Government Information and Communication Service (GICS)

29. Sir David Omand, 'Ethical Guidelines in Using Secret Intelligence for Public Security', *Cambridge Review of International Affairs* Vol. 19, No. 4 December 2006.

30. E.g. Charlie Edwards, *National Security for the 21st century*, (London: Demos, December 2007) recommendation 10.

31. The UK emergency system is described at <http://www.co-ordination.gov.uk/response/recovery_guidance/generic_issues/media.aspx and the extensive BBC preparations at http://www.bbc.co.uk/connectinginacrisis/index.shtml.

32. See the Wilkinson chapter.

33. Tony Blair, op. cit.

34. Onora O'Neill, *Licence to Deceive*, (London: BBC, Reith Lectures 2002), 5th Lecture.

35. Cited by David Rose, *Spies and their Lies*, New Statesman 27 September 2007.

36. Remarks on Lessons from the World of Journalism, Woodrow Wilson International Centre, Washington DC, 13 Nov 2007.

3. TERRORISM AND THE MEDIA: THE INFORMATION WAR

1. Ayman Al-Zawahiri July 2005.

2. John Mackinlay, 'Is UK doctrine relevant to global insurgency?' The Journal of the Royal United Services Institute, April 2007.

3. Data from *Intelcenter*—available at http://www.intelcenter.com/QMS-PUB-v3-3.pdf (accessed 7 July 2008).

4. *NBC Nightly News*, 'Islamic extremist Web sites using fake video footage to present an anti-American view on the war in Iraq', 7th June 2007.

5. See http://www.secondlife.com (accessed 14 July 2008).

6. Robert O'Harrow Jr, 'Spies battleground turns virtual', *Washington Post*, February 6th 2008

7. Jason Burke, *Al Qaeda: The True Story of Radical Islam* (London: IB Tauris), 2004

8. 'A Web Q and A with Bin Laden's No. 2', *Der Spiegel*, January 15th 2008. (http://www.spiegel.de/international/world/0,1518,528680,00.html accessed 15 January 2008).

9. Editor, 'Jihadist website poll shows 95 per cent back Al-Qa'idah attack on Denmark', *BBC Monitoring*, 28 February 2008.

10. Daniel Kimmage, The Al Qaeda media nexus. An RFE/RL special report available at http://docs.rferl.org/en-US/AQ_Media_Nexus.pdf

11. Ibid.

12. BBC Monitoring, 'Jihadist forum claims USA Censoring Iraq, Afghan Insurgency Videos', *BBC Monitoring*, 29 February 2008.

13. Ibid.

14. Gordon Corera, 'Al Qaeda's 007', *The Times*, 16 January 2008; Gordon Corera, 'The World's Most Wanted Cyber-Jihadist', *BBC News Website*, 16 January 2008.

15. Leaderless Jihad by Marc Sageman (University of Pennsylvania Press 2008), p. 116.

16. John Mackinlay, 'Is UK doctrine relevant to global insurgency?', *The Journal of the Royal United Services Institute*, April 2007.

4. GOOD ANTHROPOLOGY, BAD HISTORY: AMERICA'S CULTURAL TURN IN THE WAR ON TERROR

1. The analysis, opinions and conclusions expressed or implied in his chapter are those of the author and do not necessarily represent the views of the JSCSC, the UK Ministry of Defence or any other government agency.

2. 'Army Transformation, Implications for the Future.' Statement of Major General Robert Scales, House Armed Services Committee, 15 July, 2004.

3. Saddam's pre-war decision-making has been reconstructed from new intelligence by Kevin Woods, James Lacey and Williamson Murray, 'Saddam's delusions: The View From the Inside' *Foreign Affairs* 85:3 (May/June 2006), pp. 2–28; Michael R. Gordon and Bernard E. Trainor, *Cobra II: the Inside Story of the Invasion and Occupation of Iraq* (New York, 2006), esp. pp. 55–75.

4. See Gerhard L. Weinberg, 'Hitler's Image of the United States' *American Historical Review* 69:4 (July 1964), pp. 1001–21. On how aggressors can draw false confidence from their sense of cultural supremacy, see Michael P. Fischerkeller, 'David versus Goliath: Cultural Judgments in Asymmetric Wars', *Security Studies*, 7:4 (Summer 1998), pp. 1–43.

5. Carl von Clausewitz, *On War*, 1:1, ed. and trans. Michael Howard and Peter Paret, rev. ed. (Princeton, 1984), p. 88.

6. This definition is derived from A. Macmillan, K. Booth and R. Trood, 'Strategic Culture' in K. Booth and R. Trood (eds) *Strategic Cultures in the Asia-Pacific Region* (Basingstoke, 1999), pp. 3–26, p. 8 and Alistair Johnston, *Cultural Realism: Strategic Culture and Grand Strategy in Chinese History* (Princeton, 1997), p. ix-x, p. 36: Jack Snyder, *The Soviet Strategic Culture: Implications for Limited Nuclear Operations* (Santa Monica, 1977), p. 8; Kerry Longhurst, *Germany and the Use of Force* (Manchester, 2004), pp. 17–18.

7. Sun Tzu, *The Art of War*, III.18.

8. See Tim Benbow, *The Magic Bullet? Understanding the Revolution in Military Affairs* (London, 2004), p. 80.

9. Ralph Peters, *Fighting for the Future: Will America Triumph?* (Mechanicsburg, 1999), p. 30.

10. Tony Corn, 'Clausewitz in Wonderland' *Policy Review* (September 2006), at http://www.policyreview.org/000/corn2.html, (accessed 2 October 2006); see

also Montgomery McFate, 'Anthropology and Counterinsurgency: The Strange Story of their Curious Relationship' *Military Review* 85 (March-April 2005), pp. 24–38.

11. FM 3–24 *Counterinsurgency* (December 2006), foreword, David H. Petraeus and James F. Amos.

12. Robert H. Scales, 'Culture-centric Warfare' *Proceedings of the United States Naval Institute* 130:10 (October 2004), pp. 32–36.

13. Leo Docherty, *Desert of Death: A Soldier's Journey from Iraq to Afghanistan* (London, 2007), pp. 191–2.

14. Secretary of Defense Memo, 'Defence Capabilities to Transition to and from Hostilities' 8 October 2004, cited in Steven C. Boraz, 'Behind the Curve in Culture-centric skills' *Proceedings of the United States Naval Institute* 131:6 (June 2005), pp. 41–45.

15. 'Knowing the Enemy: Can Social Scientists redefine the 'war on terror'? *New Yorker* (December 2006), pp. 40–69.

16. M. McFate, 'The military utility of understanding adversary culture', *Joint Force Quarterly* (July 2005) 38: pp. 42–48, p. 43.

17. Raphael Patai, *The Arab Mind* (New York, 1971, 2002 edn); Matthew B. Stannard, 'Montgomery McFate's Mission: Can one Anthropologist possibly steer the course in Iraq?' *San Francisco Chronicle* 29 April, 2007.

18. John McCain, 'An Enduring Peace Built on Freedom' *Foreign Affairs* (Nov/Dec 2007), pp. 19–34.

19. Ryan Dilley, 'Lessons from Lawrence of Arabia' *BBC News* 9 April 2004 at http://news.bbc.co.uk/1/hi/magazine/3605261.stm, (accessed 19 January, 2007).

20. 'Can a lull be turned into a real Peace?' *Economist* 15 December 2007, p. 30.

21. Robert D. Kaplan, 'A Historian for Our Time' *Atlantic Monthly* (Jan/Feb 2007), pp. 78–84.

22. John Keegan, *A History of Warfare* (London, 1993), p. 387.

23. John Keegan, 'In this war of civilisations, the West will prevail' *Telegraph* 8 October, 2001.

24. Geoffrey Parker, *The Cambridge History of Warfare* (Cambridge, 2005), esp. pp. 1–15.

25. Paul Bracken, *Fire in the East: The Rise of Asian Military Power and the Second Nuclear Age* (New York, 1999), p. 130.

26. Victor Davis Hanson, *Carnage and Culture: Landmark Battles in the Rise of Western Power* (New York, 2001), esp. pp. 1–27.

27. John Poole, *Tactics of the Crescent Moon* (Emerald Isle, NC.: Posterity Press, 2001), xxviii, p. 5.

28. William Lind, foreword to J. Poole, *Phantom Soldier: The Enemy's Answer to US Firepower* (2001).

29. Robert M. Cassidy, *Counterinsurgency and the Global War on Terror: Military Culture and Irregular War* (London, 2006), p. 3.

30. This oversimplified view appears in Richard H. Shultz Jr. and Andrea J. Dew, *Insurgents, Terrorists and Militias: The Warriors of Contemporary Combat* (New York, 2006), pp. 5–6:

31. 'Army Transformation, Implications for the Future.' Statement of Major General Robert Scales, House Armed Services Committee, 15 July, 2004.

32. T.E. Lawrence, *Seven Pillars of Wisdom: A Triumph* (New York, 1935), p. 38.

33. Statement by Thomas E. Ricks paraphrasing French counterinsurgency expert David Galula, 'In Iraq, Military Forgot Lessons of Vietnam: Early Missteps by US Left Troops Unprepared for Guerrilla Warfare', *Washington Post,* 23 July 2006, A01.

34. Patrick Devenny, Robert McLean, 'The Battle for Basra' *The American Spectator,* 1 November 2005.

35. Mona Mahmoud, Maggie O'Kane and Ian Black, 'UK has left behind murder and chaos, says Basra police chief', *Guardian*, 17 December 2007.

36. See Felix Gilbert, 'Machiavelli: The Renaissance of the Art of War' *Makers of Modern Strategy: From Machiavelli to the Nuclear Age* (Princeton University Press, 1986), pp. 11–31.

37. Niccolo Machiavelli, *Discourses on the First Ten Books of Titus Livius*, 7:XL.

38. As Christopher Lynch suggests, 'Interpretive Essay', in his translation of Niccolo Machiavelli, *Art of War* (Chicago, 20030, pp. 179–226, esp. 195–200.

39. Martin van Creveld, *The Transformation of War* (New York, 1991); for similar arguments, see Ralph Peters, 'The New Strategic Trinity' *Parameters* 28:4 (1998–9), pp. 73–9.

40. Stuart Kinross, 'Clausewitz and Low-Intensity Conflict', 27:1 *Journal of Strategic Studies* (March 2004), pp. 35–58; M.L.R. Smith, 'Strategy in an Age of 'Low-Intensity' Warfare' in Isabelle Duyvesteyn and Jan Angstrom (eds), *Rethinking the Nature of War* (London, 2005), pp. 28–64.

41. Carl von Clausewitz, *On War*, 6:26, ed. and trans. Michael Howard and Peter Paret, rev. ed. (Princeton University Press, 1984), p. 479.

42. For the influence of Clausewitz and appeals to his philosophy, see Michael I. Handel, *Masters of War: Classical Strategic Thought* (London, 1992, 1996 edn.), esp. pp. 1–17.

43. Alistair Johnston, *Cultural Realism: Strategic Culture and Grand Strategy in Chinese History* (Princeton, 1995), esp. pp. 175–242.

44. Jack Kelly, 'Al Qaeda fragmented, smaller, but still deadly', *USA Today*, 9 September 2002.

45. See Jessica Stern, 'When Bombers are Women' *Washington Post* 18 December 2003; Debra D. Zedalis, 'Female Suicide Bombers' *Strategic Studies Institute* (June 2004); Diaa Hadid, 'al Qaida uses women as suicide attackers' *Associated Press* 4 January 2008.

46. Arnon Regular, 'Mother of Two Becomes First Female Suicide Bomber for Hamas', *Haaretz* 16 January 2004, also discussed in Debra Zedalis, 'Female Suicide Bombers', *Strategic Studies Institute.*

47. Farhana Ali, 'Muslim Female Fighters: An Emerging Trend' *Terrorism Monitor: An In-Depth Analysis of the War on Terror* 3:21 (3 November, 2005), pp. 9–11, p. 10.

48. Harry G. Summers, Jr., *On Strategy: A Critical Analysis of the Vietnam War* (Novato, Calif.: Presidio Press, 1982), 1.

49. Quote from Philip Sabin, *Lost Battles: Reconstructing the Great Clashes of the Ancient World* (London, 2007), xi, also p. 29.

50. Peter Krentz, 'Deception in Archaic and Classical Greek Warfare' in Hans van Wees (ed.), *War and Violence in Ancient Greece* (London, 2000), pp. 167–200.

51. J.F. Verbruggen, *The Art of Warfare in Western Europe during the Middle Ages* (1977), pp. 327–335; Sean McGlynn, 'The Myths of Medieval Warfare', 44:1 *History Today* (1994), pp. 28–34.

52. Peter Layton, 'A new Arab Way of War' *US Naval Institute Proceedings* 129:3 (March 2003), pp. 62–65.

53. Jonathan Mirsky, 'John Keegan tells us that westerners 'fight face to face' while Orientals prefer 'ambush and deceit.' Really?' *The Guardian* 10 October 2001.

54. Cited in P.H. Liotta, 'Chaos as Strategy', *Parameters* (Summer, 2002), pp. 47–56, 51.

55. John Poole, *Tactics of the Crescent Moon: Militant Muslim Combat Methods* (Emerald Isle, 2004), pp. 3–19; Michael Dewar, *The Art of Deception in Warfare* (David and Charles, 1989), pp. 38–39.

56. American Anthropological Association, *Commission on the Engagement of Anthropology with the US Security and Intelligence Communities, Final Report,* November 4, 2007, p. 22.

57. As Colin Gray argues, 'Out of the Wilderness: Prime Time for Strategic Culture' *Comparative Strategy* 26 (2007), pp. 1–20, p. 16.

58. See Jeffrey Record on this point, 'The Use and Abuse of History: Munich, Vietnam and Iraq' *Survival* 49:1 (Spring 2007), pp. 163–180.

59. A point also made by Michael Desch, 'Culture versus Structure in Post-9/11 Security Studies' *Strategic Insights* IV:10 (October 2005),

60. Martin J. Muckian, 'Structural Vulnerabilities of Networked Insurgencies: Adapting to the New Adversary' *Parameters* (Winter 2006/7), pp. 14–25; Stephen Biddle, 'Seeing Baghdad, Thinking Saigon' *Foreign Affairs* (March/April 2006).

61. Alon Ben-David, 'Debriefing Teams Brand IDF Doctrine 'Completely Wrong,'' *Jane's Defence Weekly*, 3 January 2007, p. 7

5. OPEN SOURCE INTELLIGENCE AND NUCLEAR SAFEGUARDS

1. *Report to the President of the United States, The Commission on the Intelligence Capabilities of the United States Regarding Weapons of Mass Destruction,* 31 March 2005, p. 377.

2. OSC builds 'on the established expertise of the CIA's Foreign Broadcast Information Service (FBIS)—an organization that enjoys a long history of providing the

US government highly valued open source products and services. The Center's functions will include collection, analysis and research, training, and information technology management to facilitate government-wide access and use'. See: 'Establishment of the DNI Open Source Center', Central Intelligence Agency, 8 November 2005 (https://www.cia.gov/news-information/press-releases-statements/press-release-archive-2005/pr11082005.html).

3. *IAEA Safeguards: Staying Ahead of the Game*, IAEA, July 2007, pp. 6–7
4. Ibid., pp. 6–7
5. Ibid., pp. 6–7
6. Ibid., pp. 12–13.
7. Ibid., p. 16.
8. Ibid., pp. 20–21.
9. *Article VIII: Exchange of information, Statute of the International Atomic Energy Agency*.
10. L. Bevaart, F. Claude, J. Lepingwell, M. Nicholas, H. Rilakovic, P. Caulfield, 'Safeguards Information Analysis: Progress, Challenges and Solutions', in the *Proceedings of the IAEA Conference on Addressing Verification Challenges*, IAEA-CN-148/26, 16–20 October 2006, IAEA, 2007, pp. 59–61.
11. Ibid., pp. 59–61.
12. *Energy Information Administration*, US Department of Energy (http://www.eia.doe.gov/).
13. Economist Intelligence Unit (http://www.eiu.com/).
14. L. Bevaart et al., 'Safeguards Information', pp. 59–61.
15. ISI Web of Science (http://scientific.thomson.com/products/wos/).
16. Elsevier Science Direct (http://www.sciencedirect.com/).
17. See: W.Q. Bowen and J. Kidd, 'Open Source Research and Nuclear Safeguards', in the *Proceedings of the IAEA Conference on Addressing Verification Challenges*, IAEA-CN-148/27, 16–20 October 2006, IAEA, 2007.
18. Internet Archive (http://www.archive.org/about/about.php).
19. *IAEA Safeguards: Staying Ahead of the Game*, IAEA, pp. 20–21.
20. Ibid., pp. 20–21.
21. L. Bevaart, et al, 'Safeguards Information', pp. 59–61.
22. For information on the IAEA's on-going investigation of Iran's nuclear programme, please see the regular reports presented by the Director General to the IAEA Board of Governors located on the Agency's website (http://www.iaea.org/NewsCenter/Focus/IaeaIran/index.shtml).
23. L. Bevaart, et al., 'Safeguards Information', pp. 59–61.
24. *Implementation of the NPT Safeguards Agreement in the Arab Republic of Egypt*, Report by the Director General, International Atomic Energy Agency, to the Board of Governors, GOV/2005/9, 14 February 2005, pp. 1–2 (http://www.globalsecurity.org/wmd/library/report/2005/egypt_iaea_gov-2005-9_14nov2005.pdf).
25. Ibid., pp. 1–2

26. Ibid., p. 5
27. See W.Q. Bowen and J. Kidd, 'Open Source Research'.
28. W.Q. Bowen, 'Tracking and Assessing Nuclear Issues in Open Sources: the Case of Libya', in James A. Russell (ed.), *Proliferation of Weapons of Mass Destruction in the Middle East: Directions and Policy Options in the New Century*, Basingstoke: Palgrave Macmillan, 2006, pp. 145–163,
29. Ibid., pp. 149, 153–155.
30. For a detailed account of Libya's nuclear weapons programme see: W.Q. Bowen, *Libya and Nuclear Proliferation: Stepping Back from the Brink*, Adelphi Paper 380, International Institute for Strategic Studies London: Routledge, May 2006, p. 103.
31. W.Q. Bowen, *Libya and Nuclear Proliferation*, pp. 149, 153–155.
32. *IAEA Safeguards: Staying Ahead of the Game*, pp. 20–21.
33. J. Baute, 'Safeguards Information Challenges' in the *Proceedings of the IAEA Conference on Addressing Verification Challenges*, IAEA-CN-148/25, 16–20 October 2006, IAEA, 2007, p. 53.
34. IAEA Safeguards: Staying Ahead of the Game, pp. 20–21.
35. L. Bevaart, et al., 'Safeguards Information', pp. 59–61.
36. J. Baute, 'Safeguards Information Challenges', p. 53.

6. ALL THE SECRETS THAT ARE FIT TO PRINT? THE MEDIA AND US INTELLIGENCE SERVICES BEFORE AND AFTER 9/11

1. The authors thank The Leverhulme Trust for its support of the research for this essay.
2. Lorenzo Semple Jr. and David Rayfiel, *Three Days of the Condor*, Screenplay, 1975.
3. See, for example, Mervyn Le Roy, director, *The FBI Story*, 1959; ABC, *The F.B.I.*, *1965–1974*; J. Edgar Hoover, *Masters of Deceit: The Story of Communism In America and How to Fight It*, New York: Henry Holt and Company, 1958; J. Edgar Hoover, *Persons in Hiding*, New York: Little, Brown and Co., 1938. For a depiction at Hoover's efforts to control depictions by Walt Disney of the FBI in the early 1960s see Marc Eliot, *Walt Disney: Hollywood's Dark Prince*. London: Andre Deutsch, 1993, 243.
4. *Time*, 3 August 1953, http://www.time.com/time/covers/0,16641,19530803,00. html (accessed 25 June 2008).
5. See Stella Rimington, *Open Secret: The Autobiography of the Former Director-General of MI5* London: Arrow Books Ltd., 2002; Jamie Doward, 'MI5 Chief Told Agents: 'Call Me Bob'', *The Observer*, 11 March 2007.
6. For the description of such a relationship see David Rose, 'Spies and their Lies', *New Statesman*, 27 September 2007.
7. See, for example, James Reston, 'The Invisible War Rises to the Surface', *New York Times*, 13 May 1956.

8. David Stafford, *Spies Beneath Berlin—the Extraordinary Story of Operation Stop-watch/Gold, the CIA's Spy Tunnel Under the Russian Sector of Cold War Berlin*, London: Overlook Press, 2002.

9. Bob Woodward, *Bush at War*, New York: Pocketbooks, 2003; Bob Woodward, *Plan of Attack*, New York: Pocketbooks, 2004; Bob Woodward, *State of Denial*, New York: Pocketbooks, 2007.

10. Lawrence Joffe, 'Obituary: Abul Haq,' *Guardian*, 29 October 2001.

11. A more thoughtful examination of the consequences of CIA support for certain factions in Afghanistan pre-9/11 was written by a *Washington Post* colleague of Woodward's. See Steve Coll, *Ghost Wars: The Secret History of the CIA, Afghanistan and Bin Laden*, New York: Penguin Books Ltd., 2005.

12. For a history of the CIA's use of individual reporters and news' executives, see Carl Bernstein, 'The CIA and the Media,' *Rolling Stone*, 20 October 1977.

13. 'A Look Back...Truman Appoints First DCI, 1946,' Central Intelligence Agency, https://www.cia.gov/news-information/featured-story-archive/truman-appoints-first-dci.html (accessed 1 July 2008).

14. Rhodri Jeffreys-Jones, *The CIA and American Democracy*, New Haven and London: Yale University Press, 2003, pp. 53–4; John Ranelagh, *The Agency: The Rise and Decline of the CIA*, London: Weidenfeld and Nicolson, 1986, p. 114.

15. Jeffreys-Jones, *The CIA and American Democracy*, 63.

16. For an incisive examination of the CIA's attempt in the early Cold War to influence the media, both through its support of individual journalists and its planting of 'news', see Hugh Wilford, *The Mighty Wurlitzer: How the CIA Played America*, Cambridge MA: Harvard University Press, 2008, pp. 225–248.

17. Ranelagh, *The Agency*, pp. 238–41.

18. Ibid., pp. 377–8.

19. For a partial defence of the CIA regarding its pre-9–11 failures against Al Qaeda, see Reuel Marc Gerecht, 'The Myth of Counter-Terrorism,' *The Atlantic Monthly*, August-September 2001. For a partial defence of the CIA surrounding its pre-Iraq war intelligence, see Paul R. Pillar, 'Intelligence, Policy, and the War in Iraq,' *Foreign Affairs*, March/April 2006.

20. See the special *Vanity Fair* pictorial feature on the Bush Administration in January 2002.

21. Woodward, *Bush at War*, pp. 141–3; 'CIA's License To Kill,' CBS News, http://www.cbsnews.com/stories/2002/12/03/attack/main531596.shtml, 4 December 2002 (accessed 1 July 2008).

22. Walter Pincus and Dana Priest, 'Some Iraq Analysts Felt Pressure From Cheney Visits,' *Washington Post*, 5 June 2003; Seymour Hersh, 'The Stovepipe: How conflicts between the Bush Administration and the intelligence community marred the reporting on Iraq's weapons,' *New Yorker*, 12 October 2003.

23. Jane Mayer, 'The Manipulator; Ahmad Chalabi pushed a tainted case for war. Can he survive the occupation?' *New Yorker*, 7 June 2004.

24. For more on the American media's propaganda role, see Oliver Boyd-Barrett, 'Judith Miller, The New York Times, and the Propaganda Model,' *Journalism Studies* 5, 4 (2004), pp. 435–49; Michael Massing, *Now They Tell Us: The American Press and Iraq*, New York: New York Review Books, 2004.

25. 'Report of the Select Committee on Intelligence on the US Intelligence Community's Prewar Intelligence Assessments on Iraq,' United States Senate, 9 July 2004, http://www.gpoaccess.gov/serialset/creports/pdf/s108–301/sec12.pdf (accessed 5 July 2008).

26. Seymour M. Hersh, 'Selective Intelligence,' *New Yorker*, 12 May 2003; Hersh, 'The Stovepipe'; 'Report on Intelligence Activities Relation to Iraq Conducted by the Policy Counterterrorism Evaluation Group and the Office of Special Plans within the Office of the Under Secret of Defense for Policy,' United States Senate, June 2008, http://intelligence.senate.gov/080605/phase2b.pdf (accessed 30 June 2008).

27. Thom Shanker and James Risen, 'Rumsfeld Weighs New Covert Acts by Military Units,' *New York Times*, 12 August 2002; James Risen, 'Threats and Responses: The Intelligence Dispute: CIA Rejects Call for Iraq Reports,' *New York Times*. 3 October 2002; Seymour M. Hersh, 'The Coming Wars: What the Pentagon Can Now Do in Secret,' *New Yorker*, 24 January 2005.

28. 'Powell: Iraq Hiding Weapons, Aiding Terrorists,' CNN, 6 February 2003, http://edition.cnn.com/2003/US/02/05/sprj.irq.powell.un/(accessed 12 June 2008).

29. 'Former Aide: Powell WMD Speech 'lowest point in my life',' CNN, 19 August 2005, http://edition.cnn.com/2005/WORLD/meast/08/19/powell.un/(accessed 8 July 2008).

30. John Prados, 'The Record on Curveball,' National Security Archive, 5 November 2007, http://www.gwu.edu/~nsarchiv/NSAEBB/NSAEBB234/index.htm (accessed 16 June 2008); Powell would later describe his U.N. briefing as a 'blot' on his reputation. 'Colin Powell on Iraq, Race, and Hurricane Relief,' ABC News, 8 September 2005, http://abcnews.go.com/2020/Politics/story?id=1105979&page=1 (accessed 24 June 2008).

31. Michael White and Brian Whitaker, 'UK War Dossier A Sham, Say Experts,' *The Guardian*, 7 February 2003; 'Straw Says Dossier Was Embarrassing,' *BBC News*, 24 June 2003, http://news.bbc.co.uk/1/hi/uk_politics/3015272.stm (accessed 8 July 2008).

32. 'Timeline: The 45–Minute Claim,' BBC News, 13 October 2004, http://news.bbc.co.uk/1/hi/uk_politics/3466005.stm (accessed 9 July 2008).

33. The creation of the letter by the CIA is revealed in Ron Suskind, *The Way of the World: A Story of Truth and Hope in an Age of Extremism*, New York: Harper, 2008; Con Coughlin, 'Terrorist Behind September 11 Strike Was Trained by Saddam,' *Daily Telegraph*, 13 December 2003, http://www.telegraph.co.uk/news/worldnews/middleeast/iraq/1449442/Terrorist-behind-September-11–strike-was-trained-by-Saddam.html (accessed 10 August 2008).

34. 'Leaked report rejects Iraqi Al Qaeda link,' *BBC News*, 5 February 2003, http://news.bbc.co.uk/1/hi/uk/2727471.stm, (accessed 2 July 2008).

35. 'Revealed: US Dirty Tricks to Win Vote on Iraq War,' *Observer*, 2 March 2003. The memo can be read at: http://www.guardian.co.uk/world/2003/mar/02/iraq.unitednations1 (accessed 1 July 2008). For more on the Gun case, see Marcia and Thomas Mitchell, *The Spy Who Tried to Stop a War: Katharine Gun and the Secret Plot to Sanction the Iraq Invasion*, London: Polipoint Press, 2008.

36. See, for example, Jonathan S. Landay, 'Lack of Hard Evidence of Iraqi Weapons Worries Top US Officials,' *Knight Ridder News Service*, 6 September 2002, http://www.mcclatchydc.com/reports/intelligence/story/8546.html (accessed 11 August 2008); Warren P. Strobel and Jonathan S. Landay, 'Infighting Among U.S Intelligence Agencies Fuels Dispute Over Iraq,' *Knight Ridder News Service*, 24 October 2002, http://www.mcclatchydc.com/reports/intelligence/story/8604.html (accessed 11 August 2008)

37. Nick Davies, *Flat Earth News: An Award-winning Reporter Exposes Falsehood, Distortion and Propaganda in the Global Media*, London: Chatto and Windus, 2008, p. 329.

38. Woodward as quoted in Howard Kurtz, 'The Man with the Inside Scoop,' *Washington Post*, 28 November 2005, http://www.washingtonpost.com/wp-dyn/content/article/2005/11/27/AR2005112701140_pf.html (accessed 11 August 2008).

39. Hersh, 'The Stovepipe.'

40. 'George Tenet: At the Center of the Storm', 29 April 2007, *60 Minutes*, http://www.cbsnews.com/stories/2007/04/25/60minutes/main2728375.shtml (accessed 2 October 2008)

41. Lord Hutton, 'Report of the Inquiry into the Circumstances Surrounding the Death of Dr David Kelly C.M.G.,' 28 January 2004, http://www.the-hutton-inquiry.org.uk/content/report/chapter01.htm#a2 (accessed 2 October 2008)

42. Commission on the Intelligence Capabilities of the United States Regarding Weapons of Mass Destruction, *Report to the President*, 31 March 2005, http://www.wmd.gov/report/report.html#chapter1

43. Jack Davis, 'Paul Wolfowitz on Intelligence-Policy Relations,' *Studies in Intelligence*, 1996, reprinted at http://www.au.af.mil/au/awc/awcgate/cia/intel_and_policy.htm#rft1 (access 2 October 2008)

44. 'How the Iraq Dossier Was Written', BBC News, 5 September 2003, http://news.bbc.co.uk/1/hi/uk_politics/3076692.stm (accessed 4 July 2008). For the Hutton and Butler Inquity reports see Lord Hutton, *op cit*.; Report of a Committee of Privy Counsellors, 'Review of Intelligence on Weapons of Mass Destruction,' 14 July 2004, http://news.bbc.co.uk/nol/shared/bsp/hi/pdfs/14_07_04_butler.pdf (accessed 15 June 2008).

45. Cheney appearance on *Meet the Press*, 16 September 2001, http://www.whitehouse.gov/vicepresident/news-speeches/speeches/vp20010916.html.

46. Barton Gellman and Jo Becker, 'Pushing the Envelope on Presidential Power,' *Washington Post*, 25 June 2007.

47. Bernstein, 'The CIA and the Media.'

48. Harry Truman, 'Limit CIA Role to Intelligence,' *Washington Post*, 22 December 1963.

7. BRITISH INTELLIGENCE AND THE BRITISH BROADCASTING CORPORATION: A SNAPSHOT OF A HAPPY MARRIAGE

1. S.H. Bleiweis, *The Elizabethan Intelligence Service, 1572–1585*. (PhD, Rutgers University, 1976), p. 1.

2. 'BBC Monitoring—A Brief History'. BBC Written Archives Centre (hereafter BBC): C1/181/1.

3. 'The British Broadcasting Corporation Monitoring Service', 6 December 1939. BBC: E2/407/1. On the nature and technology of monitoring, see BBC: E8/209/3.

4. 'Monitoring Service—Post War Planning', 16 August 1944. BBC: R34/479/1.

5. A copy of the report, entitled 'Proposed Future Coverage by BBC Monitoring Service' is in The National Archives (hereafter TNA), Kew: CAB 176/7.

6. 'The BBC Monitoring Service—Post War Review', 29 March 1946. BBC: R34/479/2.

7. JIC(45)59th Meeting, TNA: CAB 81/93.

8. For more see P. Cradock. *Know Your Enemy: How the Joint Intelligence Committee Saw The World*. (London: John Murray, 2002).

9. Foreign Office History Notes, *Origins and Establishment of the Foreign Office Information Research Department*. (August 1995).

10. A copy of the memorandum is in N7905/140/38. TNA: FO 371/56786.

11. For more on the former see R. Merrick, 'The Russia Committee of the British Foreign Office and the Cold War, 1946–7', *Journal of Contemporary History*, 20:3 (July 1985), pp. 453–68.

12. Foreign Office History Notes, *Origins and Establishment of the Foreign Office Information Research Department* (August 1995). p. 2.

13. JIC(46)21st Meeting, 1 May 1946. TNA: CAB 81/94.

14. 'BBC Monitoring Service: Note by Director General JIB', 17 May 1946. TNA: CAB 176/11.

15. JIC(46)29th Meeting, 24 May 1946. TNA: CAB 81/94.

16. 'Monitoring: US Monitoring Middle East and Far East—Note by Director JIB', 21 April 1947. TNA: CAB 176/14.

17. Some further details are in BBC: E1/85.

18. 'Progress Report on the Central Intelligence Group', Report by S.W. Souers, Director of Central Intelligence, 7 June 1946. Available from www.foia.cia.gov See also documentation in BBC: R34/479/3.

19. R.A.Way, 'The BBC Monitoring Service and Its US Partner', *CIA Studies in Intelligence* 2 (Summer 1958), p. 76. The author is not quite correct; there was analogous international cooperation in Signals Intelligence.
20. JIC(47)25th Meeting, 23 April 1947. TNA: CAB 159/1.
21. I.Jacob. *From Churchill's Secret Circle to the BBC.* (London: Brasseys, 1991).
22. I.Jacob to W.Hayter, 2 February 1948. TNA: CAB 176/17.
23. JIC(48)17th Meeting, 27 February 1948. TNA: CAB 159/3.
24. For example, meetings were held on 27 August 1946 and 30 August 1946. BBC: R34/479/2.
25. JIC/748/48, 19 April 1948. TNA: CAB 176/18. The GCHQ representative was Commander Clive Loehnis, a future Director of the sigint agency.
26. JIC/1080/49, 14 June 1949. TNA: CAB 176/22. For more information on the BBC/FBIS relationship, especially concerning Cyprus and the station in Cairo, see various correspondence in BBC: R34/479/3.
27. JIC(49)70th Meeting, 14 July 1949. TNA: CAB 159/6.
28. JIC(49)83rd Meeting, 25 August 1949. TNA: CAB 159/6. The current 'wordage' was 10,000 words a day, whereas it was felt the Americans wanted double or treble this amount.
29. JIC(50)72nd Meeting, 13 July 1950. TNA: CAB 159/8.
30. JIC(50)83rd Meeting, 10 August 1950. TNA: CAB 159/8.
31. JIC(51)82nd Meeting, 2 August 1951. TNA: CAB 159/10.
32. JIC(51)86th Meeting, 16 August 1951. TNA: CAB 159/10.
33. JIC(52)13th Meeting, 24 January 1952. TNA: CAB 159/11. At around the same time discussions were also made to close a TASS station in Whetstone. BBC: R28/130.
34. JIC(52)39th Meeting, 3 April 1952. TNA: CAB 159/11.
35. JIC(52) 84th Meeting, 31 July 1952. TNA: CAB 159/12.
36. JIC/2105/52, 12 September 1952. TNA: CAB 176/38.
37. JIC/2105/52, 12 September 1952. TNA: CAB 176/38.
38. JIC(52)138th Meeting, 10 December 1952. TNA: CAB 159/12.
39. JIC(52)141st Meeting, 17 December 1952. TNA: CAB 159/12. The terms of reference themselves can be found in JIC(52)79, 19 December 1952. TNA: CAB 158/14.
40. JIC(53)18th Meeting, 18 February 1953. TNA: CAB 159/13.
41. JIC(53)119th Meeting, 18 November 1953. TNA: CAB 159/14.
42. JIC(54)19th Meeting, 4 March 1954. TNA: CAB 159/15.
43. JIC(54)41st Meeting, 6 May 1954. TNA: CAB 159/15.
44. The report is in TNA: HO 256/855.
45. 'Comments on the Treasury Report on the BBC Monitoring Service', 14 October 1954. BBC: E40/235/1.
46. See the discussion in JIC(54)91st Meeting, 14 October 1954. TNA: CAB 159/17.

47. P. Fraenkel, 'The BBC External Services: Broadcasting to the USSR and Eastern Europe' in K.R.M. Short (ed.), *Western Broadcasting Behind the Iron Curtain* (London: Croom Helm, 1986), pp. 139–57. See also BBC: E40/234/1.

48. For further details on JIC(Germany) see S. Case. 'The Joint Intelligence Committee and the German Question, 1947–61' (PhD, Queen Mary, University of London, 2008).

49. P. Lashmar and J.Oliver, *Britain's Secret Propaganda War* (Gloucestershire: Alan Sutton, 1998).

50. Ibid., p. 53.

51. Cited in JIC(Germany)(M)(51)6, 108th Meeting, 17 April 1951. TNA: DEFE 41/66.

52. JIC(Germany)(M)(51)1, 103rd Meeting, TNA: DEFE 41/66.

53. JIC(Germany)(M)(51)6, 108th Meeting, 17 April 1951. TNA: DEFE 41/66.

54. JIC(Germany)(M)(51)14, 116th Meeting, 2 October 1951. TNA: DEFE 41/66.

55. (JIC)(Germany)(M)(52)1, 121st Meeting, 22 January 1952. TNA: DEFE 41/67.

56. JIC(Germany)(M)(52)5, 125th Meeting, 17 April 1952. TNA: DEFE 41/67. For more on STIB see P.Maddrell. *Spying on Science: Western Intelligence in Divided Germany, 1945–61* (Oxford University Press, 2006).

57. For more details see M.S.Goodman. *Spying on the Nuclear Bear: Anglo-American Intelligence and the Soviet Bomb.* (Stanford: Stanford University Press, 2008).

58. J.Brent and V.P.Naumov. *Stalin's Last Crime: The Plot Against the Jewish Doctors, 1948–1953.* (London: HarperCollins, 2003). p. 117.

59. Email from Dr Arnold Kramish, 11 August 2003.

60. D.E.Murphy, S.A.Kondrashev and G.Bailey. *Battleground Berlin: CIA vs KGB in the Cold War.* (London: Yale University Press, 1997). p. 15.

61. Brent and Naumov. *Stalin's Last Crime.* p. 117 and p. 137.

62. Murphy, Kondrashev and Bailey. *Battleground Berlin.* p. 15.

63. Email from Kramish, 11 August 2003.

64. H.S.Lowenhaupt, 'On the Soviet Nuclear Scent.' *CIA Studies in Intelligence.* Available at www.odci.gov/csi/index.html p. 20.

65. H.S.Lowenhaupt, 'Chasing Bitterfeld Calcium.' *CIA Studies in Intelligence.* (Spring 1973), p. 27.

66. H.S.Lowenhaupt, 'Mission to Birch Woods, Via Seven Tents and New Siberia.' *CIA Studies in Intelligence.* (Fall 1968), pp. 6–7.

67. H.Rositzke. *The CIA's Secret Operations: Espionage, Counterespionage and Covert Action.* (London: Westview Press, 1977). p. 141.

68. JIC(Germany)(M)(52)9, 129th Meeting, 10 July 1952. TNA: DEFE 41/67.

69. JIC(Germany)(M)(52)14, 134th Meeting, 21 October 1952. TNA: DEFE 41/67.

70. JIC(Germany)(M)(52)14, 134th Meeting, 21 October 1952. TNA: DEFE 41/67.

71. Brixmis is probably the most successful of these. For more see T.Geraghty, *Brixmis: The Untold Story of Britain's Most Daring Cold War Spy Mission* (London: HarperCollins, 1997).

8. BALANCING NATIONAL SECURITY AND THE MEDIA: THE D-NOTICE COMMITTEE

1. A quote from American Judge, Murray Gurfein, in his 1971 Pentagon Papers Opinion.
2. See http://www.dnotice.org.uk (accessed 14 July 2008).
3. Pre-1939 the Press Association provided and funded the Secretary.
4. See the website for details.

9. REFLECTIONS ON A LIFETIME OF REPORTING ON INTELLIGENCE AFFAIRS

1. Tube Alloys was the British codename given to the atomic bomb programme.
2. One result of this was the publication, in 1948, of my book *Into the Atomic Age*, London: Hutchinson.
3. For the definitive account of this see Margaret Gowing, *Independence and Deterrence: Britain and Atomic Energy, 1945–52*, London: Macmillan Press, 1974. Two Volumes.
4. For more information see Brundrett's obituary, *The Times*, 6 August 1974.
5. See Chapman Pincher, 'Leakers I Have Known', *The Spectator*, 12 September 1998.
6. Details are in The National Archives, Kew, London (hereafter TNA): PREM 11/2800.
7. For a useful background see http://www.dnotice.org.uk/history.htm
8. Richard Rhodes provides the best account of the wartime development: *The Making of the Atomic Bomb*, New York: Simon and Schuster, 1986.
9. See Michael S. Goodman, 'Who Is Trying to Keep What Secret from Whom and Why? MI5–FBI Relations and the Klaus Fuchs Case', *Journal of Cold War Studies*, 7, 3, 2005, pp. 124–146.
10. Details can be found in Lorna Arnold, *Britain and the H-Bomb*, London: Palgrave, 2001.
11. Details of Operation Nomination can be found in Michael S. Goodman, *Spying on the Nuclear Bear: Anglo-American Intelligence and the Soviet Bomb*, Stanford: Stanford University Press, 2008.
12. This argument is expanded in *Their Trade is Treachery*, London: Sidgwick and Jackson, 1986.
13. His own account is John Vassall, *Vassall: The Autobiography of a Spy*, London: Sidgwick and Jackson, 1975.

14. TNA: CRIM 1/4003.
15. Wynne had been involved in the running of the GRU spy Oleg Penkovsky.
16. Archival releases have revealed more details to the affair: Matthew Creevy, 'A Critical Review of the Wilson Government's Handling of the D-Notice Affair 1967', *Intelligence and National Security*, 14, 3, 1999, pp. 209–227.
17. Further details can be found in Richard Deacon, *'C': A Biography of Sir Maurice Oldfield*, London: Macdonald, 1985.
18. Chapman Pincher, *Traitors: The Labyrinths of Treason*, London: Sidgwick and Jackson, 1987.
19. The GRU was Soviet military intelligence.
20. Peter Wright, *Spycatcher: The Candid Autobiography of a Senior Intelligence Officer*, Australia: Heinemann, 1987.
21. For example see Michael S. Goodman and Chapman Pincher, 'Attlee, Sillitoe and the Security Aspects of the Fuchs Case.' *Contemporary British History*, 19, 1, 2005, pp. 67–78.
22. *The Mail on Sunday* (15 January 2006).

10. BEDMATES OR SPARRING PARTNERS?: CANADIAN PERSPECTIVES ON THE MEDIA-INTELLIGENCE RELATIONSHIP IN 'THE NEW PROPAGANDA AGE'

1. Clive Rose, *The Soviet Propaganda Network: A Directory of Organisations Serving Soviet Foreign Policy*, London: Pinter Publishers, 1988.
2. David Carment, Fen Osler Hampson, and Norman Hillmer (eds), *Canada Among Nations 2003: Coping With the American Colossus*, Don Mills, Ontario: Oxford University Press, 2003.
3. Stephen Budiansky, *Her Majesty's Spymaster*, London: Penguin Books, 2005.
4. Neil Postman, *Amusing Ourselves to Death: Public Discourse in the Age of Show Business*, New York: Viking Penguin, 1986.
5. Thomas S. Kuhn, *The Structure of Scientific Revolutions*, University of Chicago Press, 1962.
6. George Orwell, *Nineteen Eighty-Four*, USA: Penguin Group, 2003.
7. 'An informed citizenry is the bulwark of democracy' is frequently but wrongly attributed to Thomas Jefferson. However, it accurately reflects his thinking as expressed in other terms in his writing. (www.monticello.org)
8. The Statute of Westminster, 1931, 'was the logical end of years of change and nego-tiation between Britain and her Dominions (Australia, Canada, New Zealand, South Africa and Newfoundland). It made several key provisions: (1) British par-liament could no longer nullify haws in the Dominions; (2) Dominions could make their own extra-territorial laws; and (3) British law no longer applied to the Dominions. Although Canada had already acted internationally, the Statute for-mally put 'external affairs' under the authority of the federal government. Thus,

when World War II began in 1939, Canada did not automatically go to war with Britain. As an independent nation, Canada declared war six days after the British.' (www.canadiana.org) and, it might be noted, two years and three months before the United States.

9. Lord Beaverbrook's real name was Max Aitken. He is said to have been asked if Max was a short form for Maximillian and he retorted that it was actually short for 'Maximultimillion'. He was a prolific writer who published many books including *The Divine Propagandist*, New York: Duell, Sloane and Pearce, 1962.

10. Sir Campbell Stuart, *Secrets of Crewe House: The Story of a Famous Campaign*, London: Hodder and Stoughton, 1920.

11. The witticism ascribed to Oscar Wilde and George Bernard Shaw that Britain and the United States are 'two nations divided by a common language' offers an acute insight into the possibility of conflicts between allies because of language or cultural discrepancies. In negotiations with either British or American negotiators, I have often felt we Canadians would be well served by a special English-translator–and vice-versa.

12. William Stevenson, *A Man Called Intrepid: the Secret War 1939–1945*, London: Macmillan, 1976. Stevenson and Stephenson were not related.

13. Introduction by Nigel West, *British Security Coordination: The Secret History of British Intelligence in the Americas, 1940–45*, St. Ermin's Press, London, 1998.

14. New Zealand was also a regular partner of this 'Quinquepartite' or 'five eyes' alliance until American relations with New Zealand became strained by divergent nuclear policies and it evolved to being mainly 'Quadripartite'.

15. As an interesting example of how 'smaller countries' can experiment with ideas and initiatives that are harder for better established countries to try, CASIS was founded in 1985 by a small group of academics with the objective of promoting research and scholarship as well as informed public debate in the fields of security and intelligence. On a word-wide basis, CASIS remains unique in its efforts to build bridges across the distinct intelligence and security disciplines, including law enforcement, while reaching out domestically and internationally to related academic, not-for-profit, and private sector groups. (www.casis.ca)

16. Igor Gouzenko was a cipher clerk in the Soviet Embassy to Canada in Ottawa. He defected on September 5, 1945 with 109 documents on Soviet espionage activities in the West. 'The 'Gouzenko Affair' helped change the Western perception of the Soviet Union from an ally to an enemy, and is often credited as a triggering event of the Cold War.' The revelations had a necessary sobering effect on Canadian government and media understanding of intelligence as 18 of a total of 39 suspects were eventually convicted.

17. President George H.W. Bush used these terms in addressing a joint session of Congress on September 11, 1990 concerning Iraq's invasion of Kuwait. He defined the fifth of the US objectives in the Persian Gulf as the achievement of 'a new world order...in which the nations of the world...can prosper and live in

harmony...a new world is struggling to be born...'(http://www.sweetliberty.org/issues/war/bushsr.htm)

18. Francis Fukuyama, 'The End of History?', *The National Interest* (Summer, 1989).

19. Samuel P. Huntington, 'The Clash of Civilizations?', *Foreign Affairs*, (Summer 1993).

20. That intelligence as a function received so little positive attention from the Chretien government reflected several underlying factors including the ignorance and indifference of the Prime Minister about security matters.

21. Salim Jiwa, *The Death of Air India Flight 182*, Vancouver: Star Books, 1986.

22. 'Yet the patriotism, or rather the fear of not being seen as patriotic, of offending the public, could affect the way in which television news handled a story.' Paul Rutherford, *Weapons of Mass Persuasion: Marketing the war Against Iraq*, University of Toronto Press, 2004.

23. Michael Massin, 'Now They Tell Us, Part 4' *New York Review of Books* (February 26, 2004), notes that 'almost alone among national news organizations, Knight Ridder had decided to take a hard look at the administration's justifications for war'.

24. Her influential but inaccurate reports suggesting the possibility of Iraq's possessing weapons of mass destruction based on unidentified, unchallenged sources, were the main reason the *New York Times* issued an extraordinary apology on May 26, 2004 in which it said that a review of its coverage of the issue revealed 'a number of instances of coverage that was not as rigorous as it should have been'.

25. For 'un-embedded' insights into the Iraq invasion from a Canadian reporter, see Paul William Roberts, *A War Against Truth: An Intimate Account of the Invasion of Iraq*, Raincoast Books: Vancouver, 2004.

26. This has been confirmed to me by three separate confidential sources. The problem for Canadian intelligence was that not all the analytical intelligence units shared the same view. However, the Prime Minister used the 'no evidence' assessment in explaining Canada's position to President George W. Bush in September, 2002 when it was becoming evident that the US intended to attack Iraq regardless of the evidence of WMD.

27. Jeff Sallot, 'How Canada failed citizen Maher Arar', *The Globe and Mail* (September 19, 2006) reporting on the commission of inquiry headed by Mr Justice Dennis O'Connor that found that Arar was 'an innocent victim of inaccurate RCMP intelligence reports and deliberate smears by Canadian officials'.

28. Michael Herman, *Intelligence Power in Peace and War*, Cambridge University Press, 1996.

29. Ibid., pp. 10–11

30. Garth Jowett and Victoria O'Donnell, *Propaganda and Persuasion*, London: Sage Publications, 1999. p. 6.

31. Ibid., pp. 12–13.

32. Ibid., pp.17–18.

33. R.H. Shultz and Roy Godson, *Desinformatsia: Active measures in Soviet strategy*. Washington, DC: Pergamon-Brassey, 1984. p. 41.

34. Jowett and O'Donnell, *Propaganda and Persuasion*, p. 3.

35. William H. Riker, *The Art of Political Manipulation*, New Haven: Yale University Press, 1986. Riker links rhetoric, grammar and logic, 'the traditional liberal arts of language' with social choice theory or decision theory 'which is a specialized branch of economic theory and political theory'. He says on page xi 'naturally, in all these processes, strategic manipulation plays a fundamental part'.

36. Joseph S.Nye, 'Soft Power', *Foreign Policy* (1990), pp. 153–171 and 'America's Information Edge', *Foreign Affairs* (March-April 1996), p. 75.

37. Leigh Armistead (ed.), *Information Operations: Warfare and the Hard Reality of Soft Power*, Dulles, Virginia: Brassey's, Inc., 2004.

38. Michael Isikoff and David Corn, *Hubris: The Inside story of Spin, Scandal, and the Selling of the Iraq War*, New York, Three Rivers Press, 2006. For example, on p. 16 'Bush and his aides were looking for intelligence not to guide their policy on Iraq but to market it'.

39. Jowett and O'Donnell, *Propaganda and Persuasion*, pp. 217–219, quote George Creel's book *How We Advertised America: The first telling of the amazing story of the Committee on Public Information,1917–1919*, New York: Harper and Row, 1920. Creel was a peacetime journalist responsible for American wartime civilian propaganda. He saw the conflict as 'the fight for the minds of men, for 'the conquest of their convictions', and the battle-line ran through every home in the country... it was a plain publicity proposition, a vast enterprise in salesmanship, the world's greatest adventure in advertising', pp. 3–4.

40. Brian Stewart, 'Rick Hillier: Selling the Forces. Toronto: Canadian Broadcasting Corporation', http://www.cbc.ca/national/blog/video/militaryafghanistan/seling_the_forces.html (September 18, 2007)

41. Conrad Black's purchase of the Southam Press with thirty-five newspapers across Canada led to an explicit reorientation towards his conservative politics. This was followed by its subsequent sale to Canwestglobal, owned by the ardently pro-Israel Asper family, with ultimate editorial control exercised by the proprietor at the corporate headquarters in Winnipeg.

11. THE CLANDESTINE CLAPPERBOARD: ALFRED HITCHCOCK'S TALES OF THE COLD WAR

1. When he joined Paramount in 1955 he created the weekly television series *Alfred Hitchcock Presents*, and then *The Alfred Hitchcock Hour*, which ran to a total of over 400 episodes.

2. Jonathan Freedman and Richard Millington (eds), *Hitchcock's America* (New York and Oxford: Oxford University Press, 1999).

3. *The Man Who Knew Too Much* (1934), *The 39 Steps* (1935), *Secret Agent* (1936), *Sabotage* (1936), *The Lady Vanishes* (1938).
4. *Bon Voyage* and *Aventure Malgache* (1944).
5. *Foreign Correspondent* (1940), *Saboteur* (1942), *Notorious* (1946), *The Man Who Knew Too Much* (1956), *North by Northwest* (1959), *Torn Curtain* (1966), *Topaz* (1969).
6. The very first mention on screen of the CIA was made clearly but surreptitiously in British director Guy Green's crime thriller *House of Secrets* in 1956.
7. During his early days in Hollywood, Hitchcock developed and completed three espionage screenplays which never made it to the screen: there were two adaptations of John Buchan's novels, *Greenmantle* in 1943, written specially for Cary Grant and Ingrid Bergman, and *The Three Hostages* in 1964, as well as an adaptation of Laurens van der Post's *The Flamingo Feathers*, about a Soviet plot in Southern Africa, in 1956, in which James Stewart and Grace Kelly were to play the lead roles.
8. Asquith's film was groundbreaking in its study of the creation of a secret assassin who is trained to kill using 'innocent weapons', i.e. ordinary objects or his bare hands, and who ends up killing an innocent man against his will at the behest of a woman who has absolute moral power over him.
9. In May 1945, four German atomic scientists who had previously worked for the Nazi regime—Baron Manfred Von Ardenne, Nobel Prize-winner Gustav Hertz, Peter Adolf Thiessen and Max Volmer—began to recruit more than 300 German scientists to work under their supervision in Russia on the development of a Soviet atomic bomb. In June 1987 Von Ardenne joined forces with the head of the East German secret service, Markus Wolf, and the director of the KGB, Vladimir Kryuchkov, in a plot to overthrow Erich Honecker, as well as in the transformation of the 1974 operation Lightbeam (Luch) into a clandestine network designed to recruit a ring of Stasi agents who would continue to spy for Moscow after the GDR collapsed. See Andrew Jack, *Inside Putin's Russia* (London: Granta Books, 2004), p. 66; Pierre de Villemarest, *Le Coup d'état de Markus Wolf* (Paris: Stock, 1991), p. 43; Christopher Andrew and Vasili Mitrokhin, *The Mitrokin Archive* (London: Allen Lane, 1999), p. 43.
10. This was demonstrated on 1 May 1960, when, to the surprise and dismay of the CIA, a high-altitude U2 spy plane—considered invulnerable to anti-aircraft missile attack—was shot down by a Russian ground-to-air missile. The capture of the pilot, squadron leader Gary Powers, by the KGB, and the Kremlin's decision to crow about the incident, led to the abrupt break-up of the Paris summit in May 1960 between Eisenhower, Macmillan, de Gaulle and Khrushchev.
11. 'Unified Action and United Front against American Imperialism', *Red Guard*, issue no. 3, January 1967. This article was published just as the Vietnam Comités de Base were being formed, which reverberated across the world and provided the framework for the virulent Maoist movement in 1968.

12. Bolstered by the Red Army, the East German security forces gunned down 100 demonstrators and arrested more than 15,000.

13. Ralf Dahrendorf, *Society and Democracy in Germany* (London: Weidenfeld and Nicolson, 1968), p. 433.

14. However, this vision had regularly been challenged in a number of films which explored the US's wheeler-dealing diplomacy in the 1960s, in particular in George Englund's *The Ugly American* (1963) and, even more radically, in Ken Russell's *Billion Dollar Brain* (1967).

15. *Revue d'Histoire Diplomatique* 3 (1994), p. 257.

16. Hitchcock's innovations in this area, discussed above, heralded developments in 1970s cinema, in which the CIA's domestic activities gradually became a motif of espionage and conspiracy thrillers—examples include Michael Winner's *Scorpio* (1973), David Miller's *Executive Action* (1973) and Sydney Pollack's *Three Days of The Condor* (1975).

17. Cf. Thomas Powers, *Intelligence Wars: American Secret History from Hitler to Al Qaeda* (New York: New York Review of Books, 2002), p. ix.

18. Michael R. Beschloss, *The Crisis Years: Kennedy and Khrushchev, 1960–1963* (New York: HarperCollins, 1991), p. 768.

19. *Conversations with History: Reflections, with John A. McCone*, interviews conducted by Harry Kreisler at the Institute of International Studies, UC Berkeley. University of California Television, Fall 1987–Spring 1988.

20. Maurice Vaisse: 'De Gaulle's Handling of the Berlin and Cuban Crises', in Wilfried Loth (ed.), *Europe, Cold War and Coexistence, 1953–1965* (London: Frank Cass, 2004), pp. 67–71.

21. In an interview granted to Dr Charles G. Cogan by Walter Eder, John McCone's special assistant, Eder insisted, nearly forty years after the events they were discussing, that if Vosjoli had played a role in Cuba during the missile crisis, it could only have been a very marginal one. Eder claimed that Vosjoli's involvement had left very few traces because both prior to the end of August and after the end of September 1962 he had kept strictly to face-to-face contact with McCone. See Charles G. Cogan, *L'Europe et la crise de Cuba* (Paris: Armand Colin, 1993).

22. Leon Uris, *Topaz* (Montreal: Les Editions de l'Homme, and London: William Kimber, 1968).

23. 'The French Spy Scandal', *Life*, 26 April 1968.

24. Philippe Thyraud de Vosjoli, *Lamia* (Boston, MA, and Toronto: Little, Brown, 1970).

25. In 1975, the CIA reassessed the information supplied by Golitsin since 1962. The Kalaris-Tweedy Report, which was compiled shortly after James Angleton was moved off the case (he had become obsessed with Golitsin), confirmed that Golitsin was a genuine defector, but that his contribution had been less significant than his partisans claimed. Nevertheless, after the exposure of a number of espionage cases in the United States, in 1987 Golitsin received a medal from the

CIA for exceptional services rendered. See David Wise, *Molehunt: the Secret Search for Traitors that Scattered the CIA* (New York: Random House, 1991), p. 298.

26. Years of inquiries followed Golitsin's revelation, during which a number of errors were committed which destroyed the careers and besmirched the honour of a dozen agents. The mole who had been operating at the heart of the CIA since the early 1950s was finally identified as Franz Koischwitz, alias Sacha Orlov, who had died in 1982.

27. A huge amount has been written on the damage done by Angleton's hunt for moles. The pioneering article was Seymour M. Hersh, 'Angleton: the Cult of Counterintelligence', *New York Times Magazine*, 25 June 1978. Other works then began to appear, such as David C. Martin, *Wilderness of Mirrors* (New York: Harper and Row, 1980), and Tom Mangold, *Cold Warrior: James Jesus Angleton, the CIA's Master Spy Hunter* (New York: Simon and Schuster, 1991).

28. Jeanne-Marie Piquemal: *Le SDECE: une administration très spéciale* (doctoral thesis, University of Toulouse I, 1975), chapter II: 'le SDECE victime d'une trahison diplomatique: "Pâques a avoué la communication au KGB en 1961 des plans secrets des alliés pour la défense de Berlin Ouest",' p. 166.

29. Eric Merlen and Frédéric Ploquin, *Carnets intimes de la DST* (Paris: Fayard, 2003), p. 164.

30. Roger Faligot and Pascal Krop, *DST: police secrète* (Paris: Flammarion, 1999), p. 230.

31. Vosjoli 1970, p. 317.

32. See Piquemal 1975, p. 169: 'It was towards the middle of 1962 that France decided to steal from the Americans the technology which would enable their nuclear weapons programme to begin.'

33. David Freeman was hired by Universal Studios to rework the script between December 1978 and May 1979; he published the definitive version in his retrospective, *The Last Days of Alfred Hitchcock: a Memoir Featuring the Screenplay of Alfred Hitchcock's 'The Short Night'* (Woodstock, NY: Overlook, 1984).

34. According to Vasili Mitrokhin, Blake informed against several hundred Western agents, or agents working for the West, between 1951 and 1961. In May 1967 he appeared in the dignitaries' box in Moscow during the parade commemorating the fiftieth anniversary of the Russian Revolution—the very same iconic scene which appears during the opening credits of *Topaz*. See Andrew and Mitrokhin 1999, pp. 645–7.

35. Ang Lee's film *Lust-Caution*, which owes as much to Lang as it does to Hitchcock, requires a similar sequence of sexually charged sequences to give the viewer the necessary understanding of the trap and the psychological state of those caught in the trap.

36. Bailey, initially uninterested in politics, had tried in vain to talk his brother out of the CIA. Interestingly, Bailey is convinced that his brother was not much of a

patriot, suggesting that he went into espionage for the excitement: 'He was working on a PhD, and he ran off for the adventure of it' (Freeman 1984, p. 174). The same explanation is provided by the character Carla Brand—it was basically for the thrill that Brand became an agent and then a double agent.

12. FROM VAUXHALL CROSS WITH LOVE: INTELLIGENCE IN POPULAR CULTURE

1. Colin Shindler, *Hollywood Goes to War*, New York: Routledge, 1979; Jeffrey Goldstein, 'Immortal Kombat: War Toys and Violent Video Games', in Jeffrey Goldstein (ed.), *Why We Watch: The Attraction of Violent Entertainment*, New York: Oxford University Press, 1998; Karen Rasmussen and Sharon Downey, 'Dialectical Disorientation in Vietnam War Films: Subversion of the Mythology of War', *Quarterly Journal of Speech*, 77(2), 1991, pp. 176–95.

2. Christina Rowley, 'West-wing', chapter for PhD in progress, University of Bristol, 2008.

3. Jutta Weldes, 'Going cultural: Star Trek, State Action and Popular Culture', *Millennium—Journal of International Studies*, 28, 1999, pp. 17–34.

4. Laura Shepherd, 'Veiled References: Constitution of Gender in the Bush Administration's Discourse on the Attack on Afghanistan post 9–11', *International Feminist Journal of Politics*, 8 (1), 2006, pp. 19–41; Penny Griffin, 'Sexing the economy in a neo-liberal world order: Neoliberal discourse and the reproduction of heteronormative heterosexuality', *British Journal of Politics and International Relations*, 9(2), 2007, pp. 220–238.

5. Tony Blair, 'A Battle for Global Values', *Foreign Affairs*, 2007.

6. Nick Turse, *The Complex: How the Military Invades our Everyday Lives*, London: Faber and Faber, 2008, pp. 103–113.

7. Jean-Michel Valantin, *Hollywood, The Pentagon and Washington: The Movies and National Security from WWII to the Present*, London: Anthem Press, 2005, p. xii.

8. Elaine Sciolino and Stephen Grey, 'British Terror Trial Centres on Alleged Homegrown Plot', *New York Times*, 26 November 2006.

9. Slavoj Zizek, *Violence*, London: Profile Books, 2008.

10. Dimitrios Giannoulopoulous, 'Torture, Evidence and Criminal Procedure in the Age of Terrorism', in George Kassimeris (ed.), *Warrior's Dishonour* (Ashgate: Aldershot), 2006, p. 230.

11. Jane Mayer, 'Letter from Hollywood: Whatever it takes. The Politics of the Man Behind '24'', *The New Yorker*, 2007.

12. Ronald Dworkin, 'The Threat to Patriotism', *New York Review of Books*, 49(3), 2002.

13. Robin Butler, *Review of Intelligence on Weapons of Mass Destruction*, London: The Stationery Office, 2004.

14. Ronnie Janoff-Bulman, 'Erroneous Assumptions: Popular Belief in the Effectiveness of Torture interrogation', *Peace and Conflict: Journal of Peace Psychology*, 13(4), 2007, pp. 429–35.

15. M.L.R. Smith and David Martin Jones, 'The Commentariat and Discourse Failure: Language and Atrocity in Cool Britannia', *International Affairs*, 82, 2006, pp. 1077–1100; Tarak Barkawi, 'Response to David Martin Jones and MLR Smith', *International Affairs*, 83, 2007, pp. 165–170; Richard Jackson, 'Response to David Martin Jones and MLR Smith', *International Affairs*, 83, 2007, pp. 172–177.

16. Richard Cheney, (16 September 2001) The Vice-President on Meet the Press with Tim Russett (http://www.whitehouse.gov/vicepresident/news-speeches/speeches/vp20010916.html accessed 10 April 2008)

17. Adam from *Spooks* makes a very similar speech to Cheney's in Series 3 (2004), art imitating life perhaps?

18. Slavoj. Zizek, 'The depraved heroes of 24 are the Himmlers of Hollywood', *The Guardian*, 10 January 2006.

19. 'Questioning the Jack Bauer Way' *The Guardian*, 19 April 2008.

20. James Sturke, 'MI5's Warning' *The Guardian*, 10 November 2006.

21. Paul Rabinow, *The Foucault Reader*, New York: Pantheon, 1984.

22. With the exception of Spooks in Series 3.

23. Patrick Leigh Fermor, *A Time to Keep Silent*, London: John Murray, 2004; Patrick Leigh Fermor, *Mani: Travels in the Southern Peloponnese*, London: John Murray, 2004a.

24. Germaine Greer, *Sex and Destiny: The Politics of Human Fertility*, London: HarperCollins, 1984.

25. Jeremy Black, *The Politics of James Bond*, Nebraska: University of Nebraska Press, 2005, p. 107.

26. Karen Tumulty, 'The Clinton Files and the X-Files', *Time Magazine*, 13 November 2007.

27. Owen Gibson, 'Spooky Coincidences', *The Guardian*, 12 September 2005.

28. John Vidal and Dan Milmo, 'Mystery over who hired mole to dig dirt on Plane Stupid's environment activists', *The Guardian*, 9 April 2008.

29. John Vidal, *McLibel: Burger Culture on Trial*, London: Pan, 1997.

30. Nathan Hodge, 'US Army Debuts Armed Ground Robot in Iraq', *Jane's Land Forces News*, 13 August 2007.

AFTERWORD

1. Carmen A. Medina, 'What to do When Traditional Models Fail', *CIA Studies in Intelligence*, 46:3 (2002).

ABOUT THE CONTRIBUTORS

Professor Richard J. Aldrich is Professor of International Security at the University of Warwick and the author of several books including *The Hidden Hand: Britain American and Cold War Secret Intelligence*, which won the Donner Book prize in 2002 and was short-listed for the Westminster Medal. Since 2008 he has been leading an AHRC-funded project entitled: 'Landscapes of Secrecy: The Central Intelligence Agency and the Contested Record of US Foreign Policy'. He has held a Fulbright Fellowship at Georgetown University in Washington DC and more recently has spent time in Canberra and Ottawa as a Leverhulme Fellow while completing a book examining the impact of globalisation upon the intelligence services.

Professor Wyn Bowen is Professor of Non-Proliferation and International Security, and Director of the Centre for Science and Security Studies, in the Department of War Studies at King's College London. In 1997–98 he served as a weapons inspector on several missile teams in Iraq with the UN Special Commission and has also worked as a consultant to the International Atomic Energy Agency. Wyn Bowen served as a Specialist Advisor to the House of Commons' Foreign Affairs Committee for inquiries into 'The Decision to go to War with Iraq' (2003) and 'Weapons of Mass Destruction' (2000). He has written widely on proliferation and security related issues.

Tony Campbell is the President of Campbell Intel Services Inc., a strategic analysis and executive development consultancy based in Ottawa, Canada. He is an adjunct professor at Royal Roads University and has held a variety of fellowship or adjunct positions at Carleton University, the University of Victoria, the University of Cambridge and Warwick University. From 2001–04 he served as Vice President and President of the Canadian Association for Security and Intelligence Studies. In his thirty-four year career in Canada's Public Service, he held increasingly senior positions in nine departments and agencies as a policy advisor, international negotiator, regulatory policy expert, educator in leadership and management, and as a manager of foreign intelligence analysis, culminating in the post of Executive Director of the Intelligence Assessment Secretariat in the Privy Council Office (1993–2000).

Gordon Corera has been a Security Correspondent for BBC News since June 2004. In that role he covers counter-terrorism, counter-proliferation and international security issues for BBC TV, Radio and Online. He was previously a foreign affairs reporter on *Today*, BBC Radio 4's flagship news programme. He has also been a State Department Correspondent based in Washington DC and the US Affairs Analyst for BBC News. He is the author of *Shopping for Bombs: Nuclear Proliferation, Global Insecurity, and the Rise and Fall of the A.Q. Khan Network*, which was published by Hurst in September 2006.

Dr Robert Dover has held academic posts at Bristol University, King's College London and is now based at Loughborough University. His research interests include the government's use of intelligence, the European arms trade and British and European foreign and defence policy. He and Philip Davies jointly hold an ESRC grant to run six one-day research workshops on 'Intelligence and Governance in the 21st Century'. In April 2008 he was awarded the Wilfrid Harrison Prize by the Political Studies Association.

Dr Michael Goodman is a Senior Lecturer in the Department of War Studies, King's College London. He joined the Department in September 2004 as a Lecturer specialising in the study of intelligence. His first book is entitled *Spying on the Nuclear Bear: Anglo-American Intelligence and the Soviet Bomb* (Stanford University Press, 2008). He has written widely on the atom spy Klaus Fuchs, and on various aspects of British intelligence history. In 2007 he was appointed, on secondment, to the Cabinet Office, where he is the Official Historian of the Joint Intelligence Committee.

Dr Steve Hewitt is a Senior Lecturer in American and Canadian Studies at the University of Birmingham. He is the author of several articles and books related to security and intelligence, including *Spying 101: The RCMP's Secret*

Activities at Canadian Universities, 1917–1997 (University of Toronto Press, 2002), and *The British War on Terror: Terrorism and Counter-Terrorism on the Home Front since 9/11* (Continuum, 2008). He is currently working on a history of the American counter-terrorism programme provisionally entitled *Rewards for Justice*.

Colonel Pierre Lethier After graduating from the Military College at Saint-Cyr, Colonel Lethier worked for France's external intelligence agency from 1978 to 1998. In his position as Director General for the External Security Chief of Staff, he was responsible for special operations and foreign relations. A recent career change has seen him move to the London Film School and then to King's College London, where he is working towards a PhD in Film Studies.

Professor Scott Lucas is Professor of American Studies, where he has worked since 1989. A specialist in US and British foreign policy, he has written and edited seven books, including *Divided We Stand: Britain, the US and the Suez Crisis*; *Freedom's War: The US Crusade Against the Soviet Union, 1945–56*; *George Orwell: Life and Times*; and *The Betrayal of Dissent: Beyond Orwell, Hitchens, and the New American Century*, and published more than thirty major articles. In addition to adjunct and visiting posts at University College Dublin, the American University in Beirut, and the University of Tehran, he is the Associate Editor of the *Journal of American Studies*. Most recently, he has launched the on-line research centre, Libertas, for contemporary publications, blogs, and podcasts on US foreign policy.

Sir David Omand has been a Visiting Professor at the Department War Studies, King's College London since 2006. He was the first UK Security and Intelligence Coordinator as Permanent Secretary in the Cabinet Office from 2002 to 2005, responsible for the professional health of the intelligence community, national counter-terrorism strategy and 'homeland security'. He served in total for seven years on the UK's Joint Intelligence Committee. He was previously Permanent Secretary of the Home Office, Director of GCHQ (the UK Signals Intelligence Agency), and the Deputy Under Secretary of State for Policy in the Ministry of Defence. His most recent publications are on national security strategy, the uses of strategy in counter-terrorism and national resilience, the relationship of the media and intelligence, and proposing a code of ethics for intelligence and security work.

Harry Chapman Pincher was born in 1914 and is a noted British journalist, who first began writing for the *Daily Express* in 1946. His work as a novelist and journalist mainly focuses on espionage and related matters, after some early books on scientific subjects. Pincher is probably best known as the author of *Their Trade is Treachery*, which alleged that the former director-general of MI5, Sir Roger Hollis, had been a spy for the Soviet Union. Pincher is noted for his strong support for the work of the intelligence agencies—including running stories that assisted the intelligence agencies.

Dr Patrick Porter is a Lecturer at the Defence Studies Department, Kings College London at the Joint Services Command and Staff College (JSCSC), Defence Academy of the UK. His forthcoming book *Military Orientalism: Eastern War through Western Eyes* will be published in 2009 by Hurst and Company, London and Columbia University Press, New York.

Rear Admiral Nick Wilkinson After forty years of service in the Royal Navy, Whitehall, NATO and the Defence Academy, Nick Wilkinson was the D-Notice Secretary 1999–2004. He is a Cabinet Office Historian, who has written a book 'Secrecy and the Media—the Official History of the UK D-Notice System', published by Routledge June 2009. He was a Press Complaints Commissioner 2005-8.

INDEX

Church Commission, 3, 20–1, 38
Churchill, Winston, 6, 136, 170, 211
CIA, 14, 19–33, 92, 106–15, 121, 130,
   156, 158, 185, 187–8, 192–9, 205,
   208, 222
Clarke, Peter, 45, 66
Clausewitz, Carl von, 44, 71–2, 80–2
Clinton, Hillary, 34
Clinton, Bill, 23–6
CNN, 9
Colby, William, 21
Cold War, 6–7, 10–25, 38, 48, 54, 106,
   108, 117, 126, 131, 137, 142, 146, 154,
   167, 170–5, 185, 187–8, 191–2, 197,
   199, 210–1, 222
computer games, 201, 215–7
Coughlin, Con, 111
counter terrorism, 10, 38–9, 41, 66, 72,
   203–4, 207–9, 213–8.
CREVICE plot, 204–5
Cuban Missile Crisis, 189, 192, 199
culture, importance of, 71–90, 201–20
Curveball, 31, 110

Dean, Patrick, 125
Dearlove, Richard, 112
Department of Defense, 108
Department of Homeland Security, 34
Department of State, 19, 26, 75, 194
Director of Central Intelligence (DCI),
   20–1, 30, 49, 55, 92, 106, 109, 113,
   196
Director of National Intelligence (DNI),
   34, 92, 113
D-Notice, 4, 8, 133–47, 153, 160
D-Notice Affair, 160
D-Notice, origins, 135–8
D-Notice, system, 138–40
dossiers (WMD/Iraq), 110–4
Drogin, Bob, 31
DST, 197
du Gardier, Roger, 194
Dulles, Allen, 106–8

The Economist, 40, 76, 96

Elcock, Ward, 178
embedded journalists, 144–5, 170–3
Evans, David, 128, 130

Facebook, 65
Falklands War, 6, 144
FBI, 24, 106, 185, 187, 213
Federation of American Scientists (FAS),
   32
Feith, Douglas, 110
films (*see* Hollywood), 185–220
First World War, 88, 136–7, 169, 180
Fleet Street, 150–4
Foot, M.R.D., 6
Foote, Alexander, 19
Foreign Broadcasting Information
   Services (FBIS), 121, 123, 132
Foreign Office, 10, 38, 119–20, 122–3,
   125–7, 157, 159–61
Forest Gate, police raid, 54
Fox News, 9
Freedom of Information (FOI), 13–5, 21,
   27–8, 55, 134
Fuchs, Klaus, 154
Fukuyama, Francis, 174

Gates, Robert, 22
GCHQ, 37, 111, 119, 122, 154, 160, 162
Gilder, Barry, 4
globalisation, 7–8, 13–35, 62, 135, 180
Goleniewski, Michael, 196
Golitsin, Anatoli, 158, 195–7
Goss, Porter, 92
Guantanamo Bay, 34, 208
Gulf War, 1, 80, 181
Gup, Ted, 27
Hamas, 62, 83, 88
Harper, Stephen, 178, 181
Hayden, Michael, 30
Heathrow Airport closure, 2004, 42–3
Helgerson, John, 30
Helms, Richard, 196
Herman, Michael, 179
Hersh, Seymour, 29, 33, 112
Hitchcock, Alfred, 185–200